Citation

OpenAI. (2024). *ChatGPT* (4) [Large language model]. https://chat.openai.com

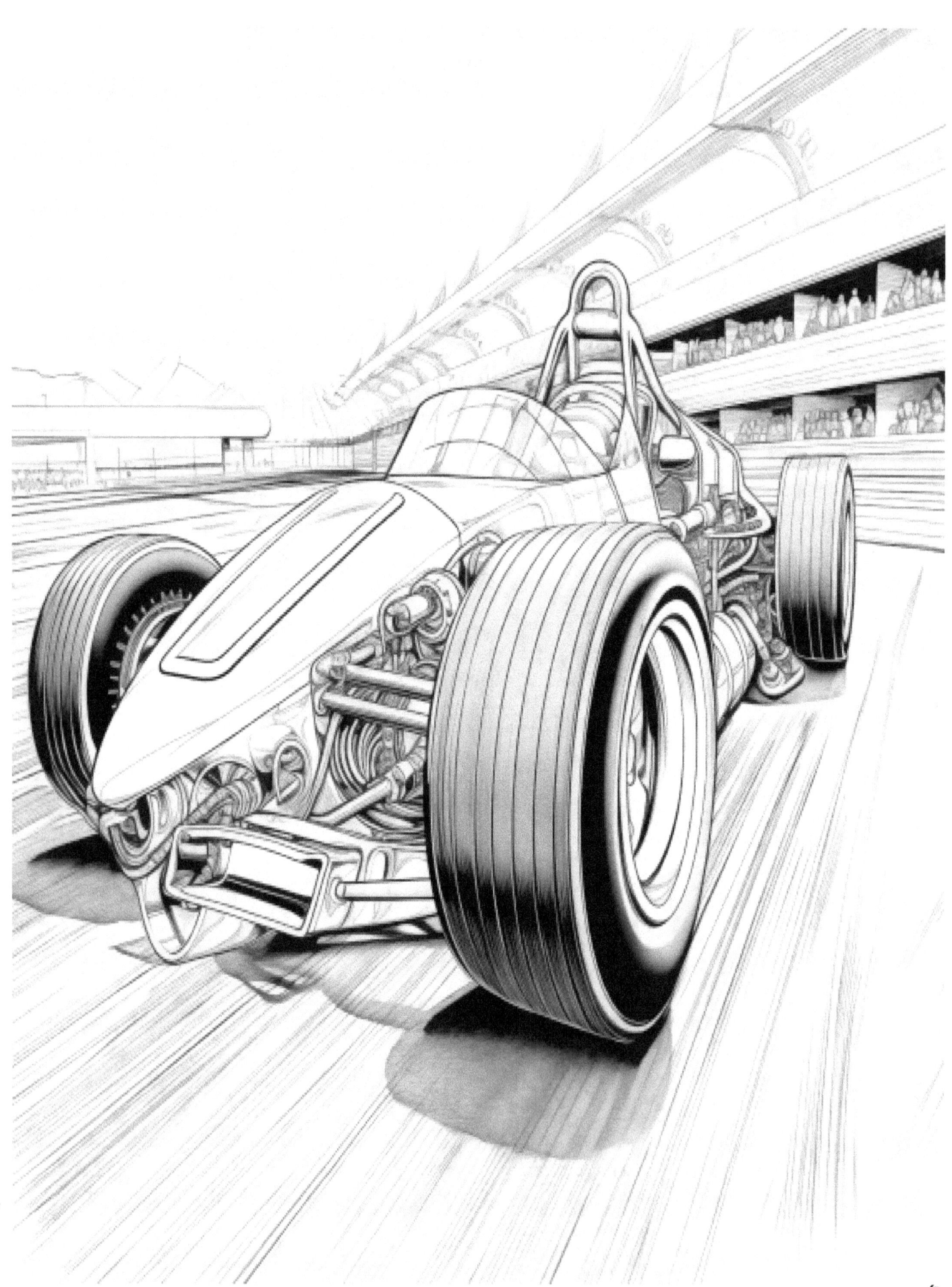

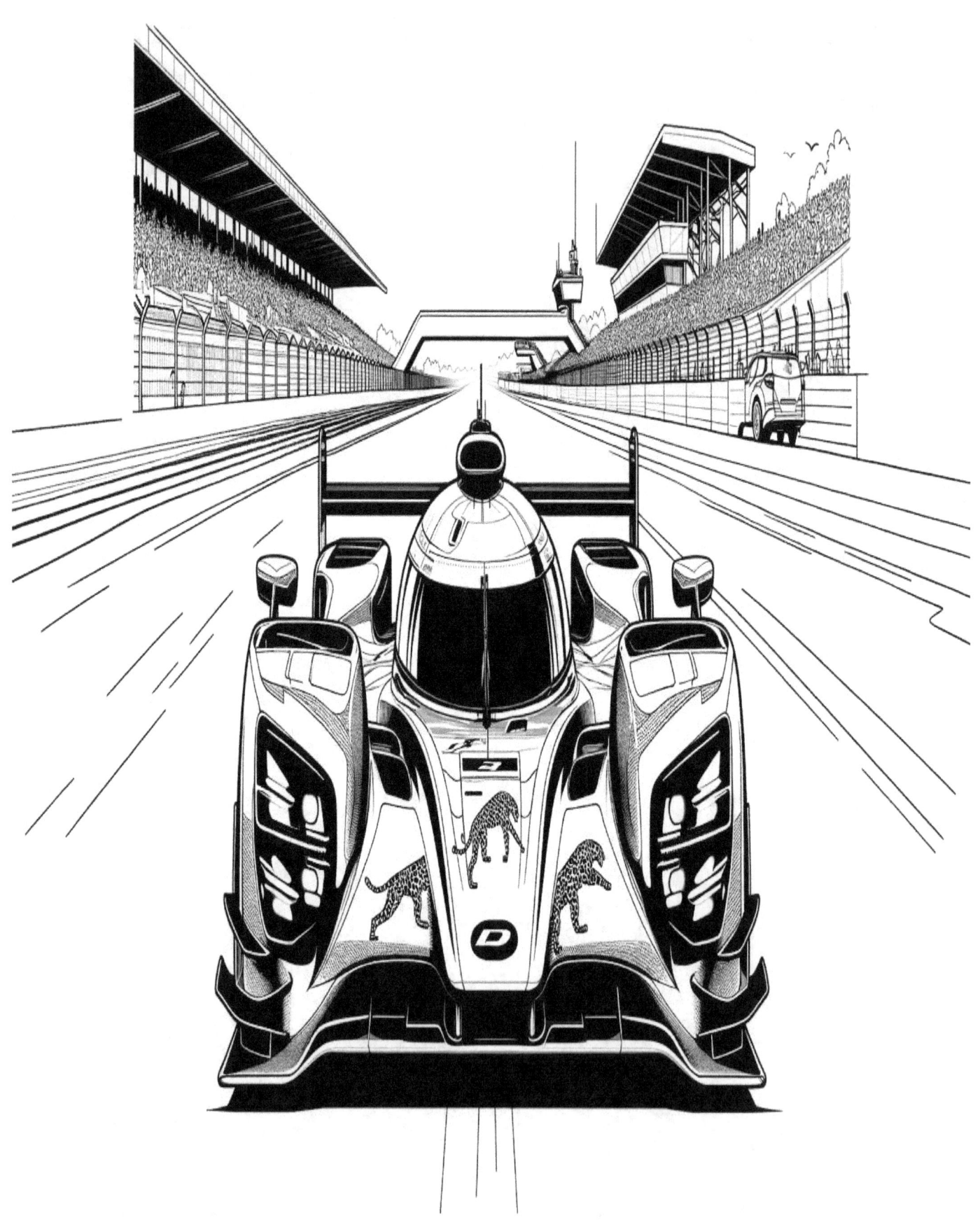

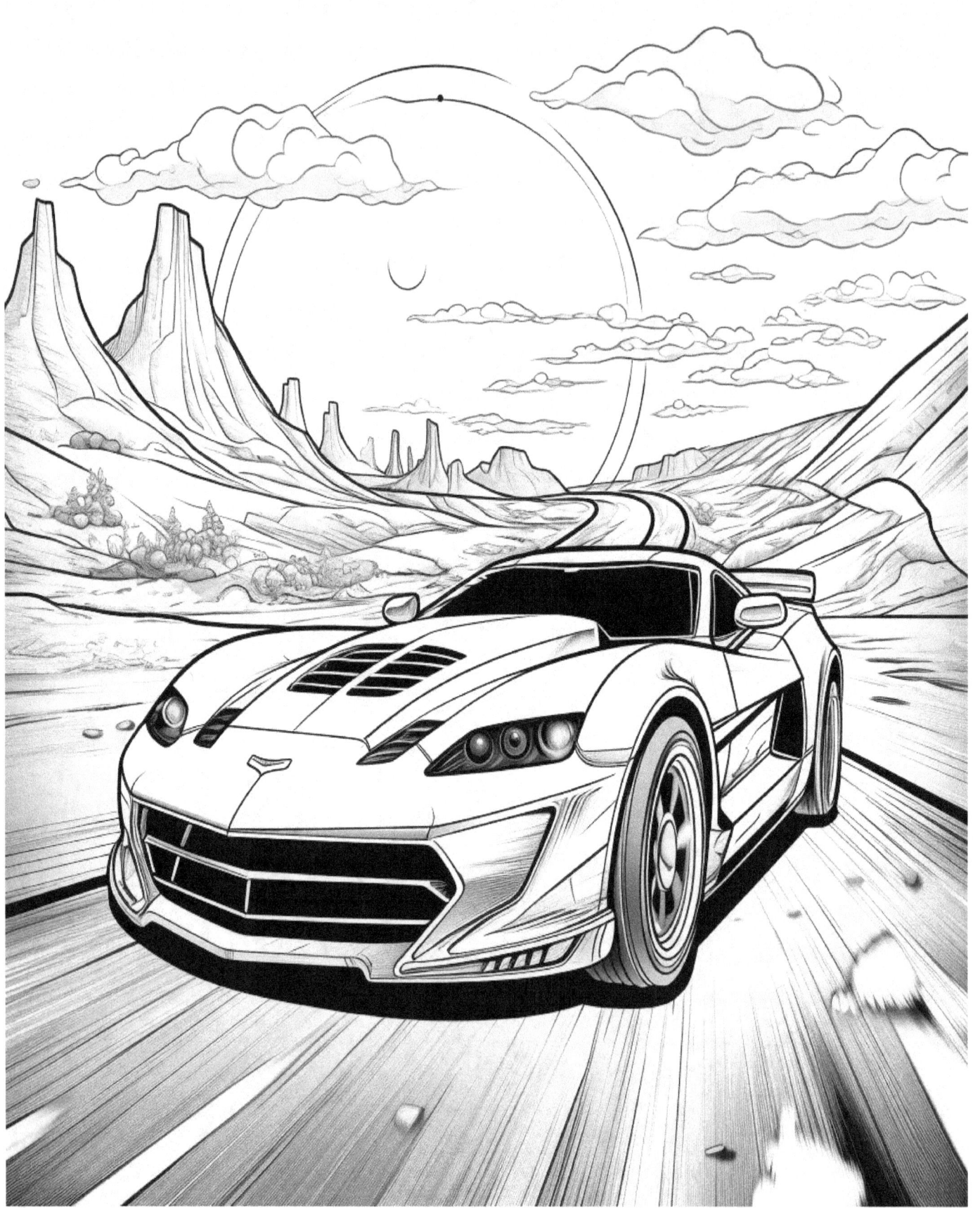

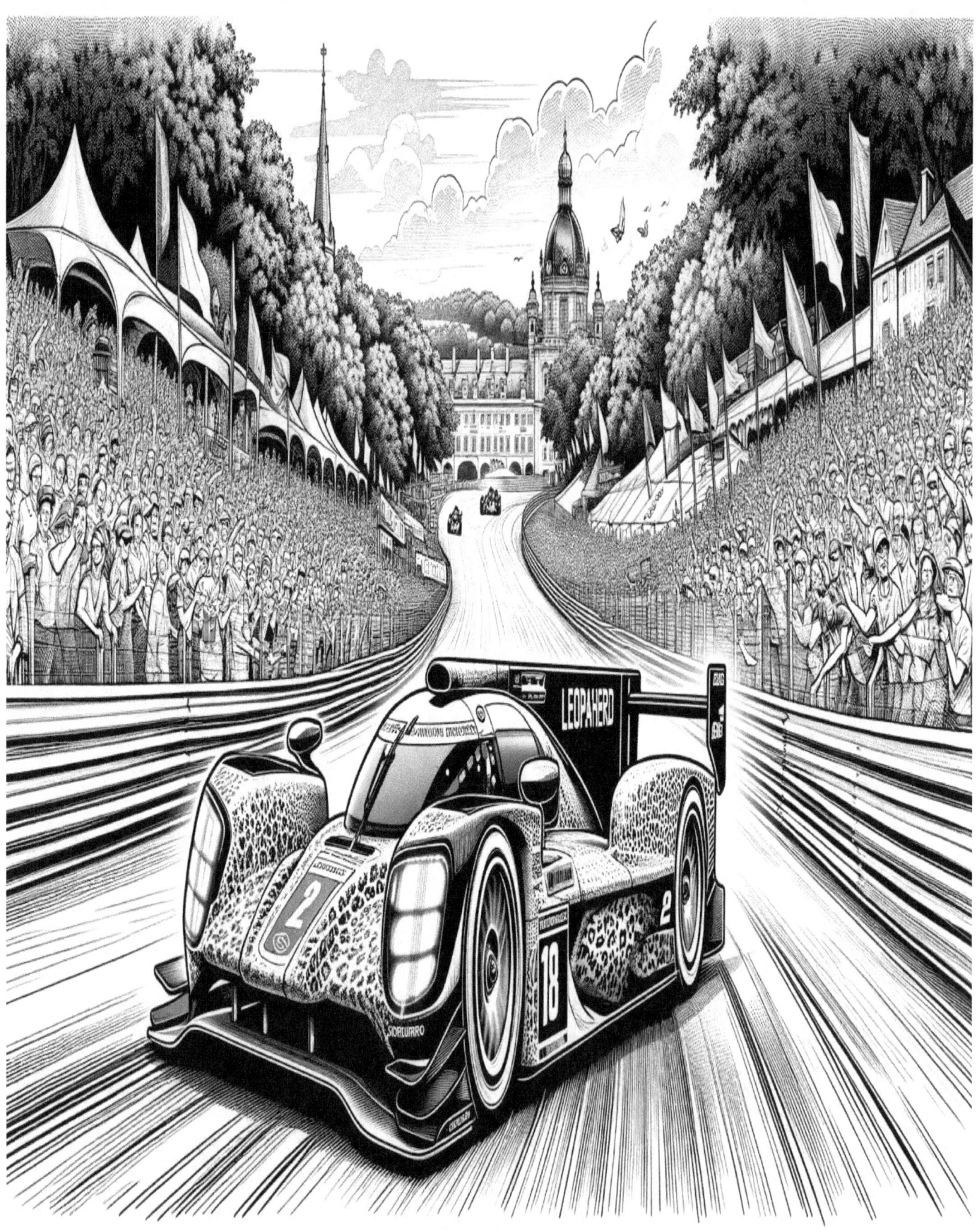

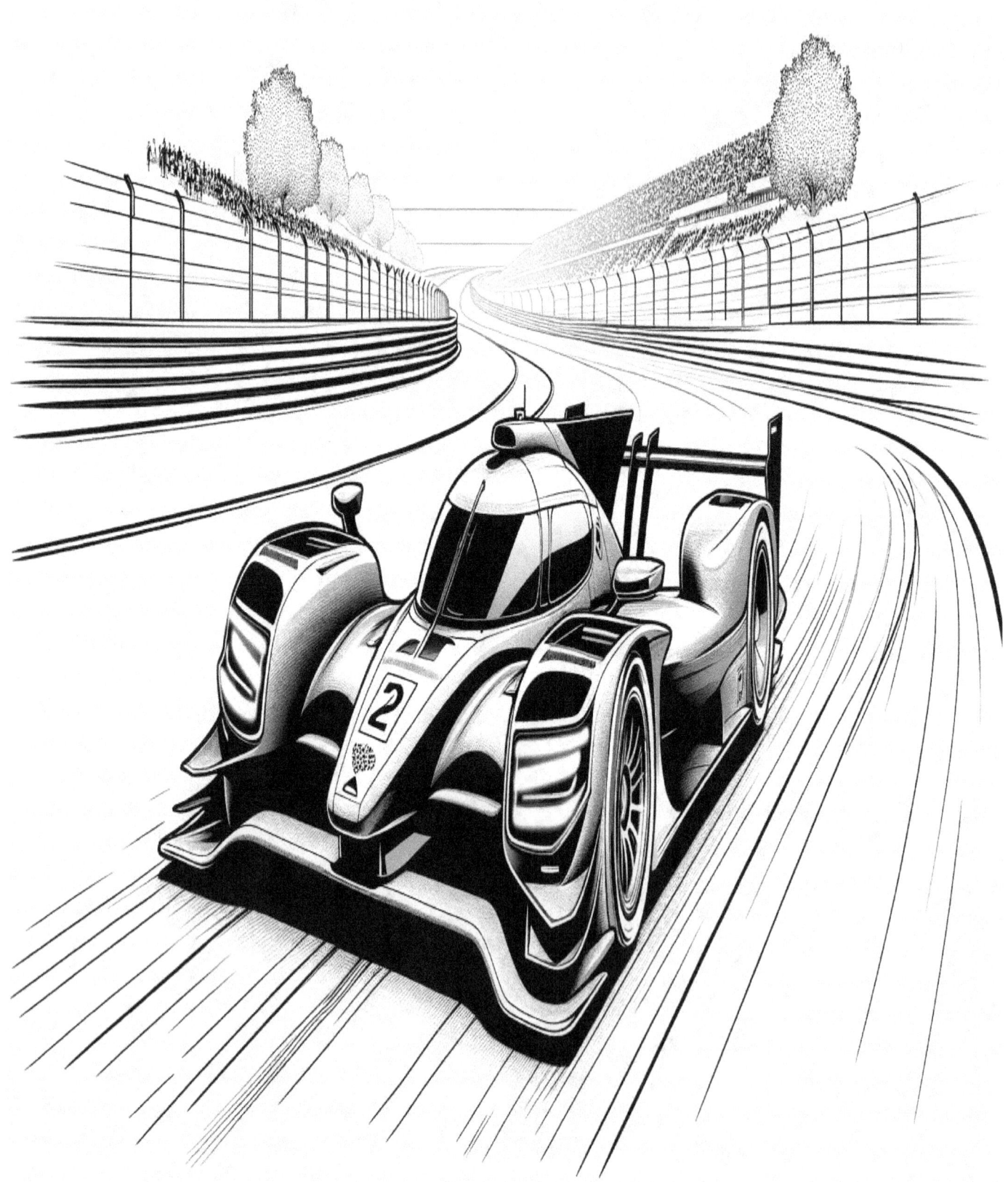

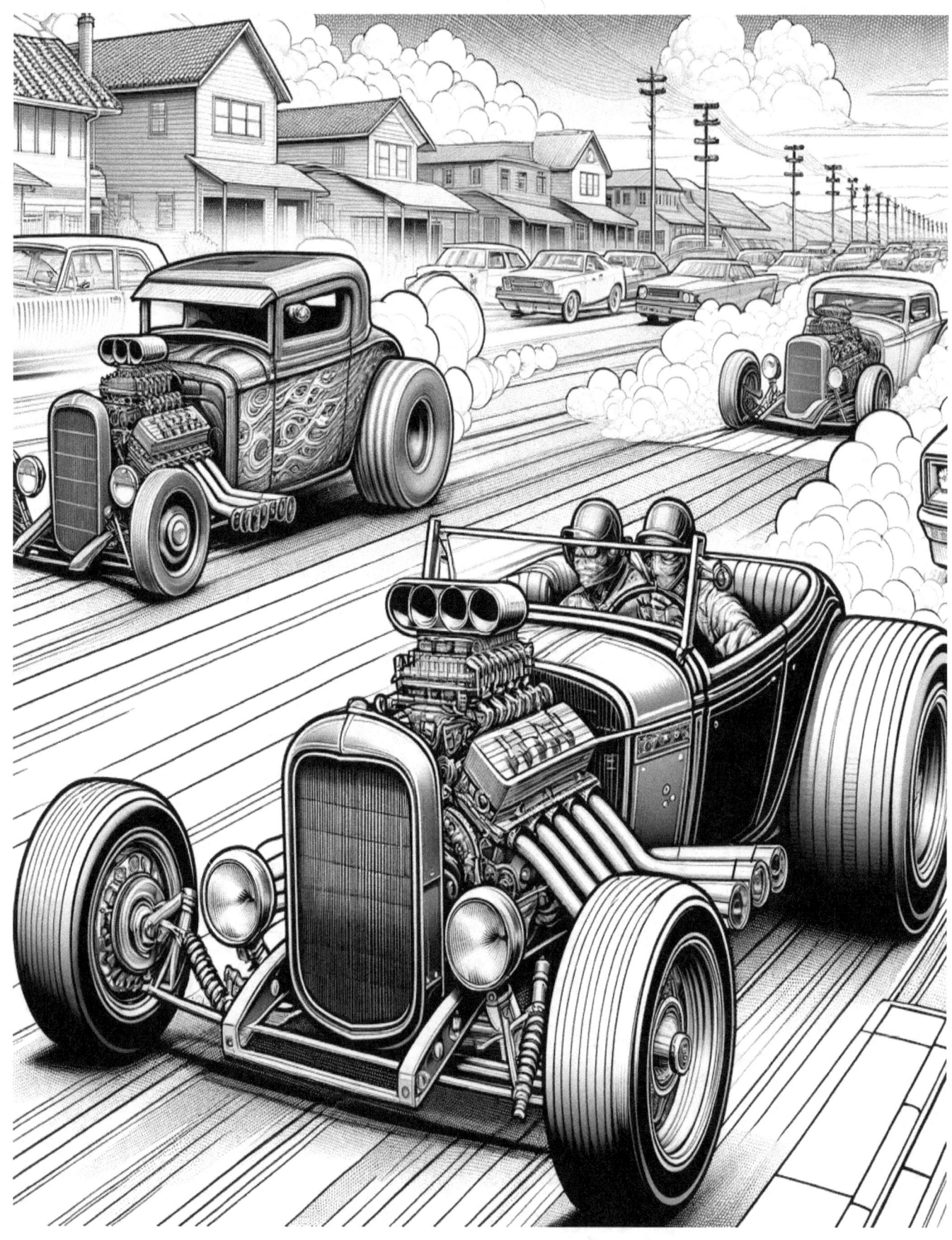

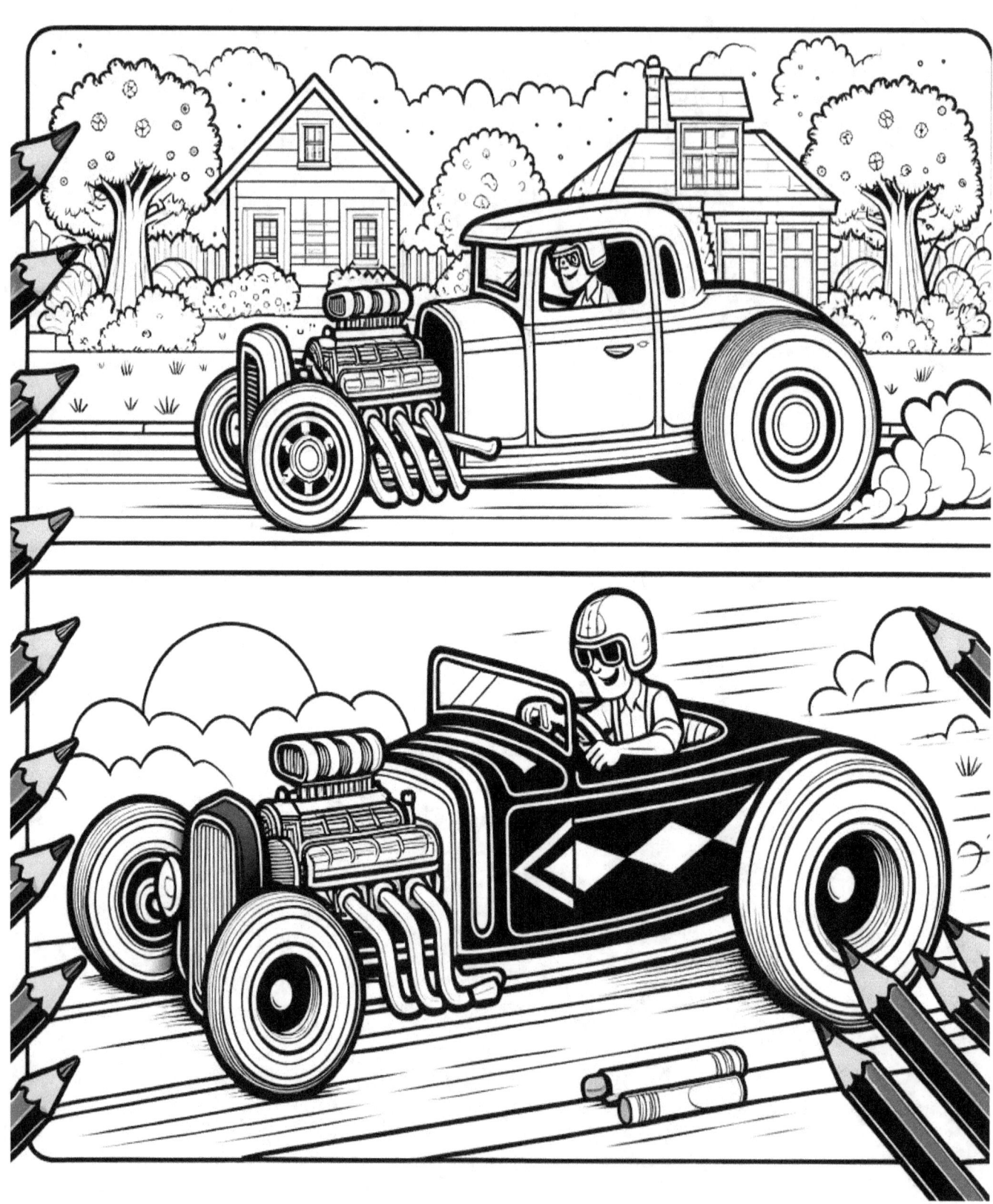

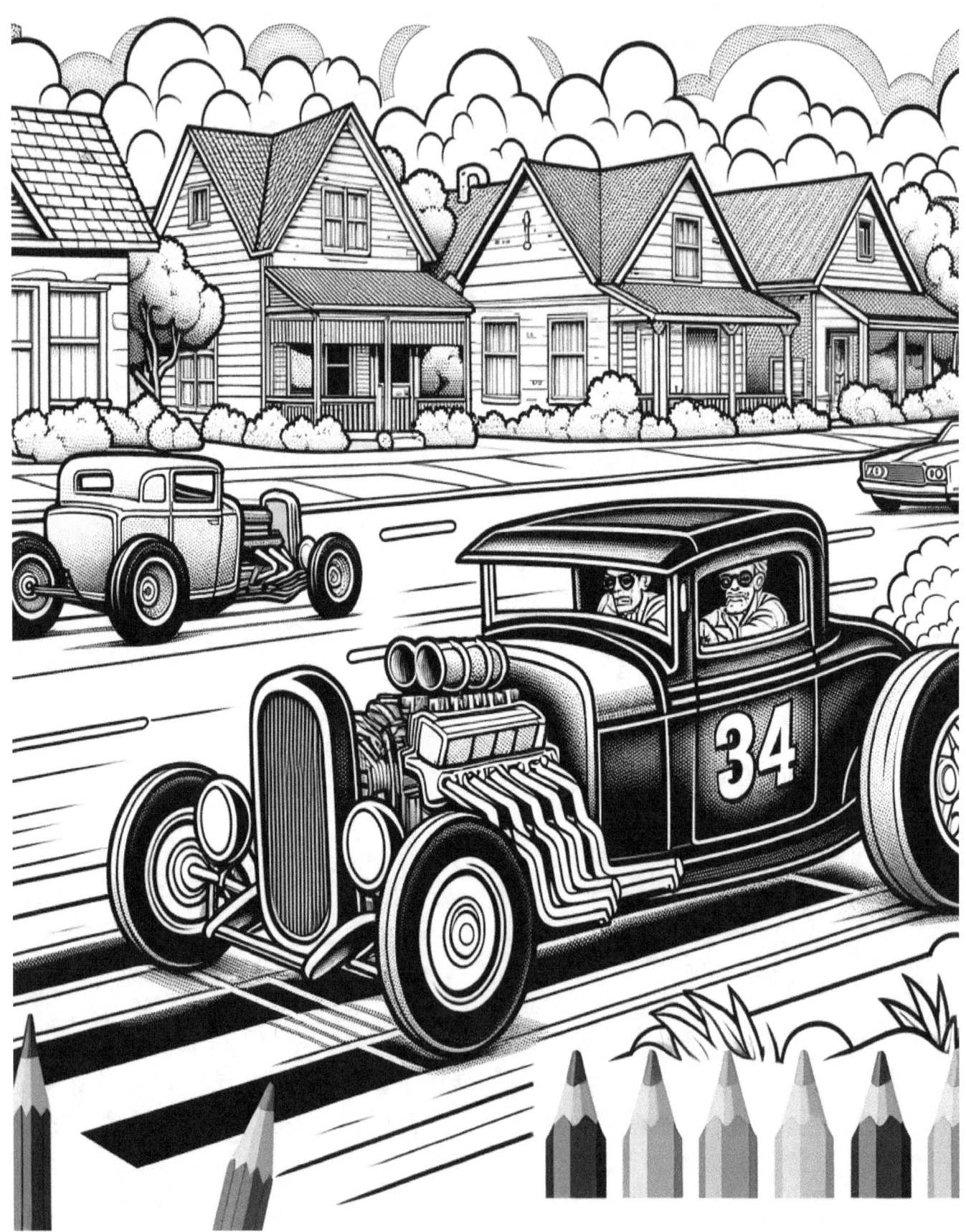

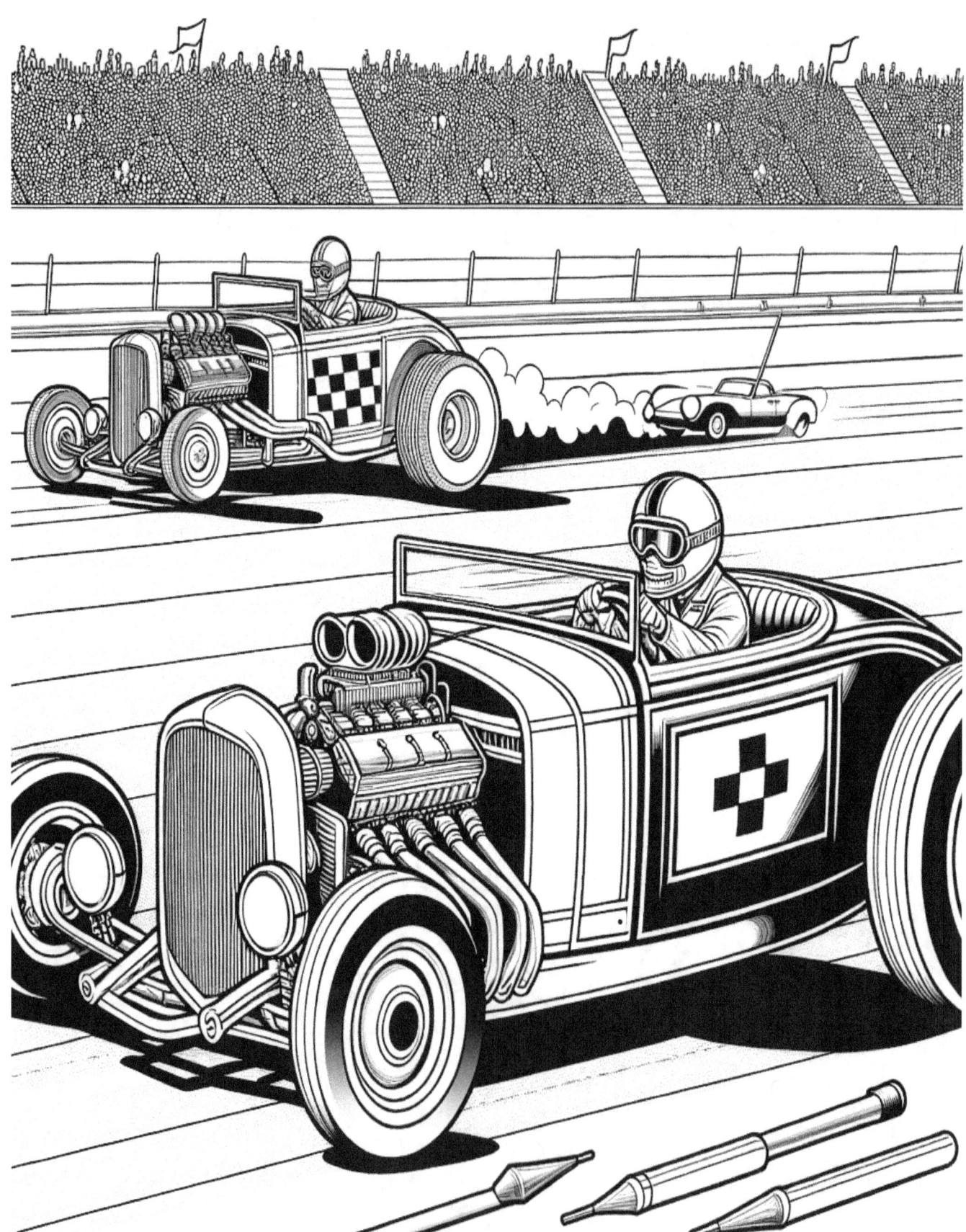

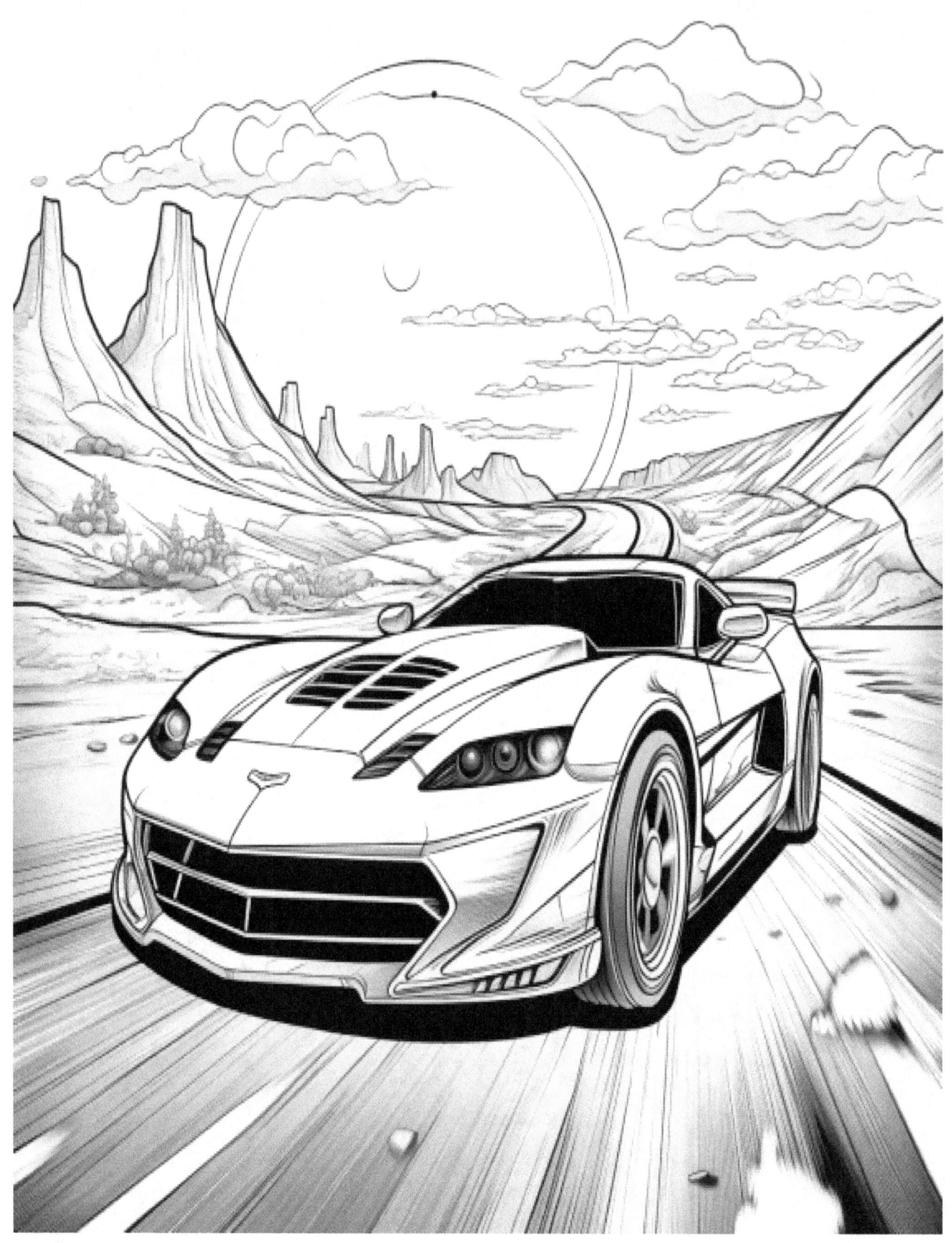

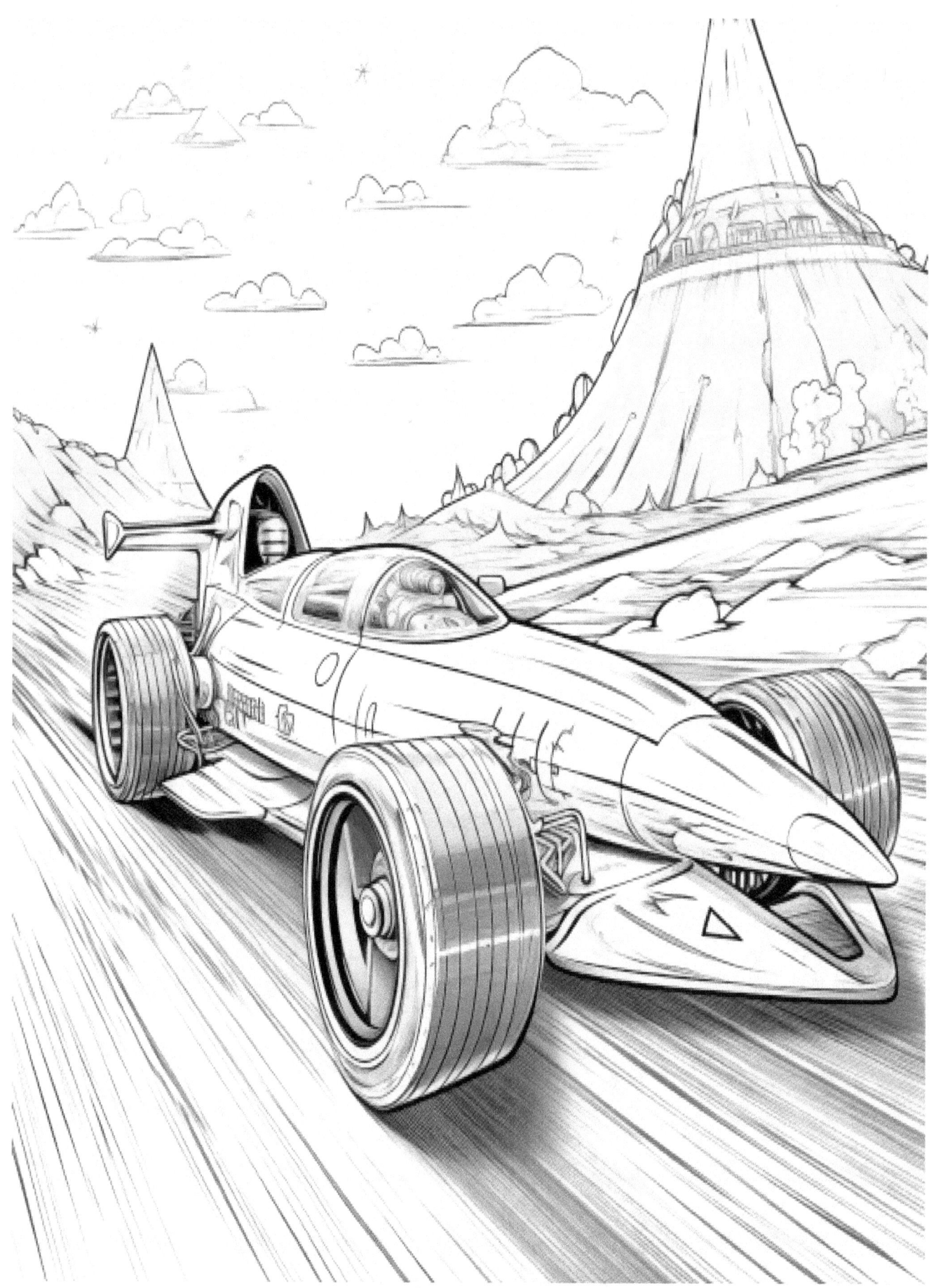

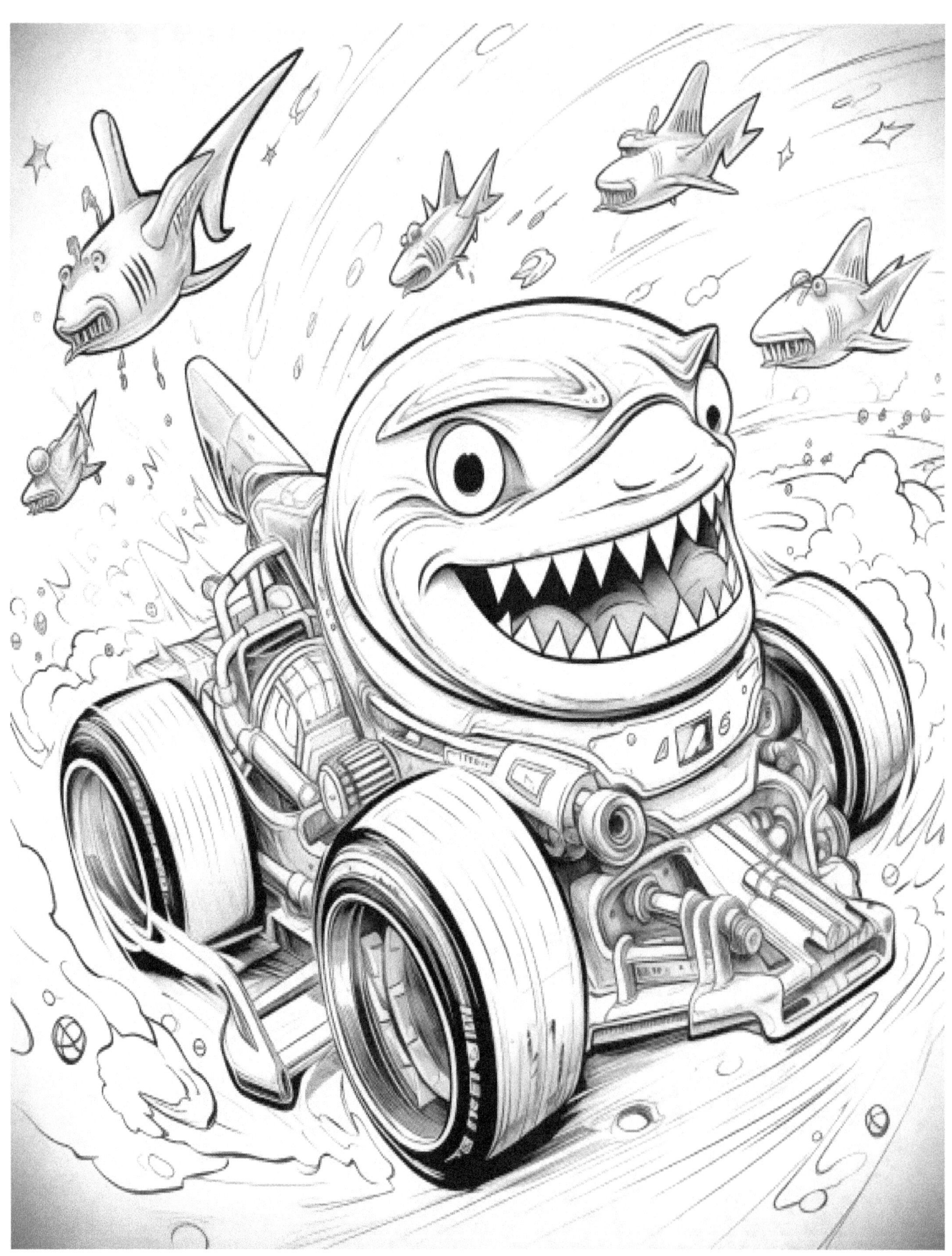

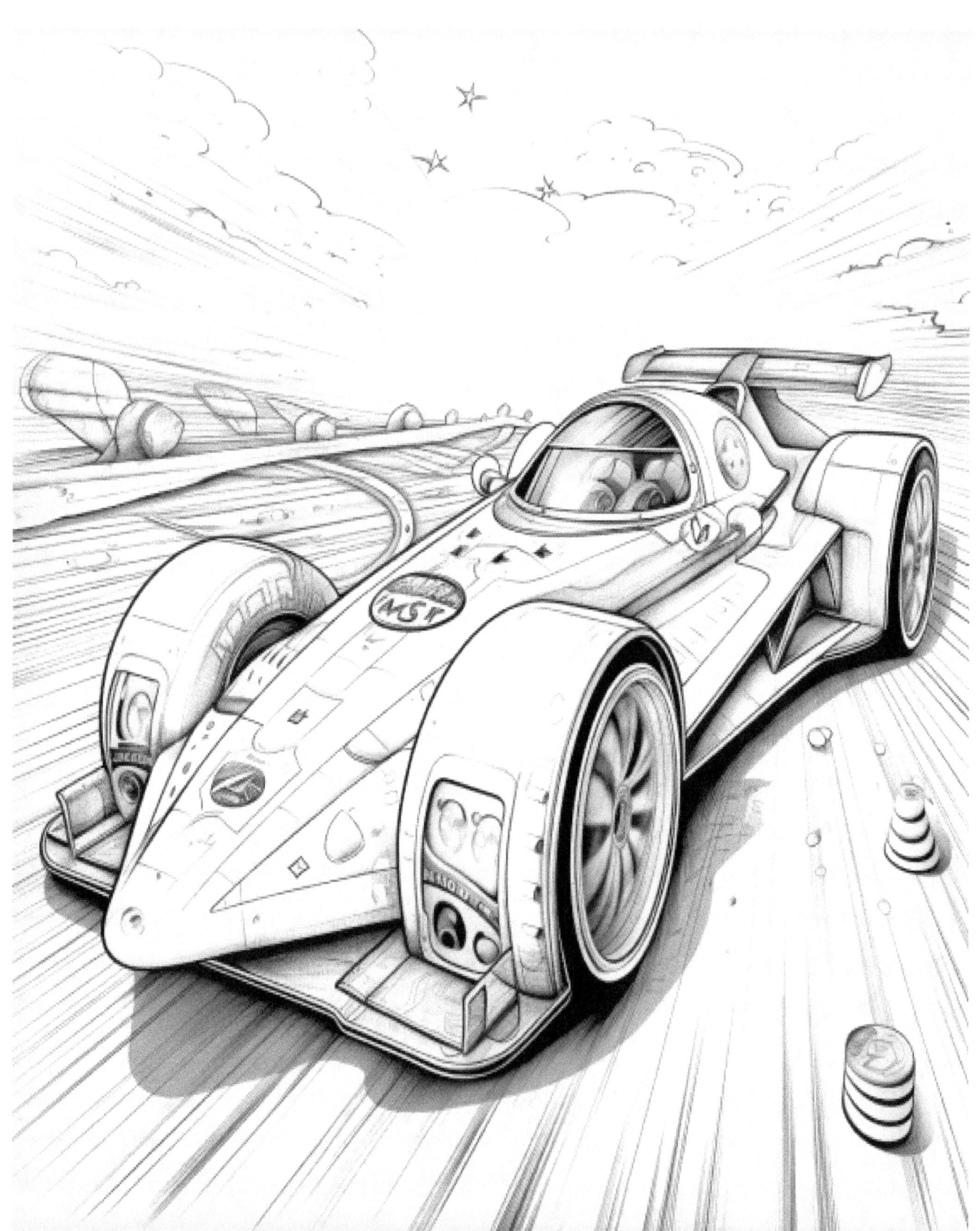

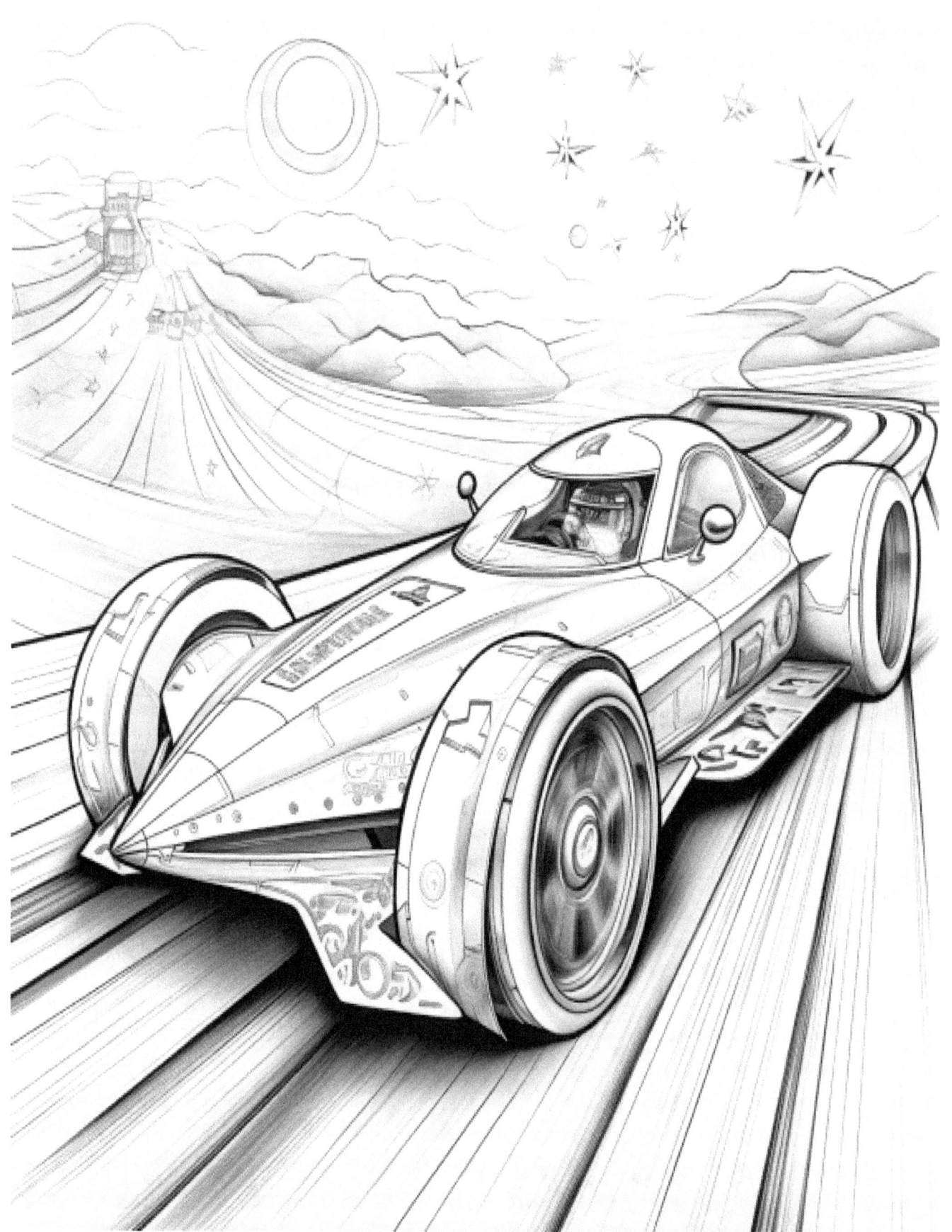

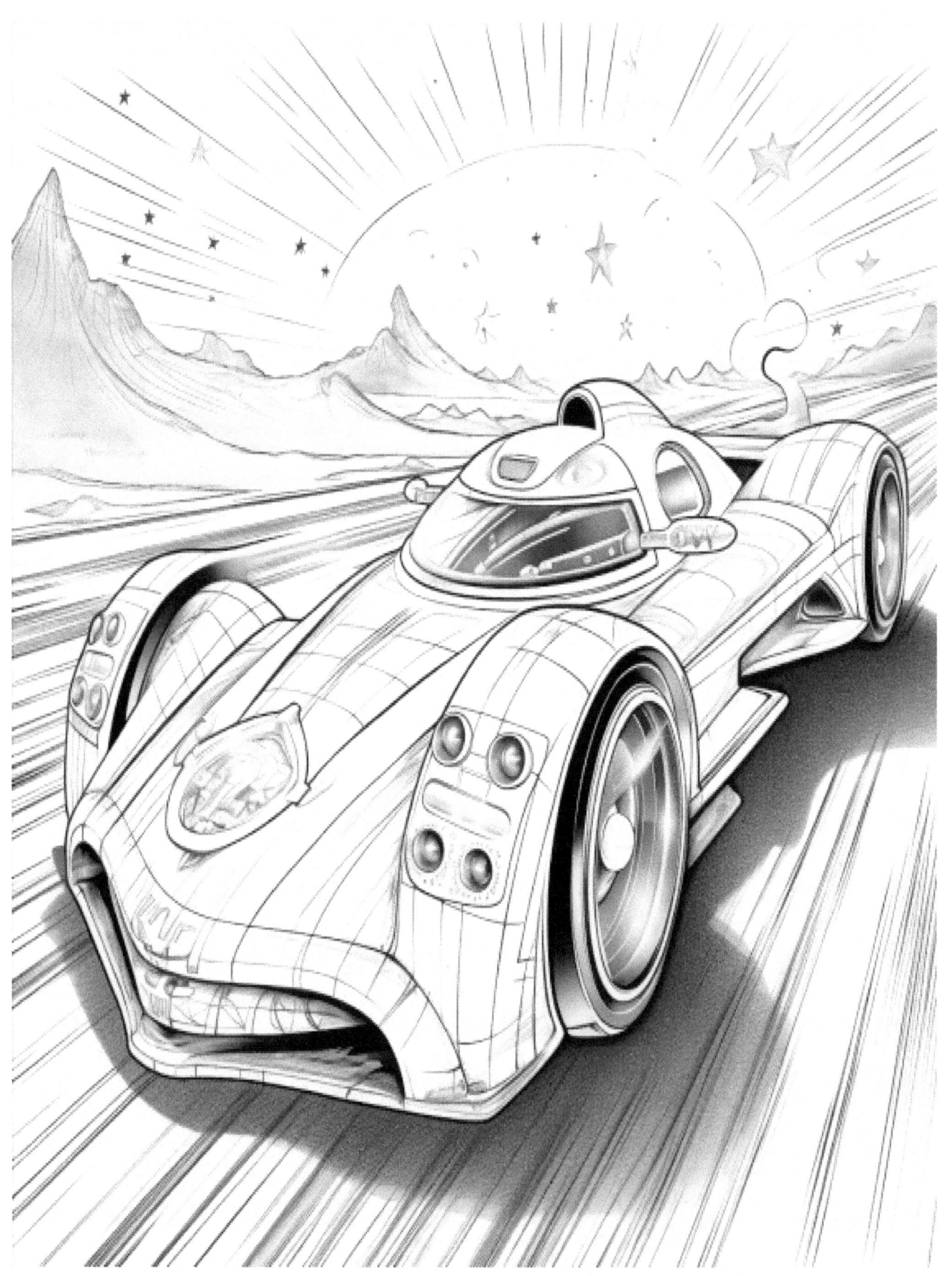

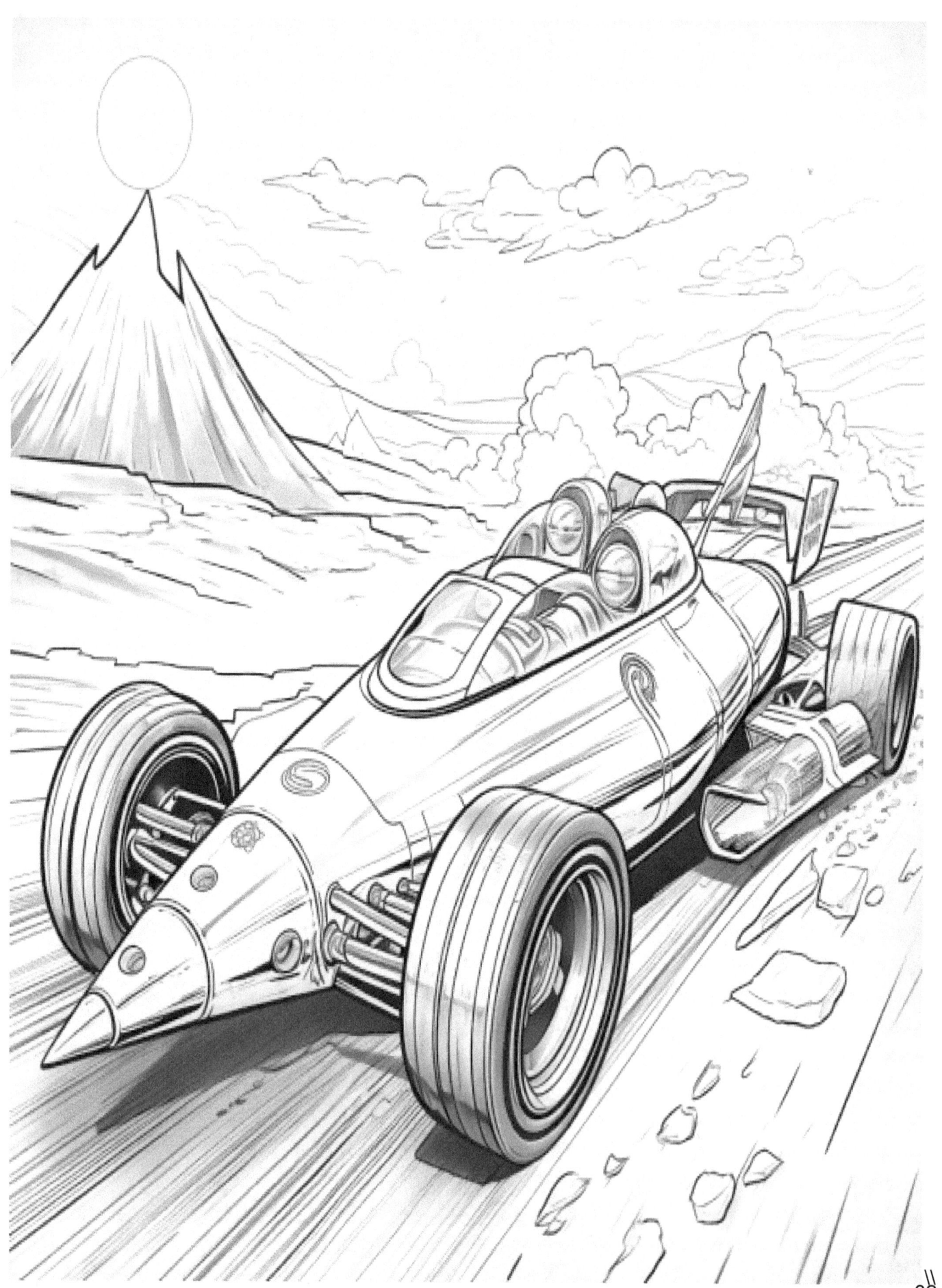

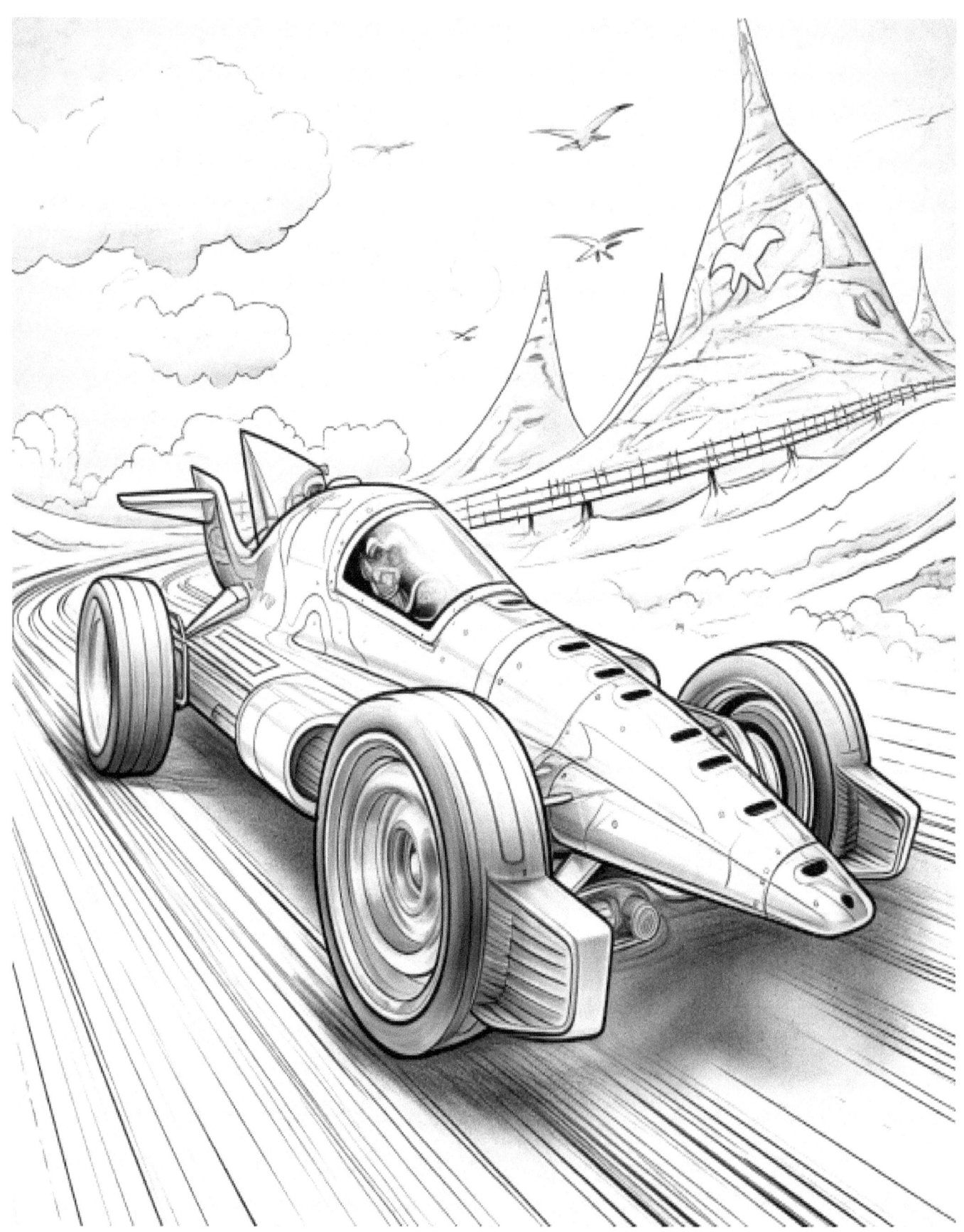

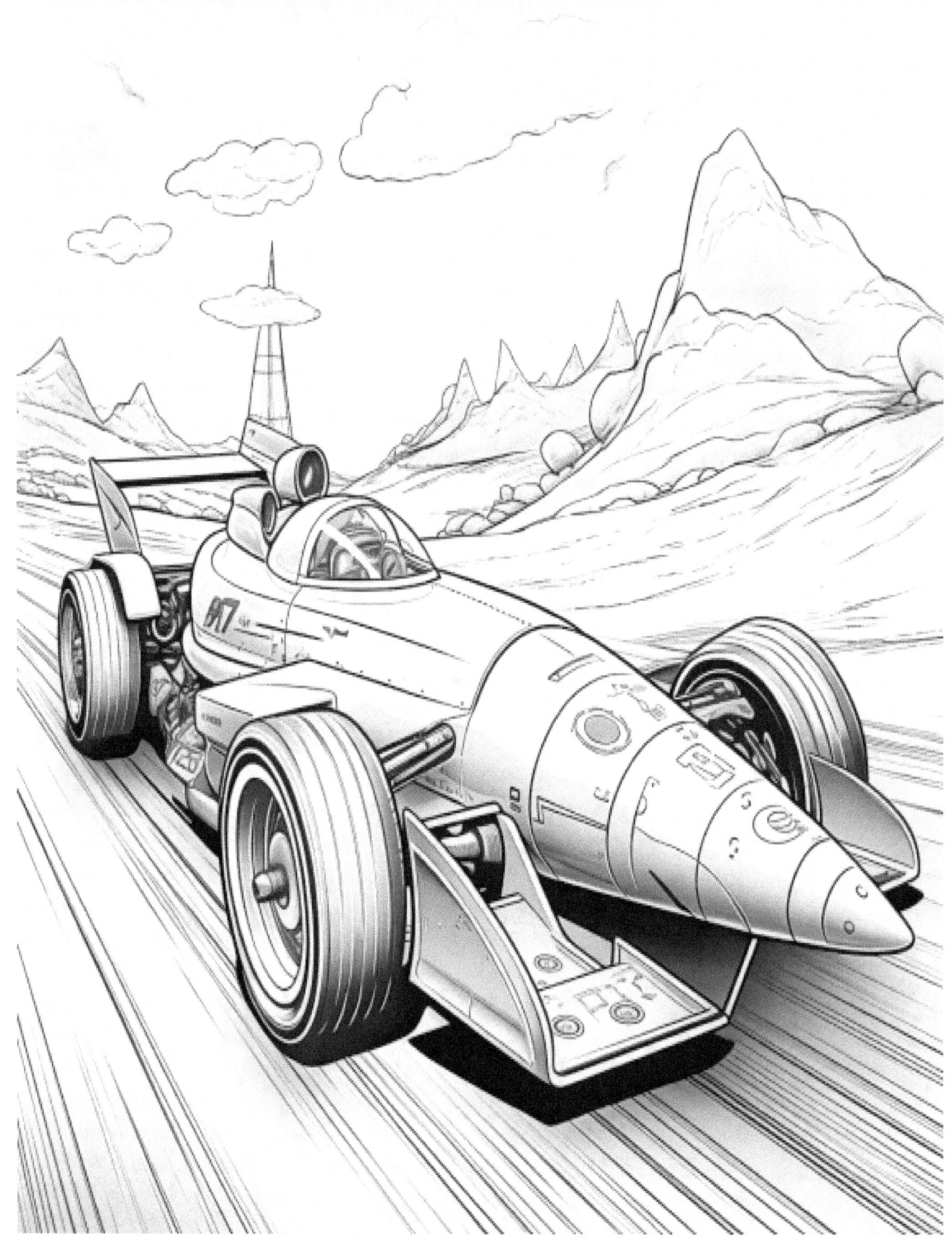

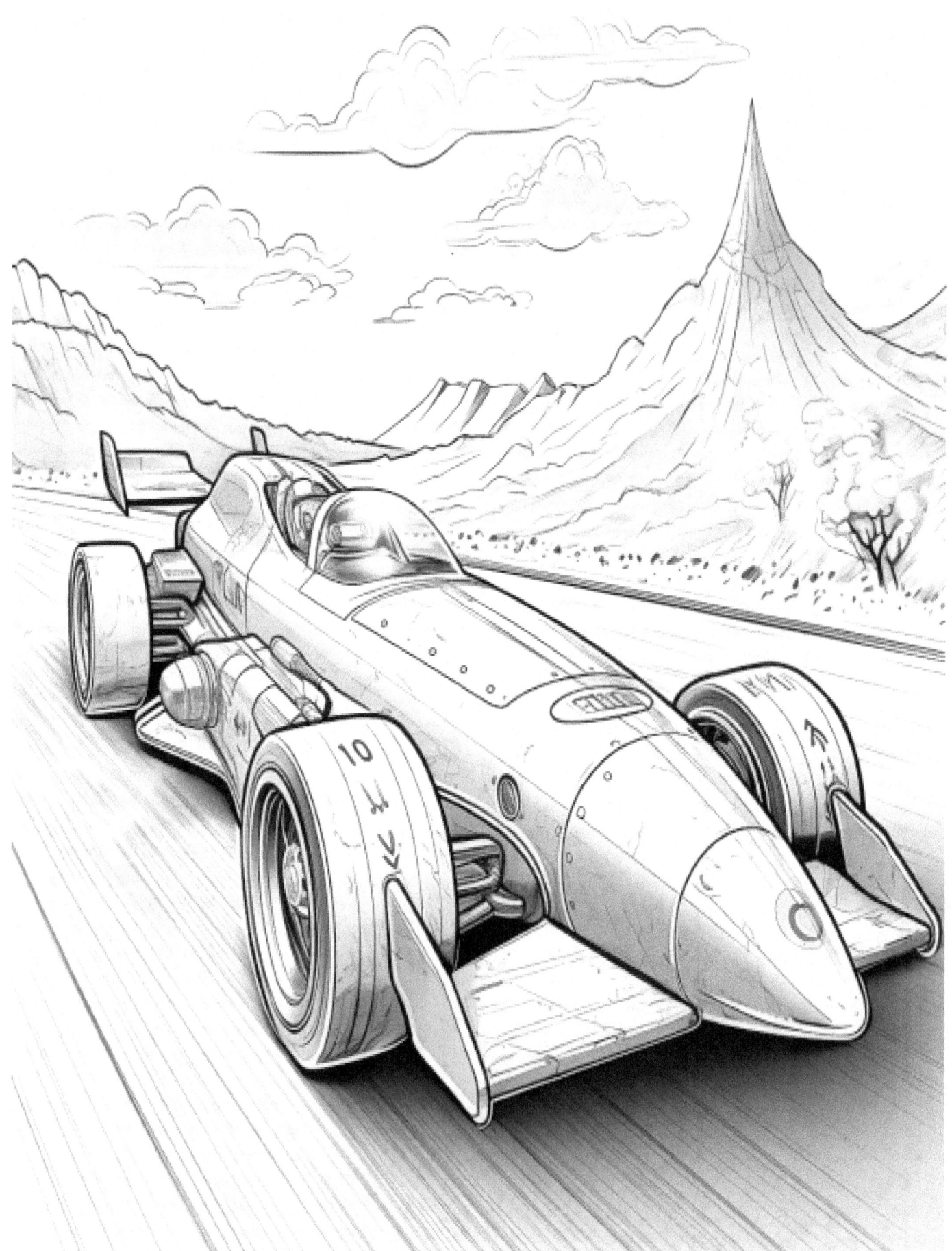

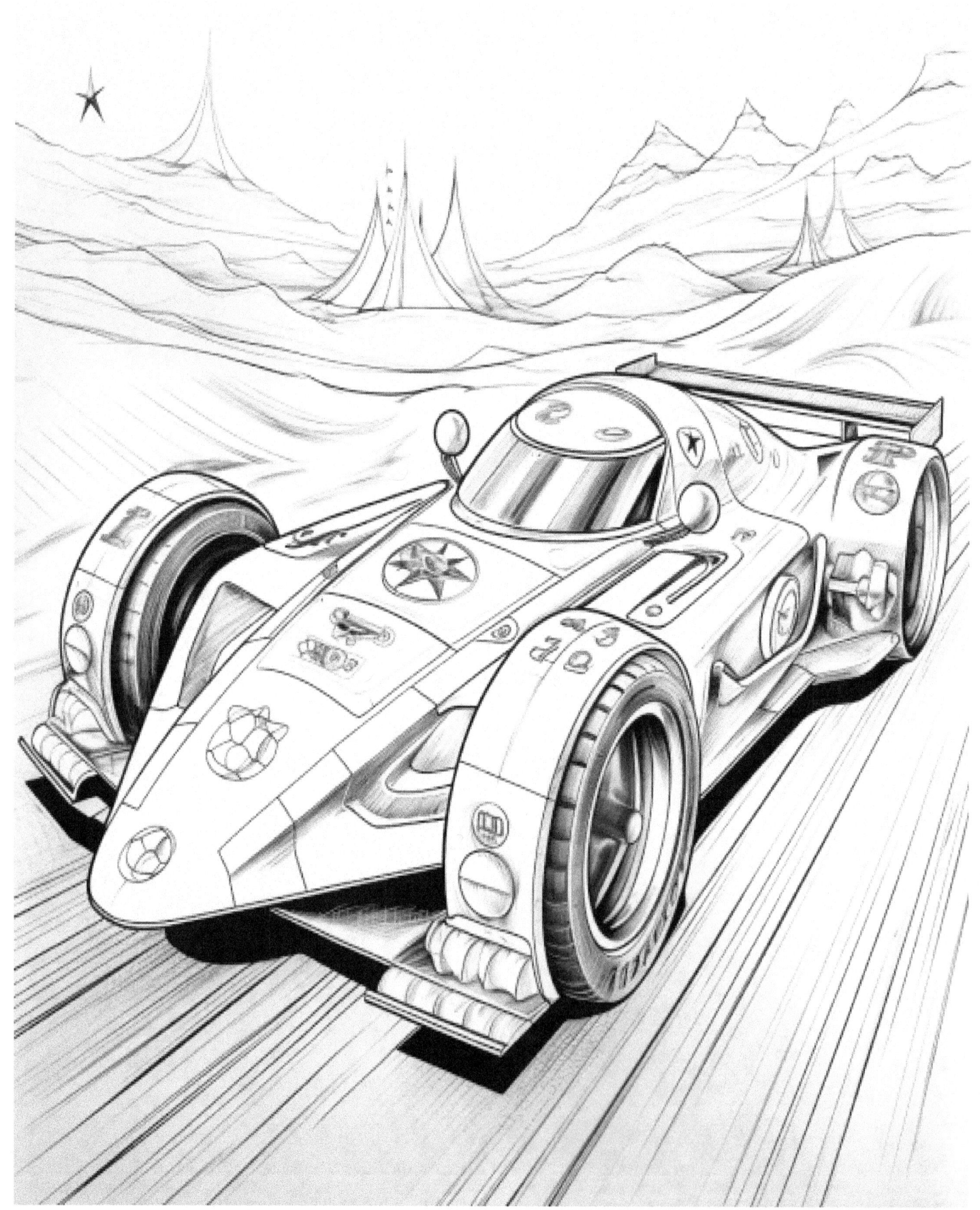

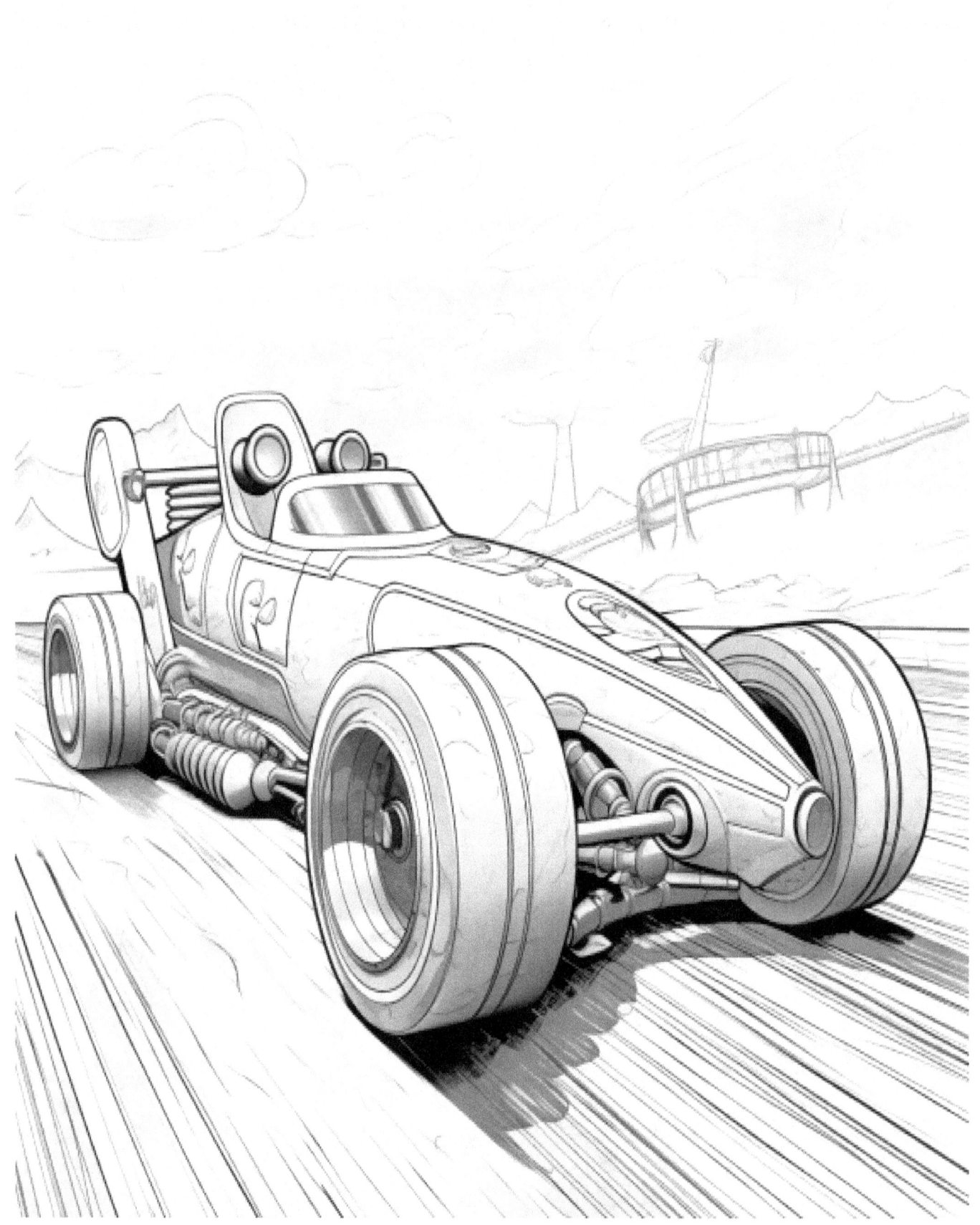

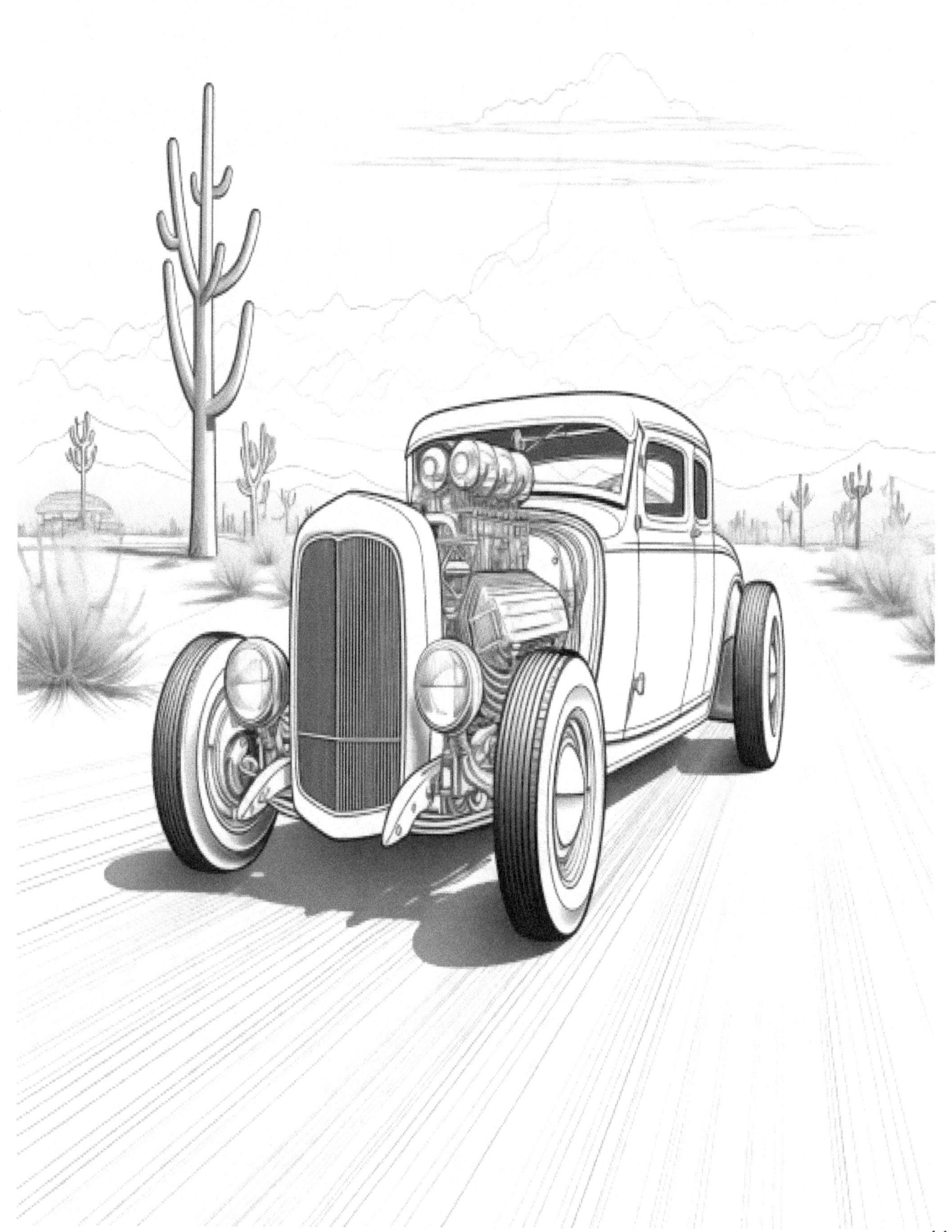

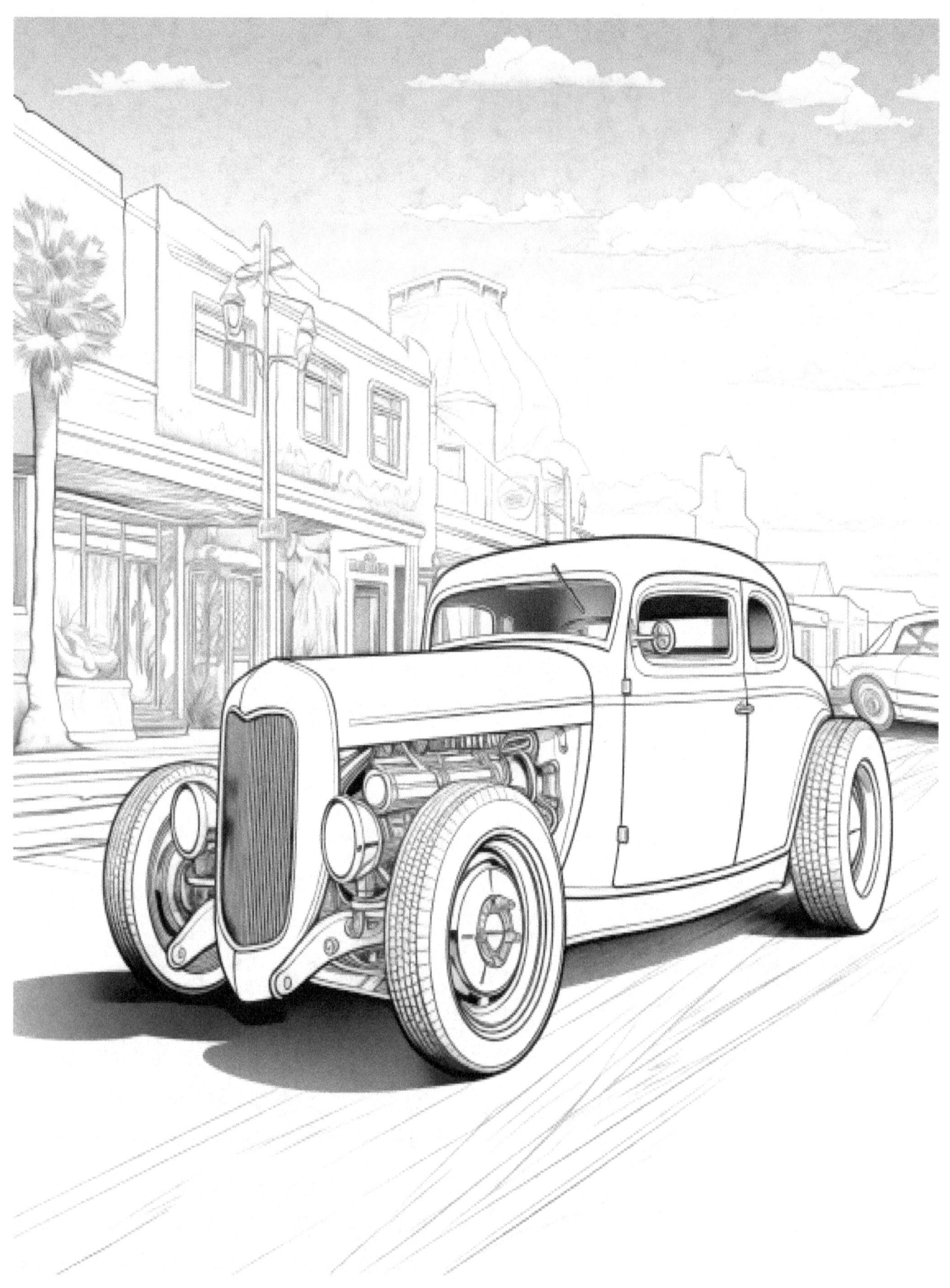

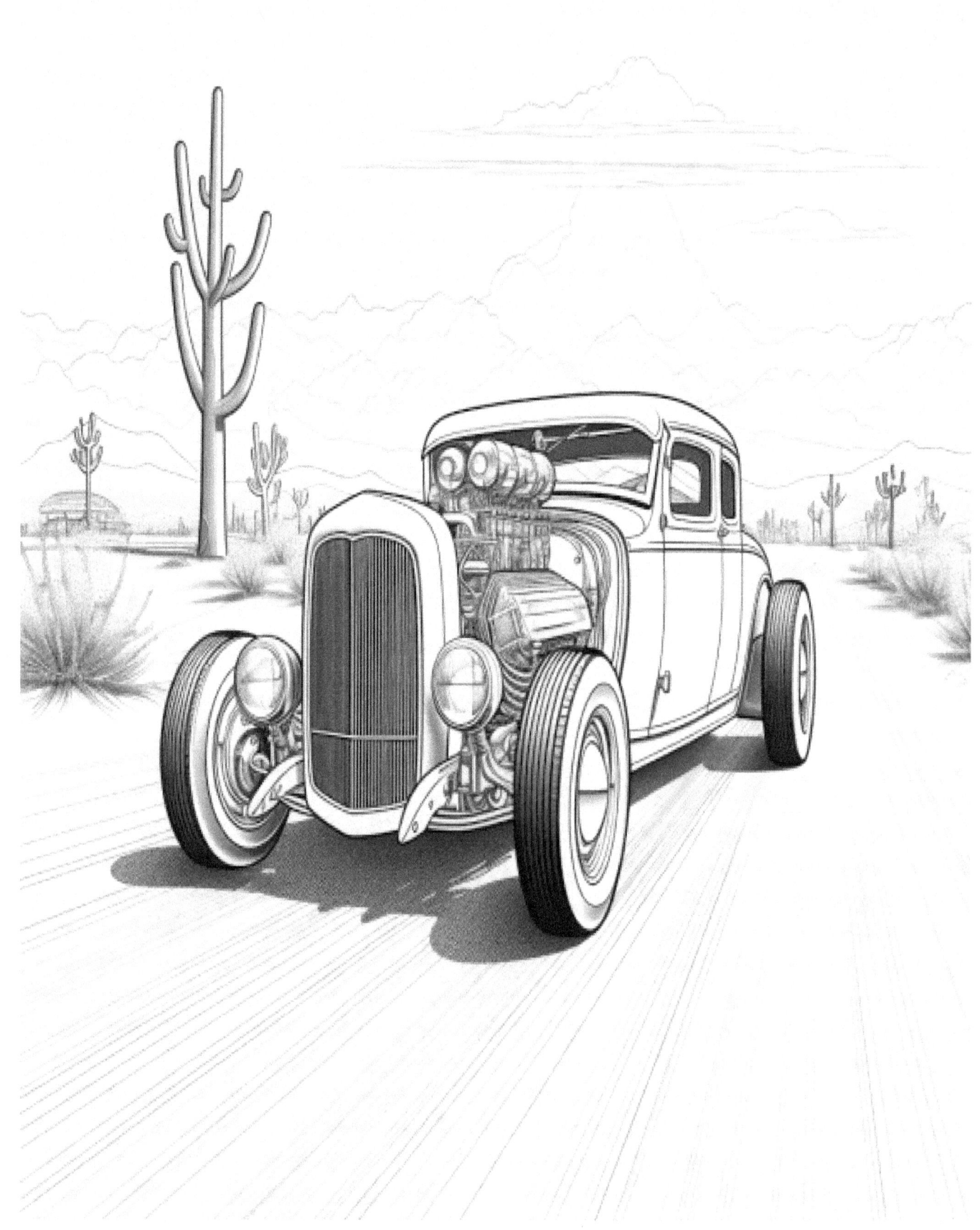

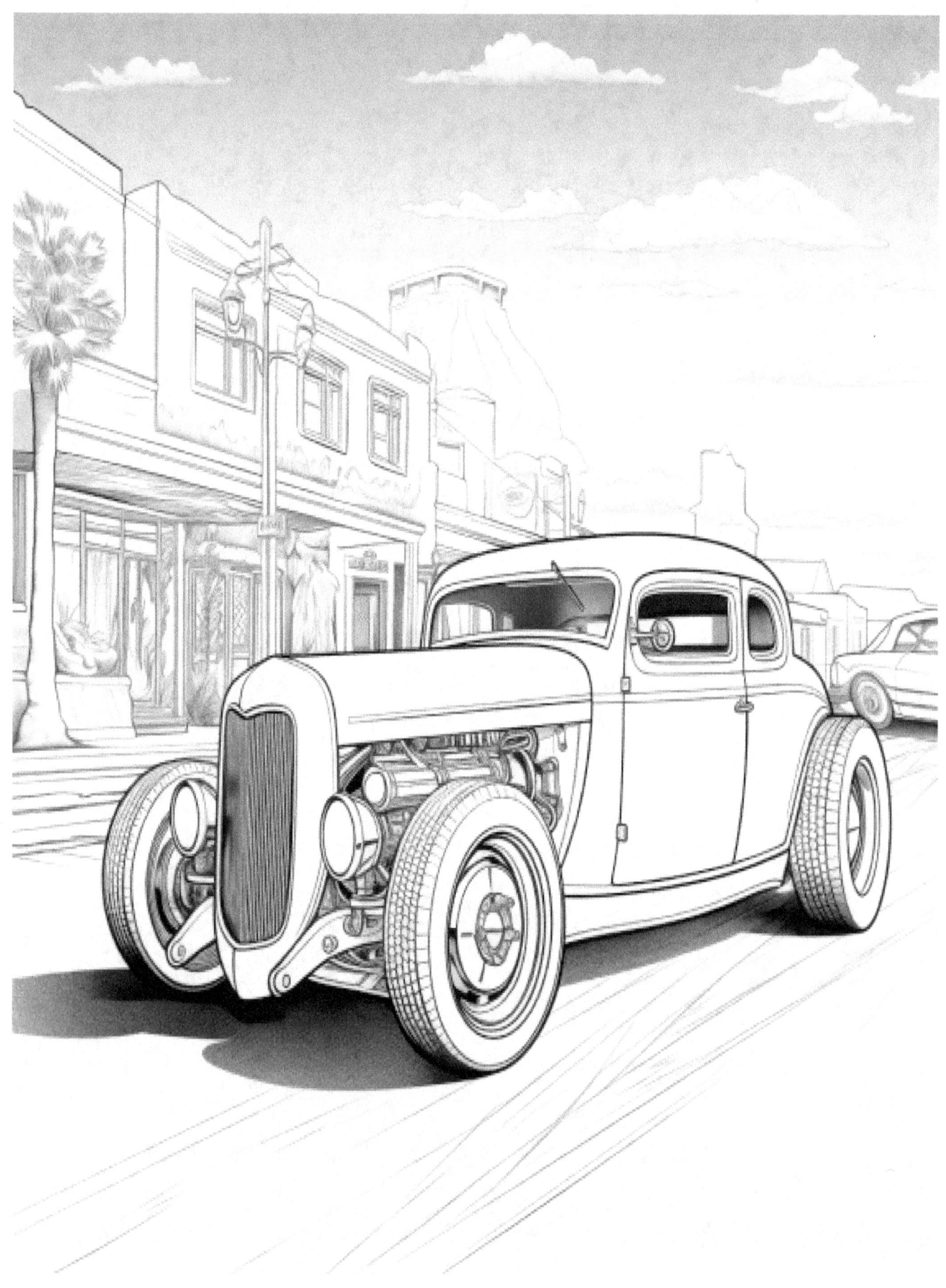

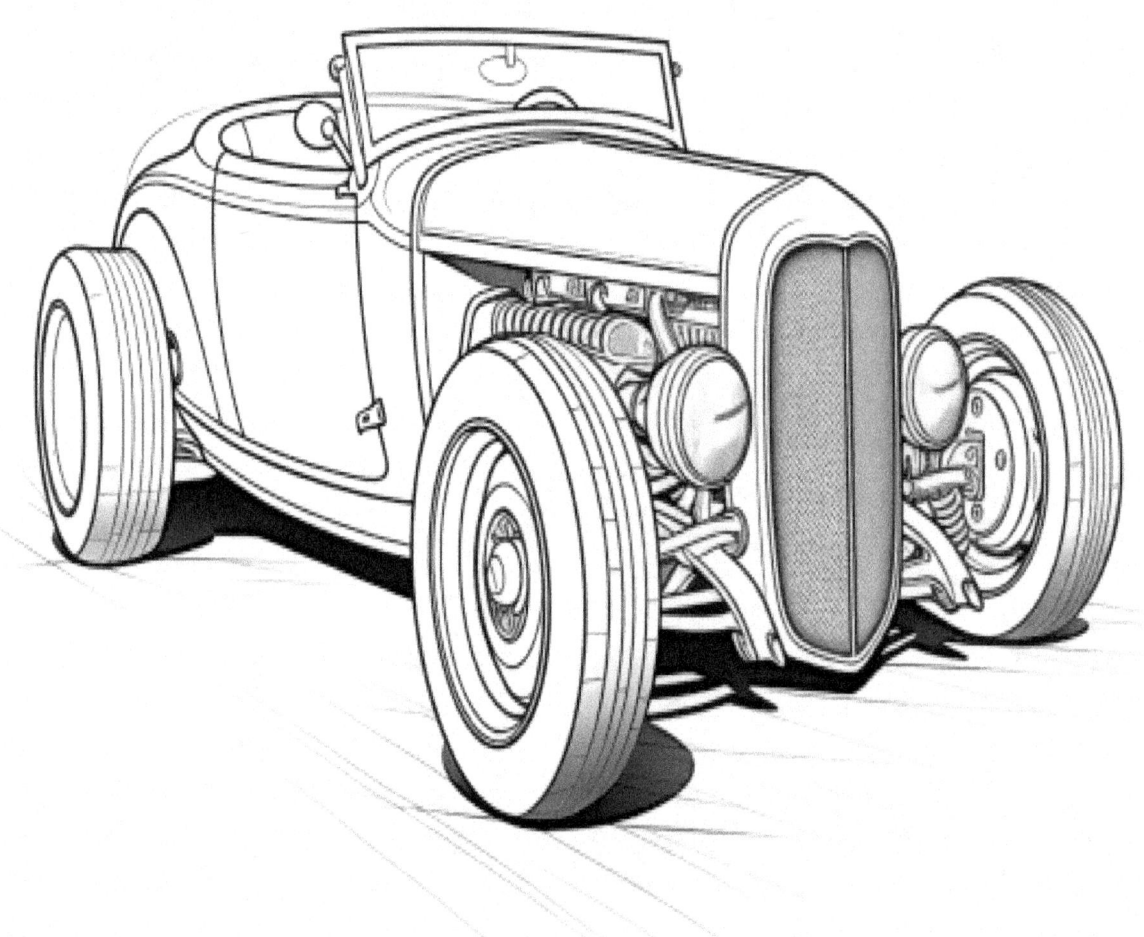

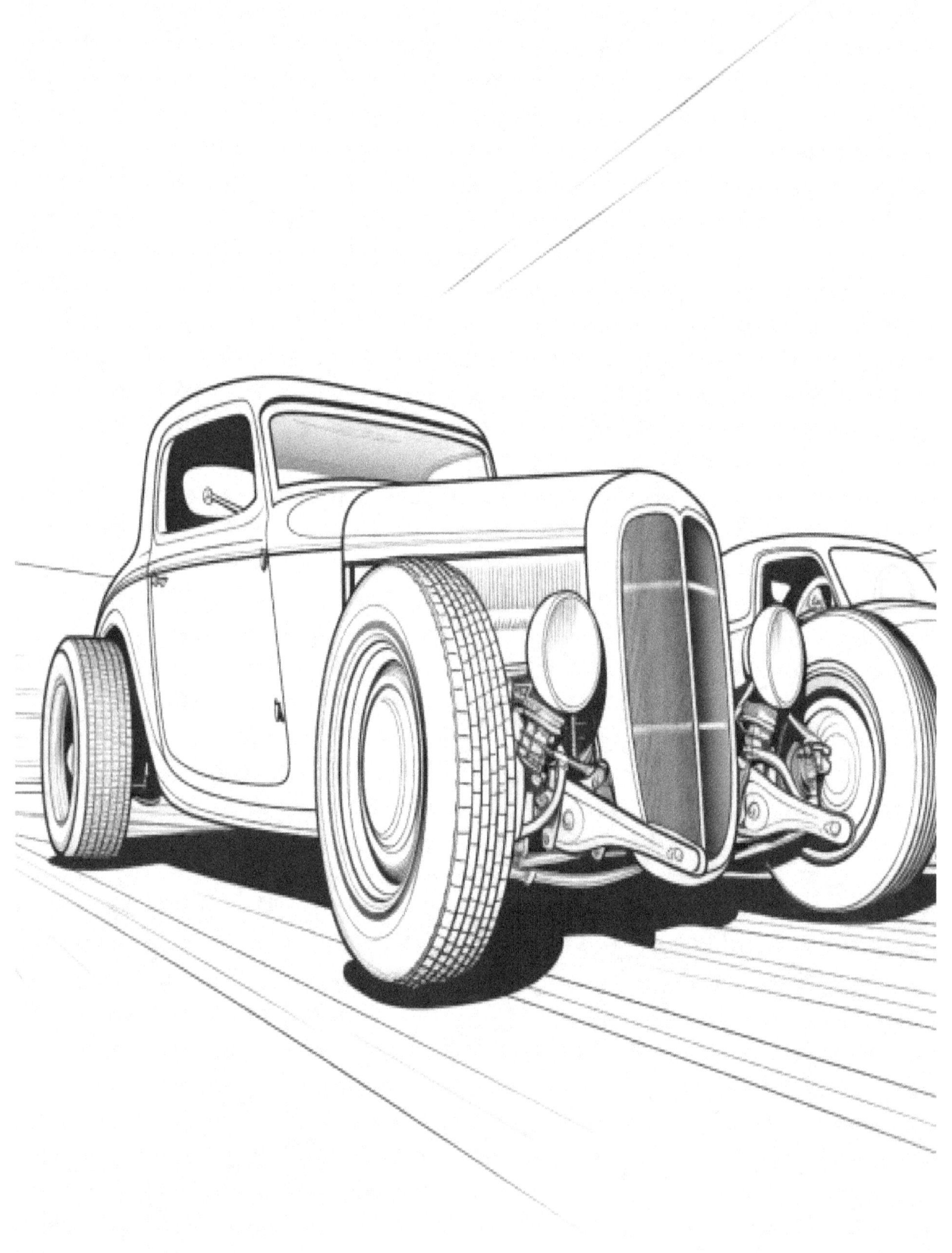

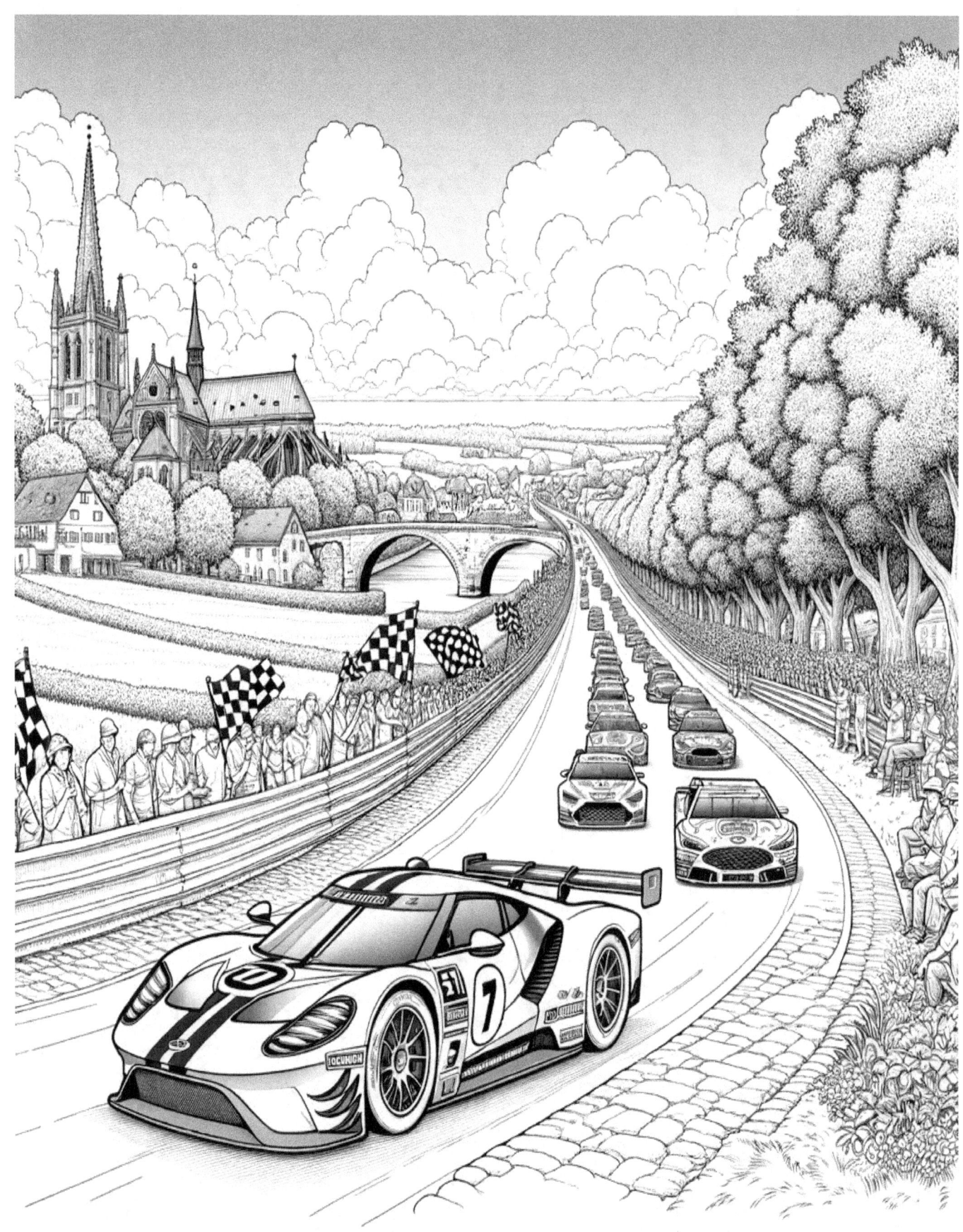

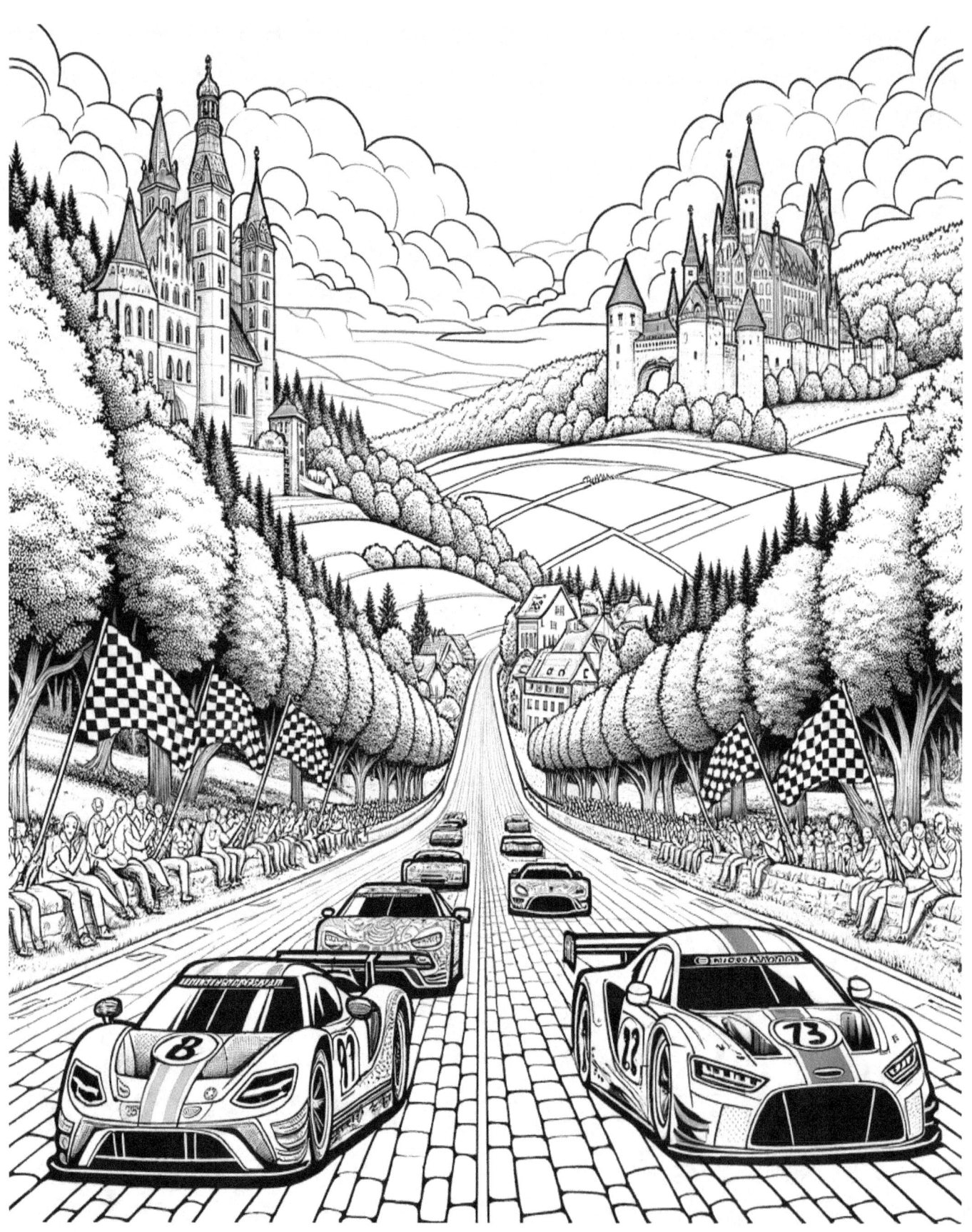

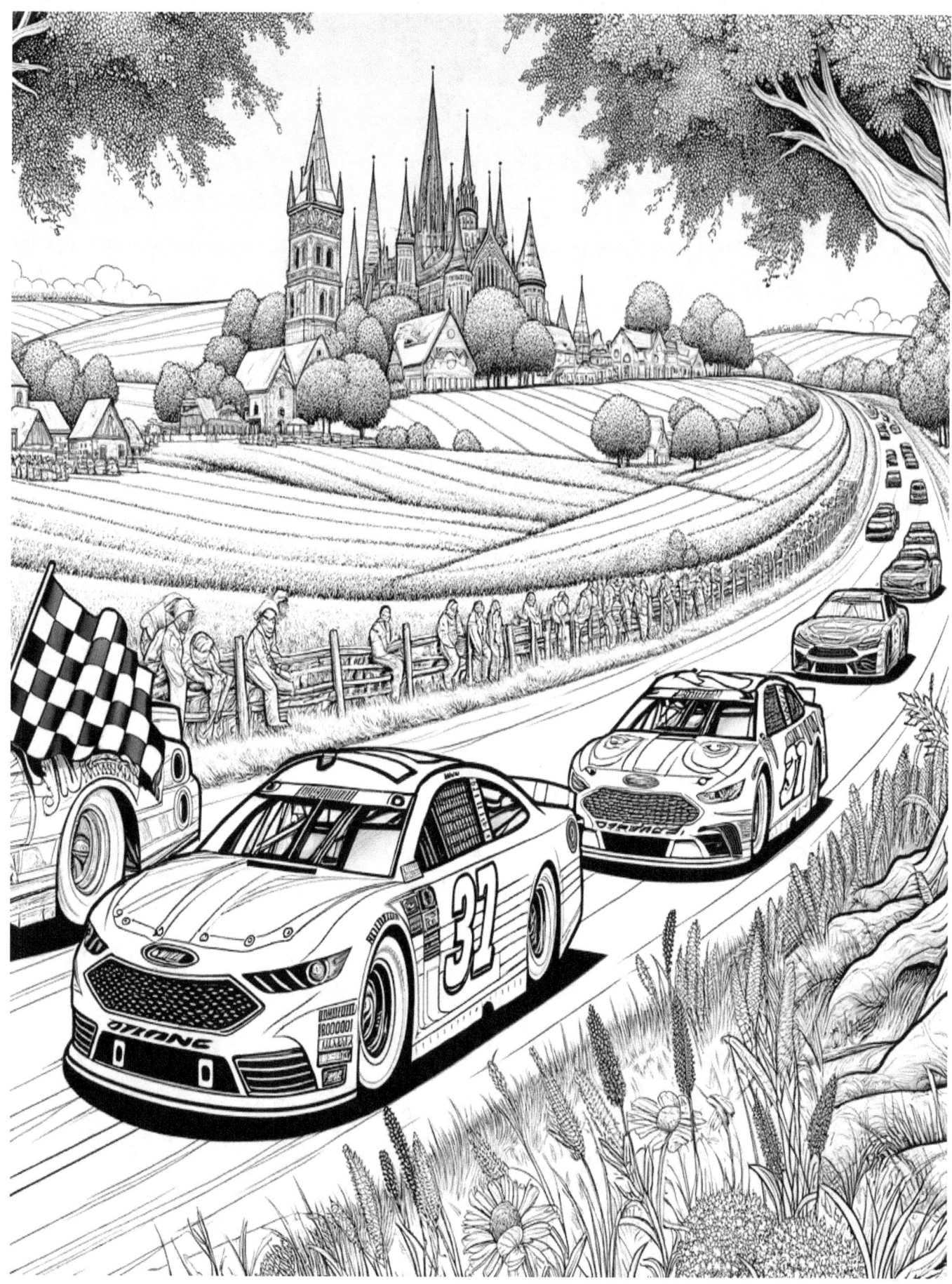

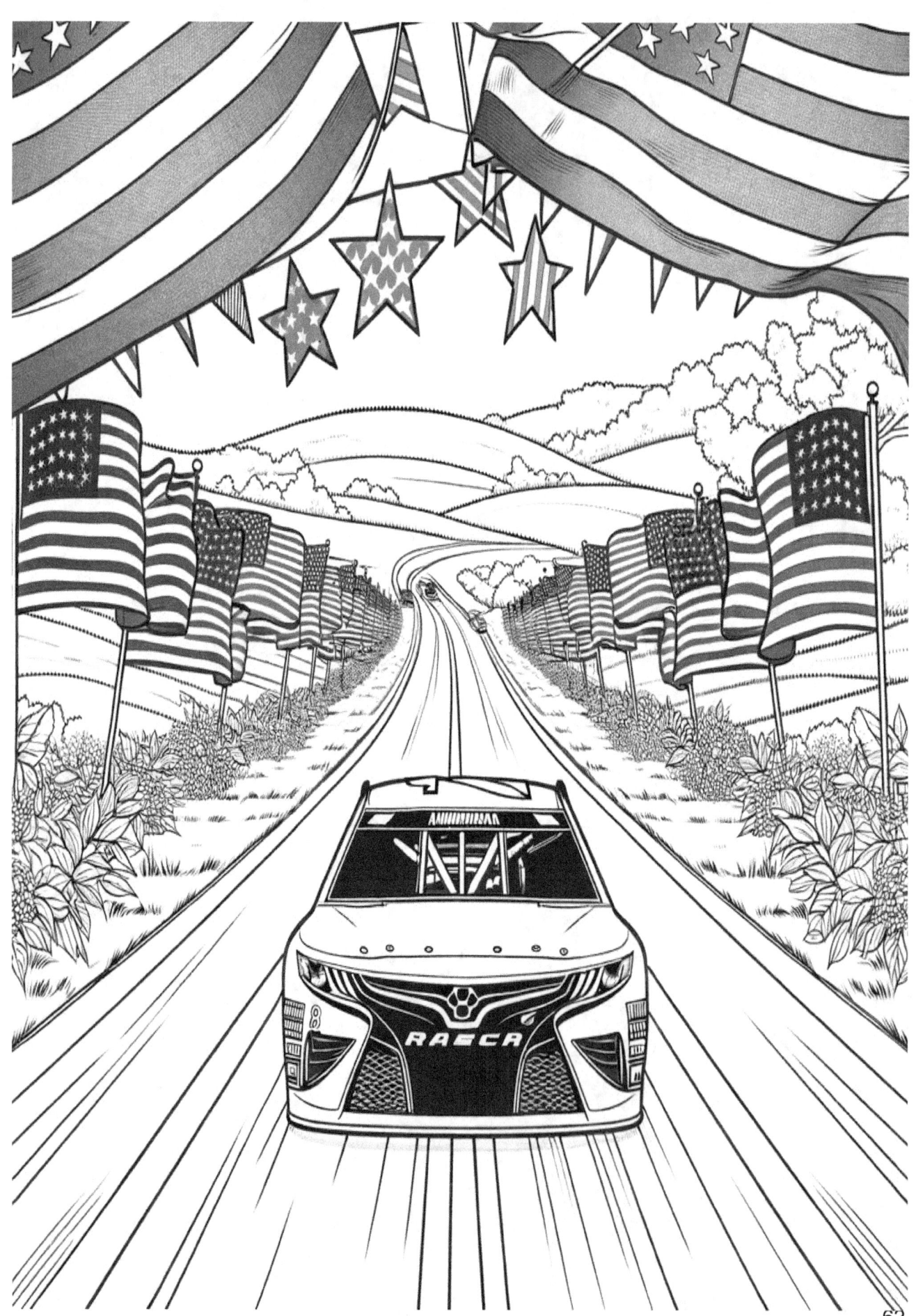

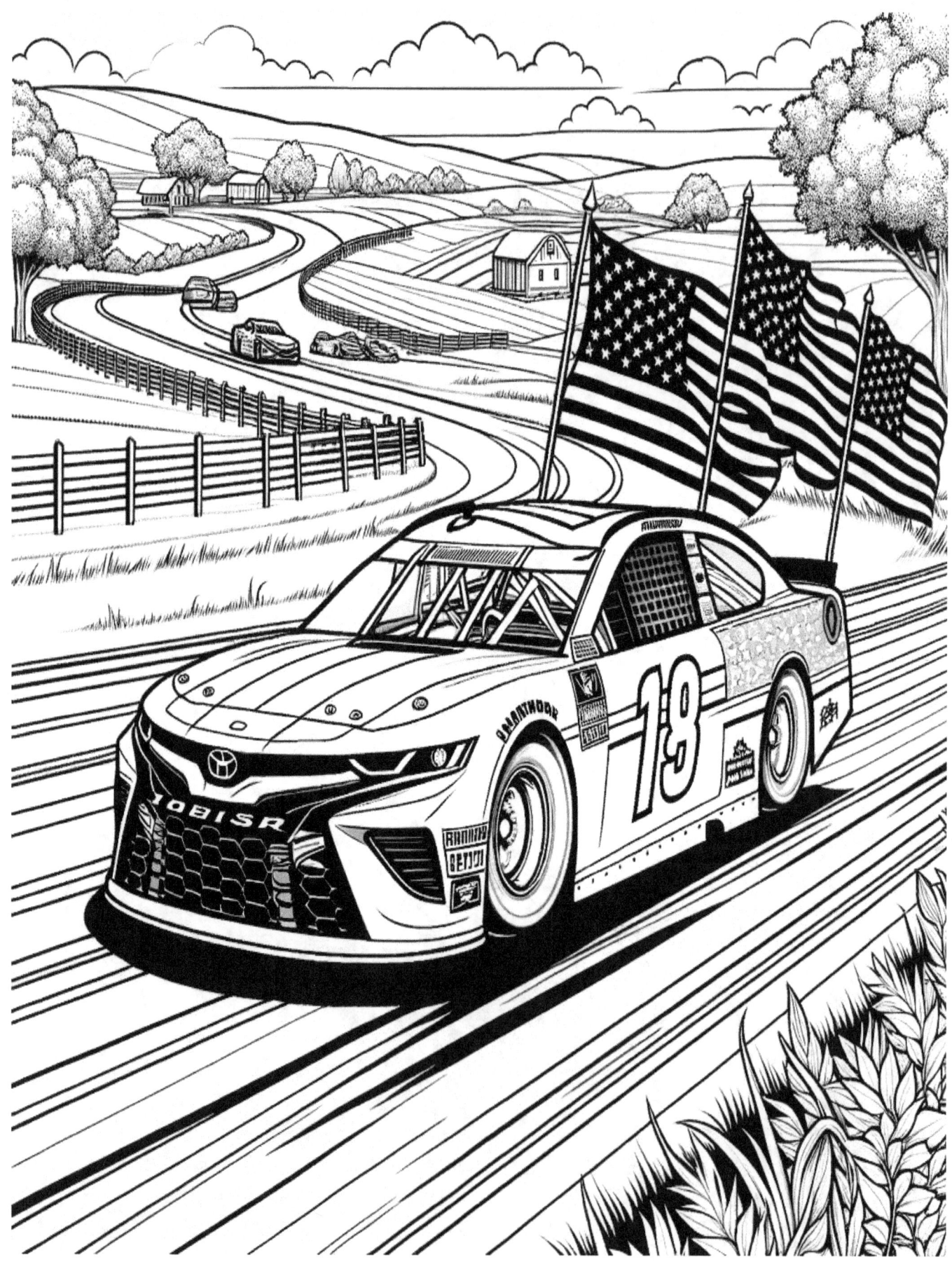

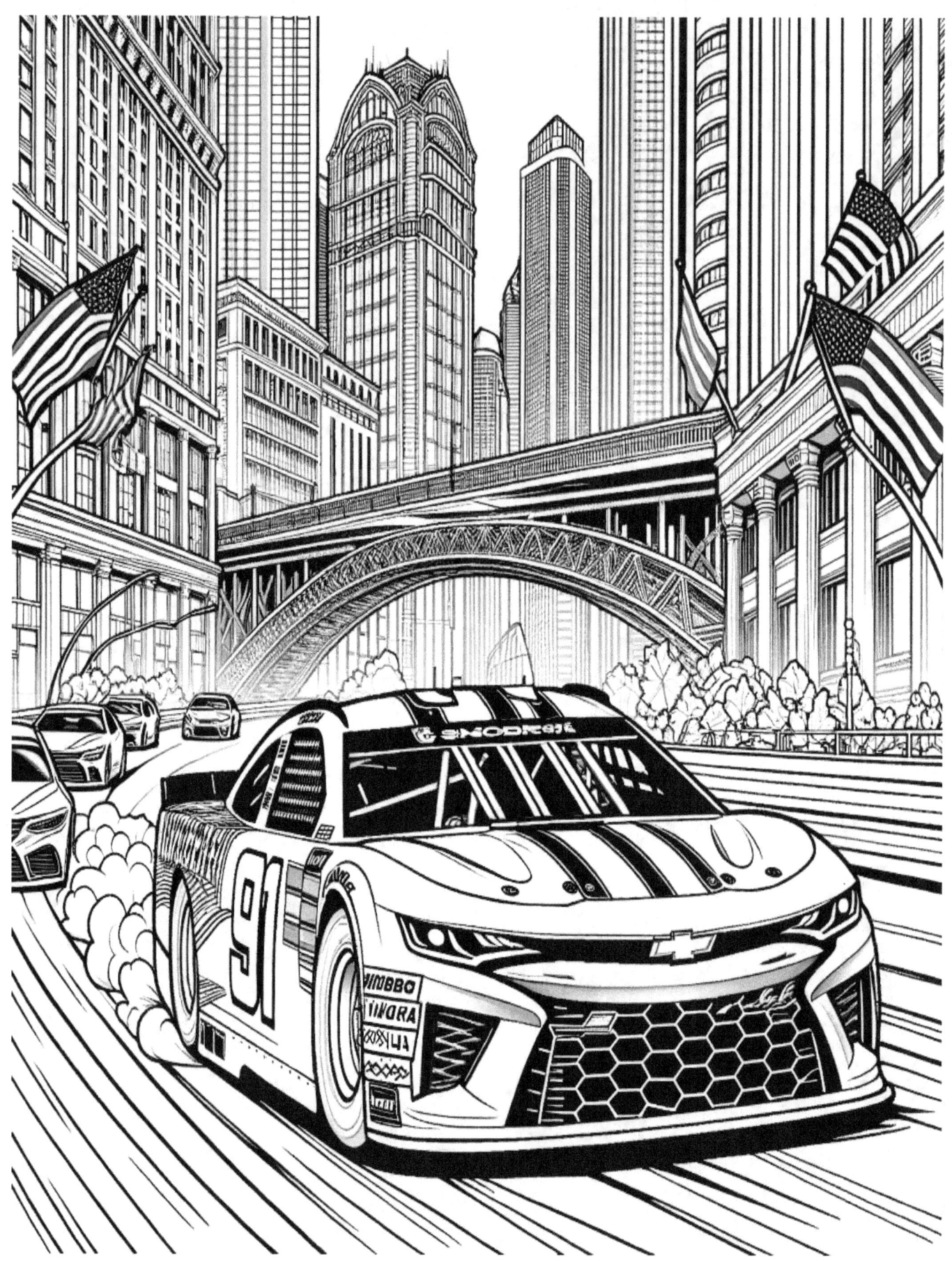

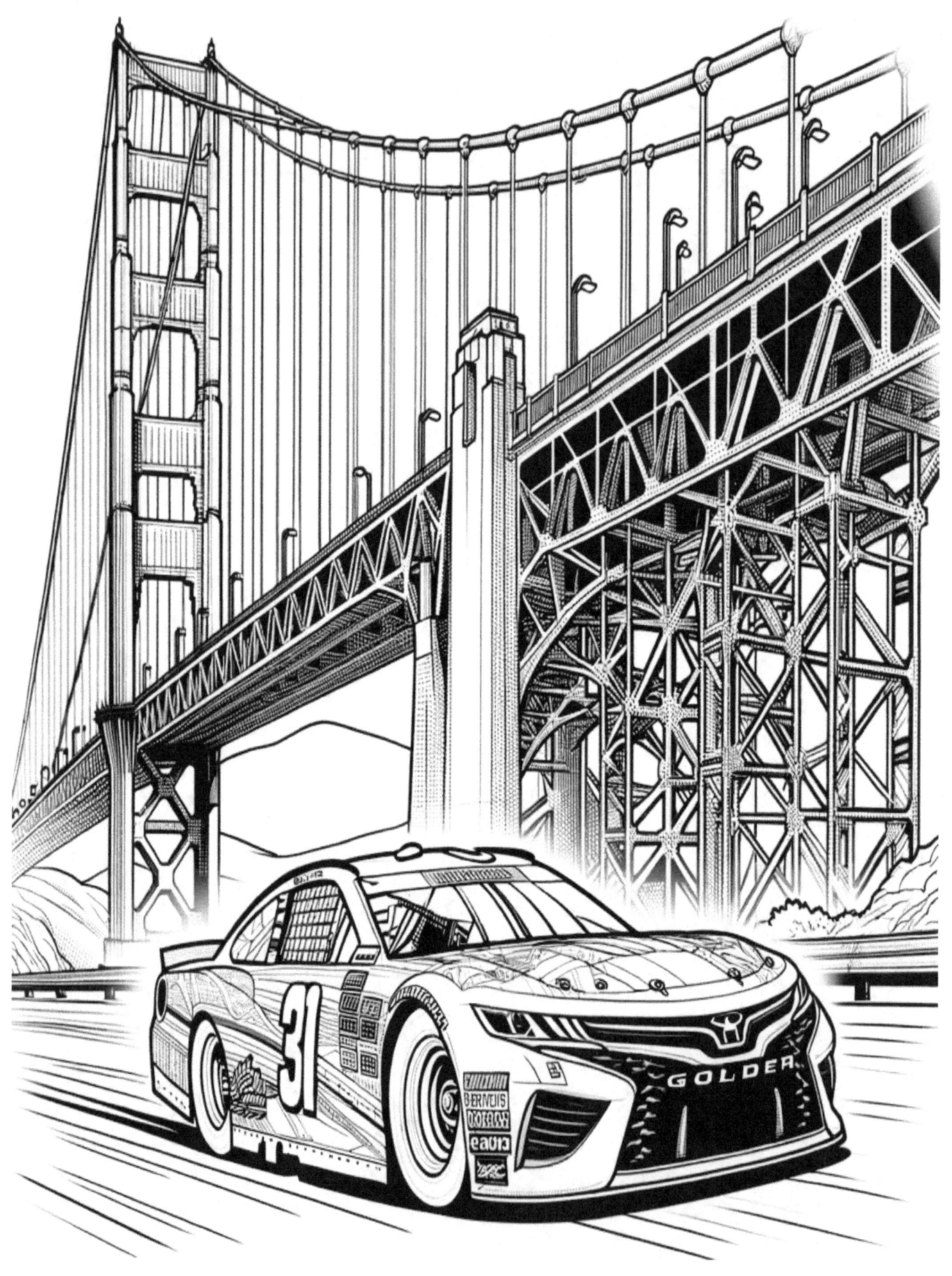

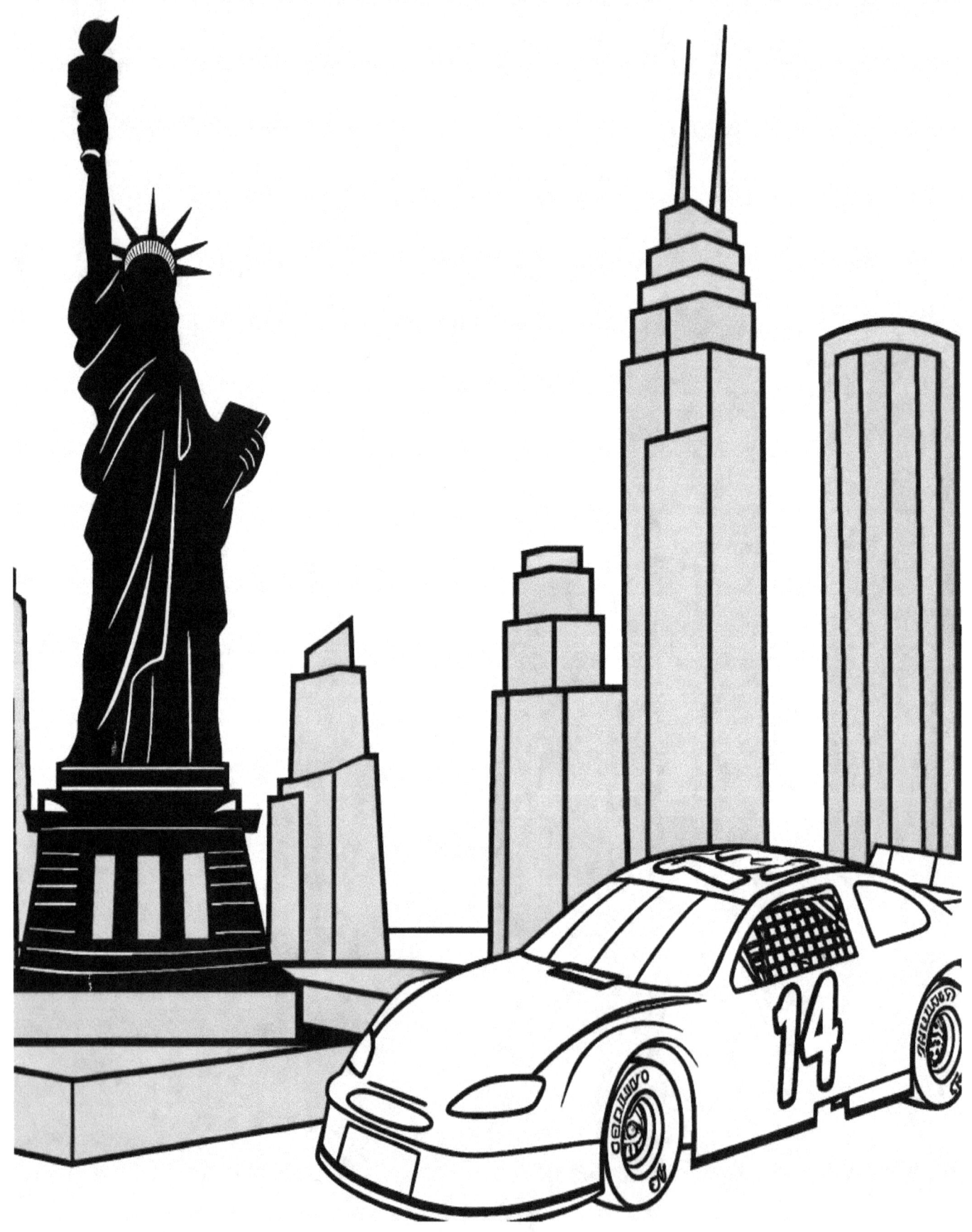

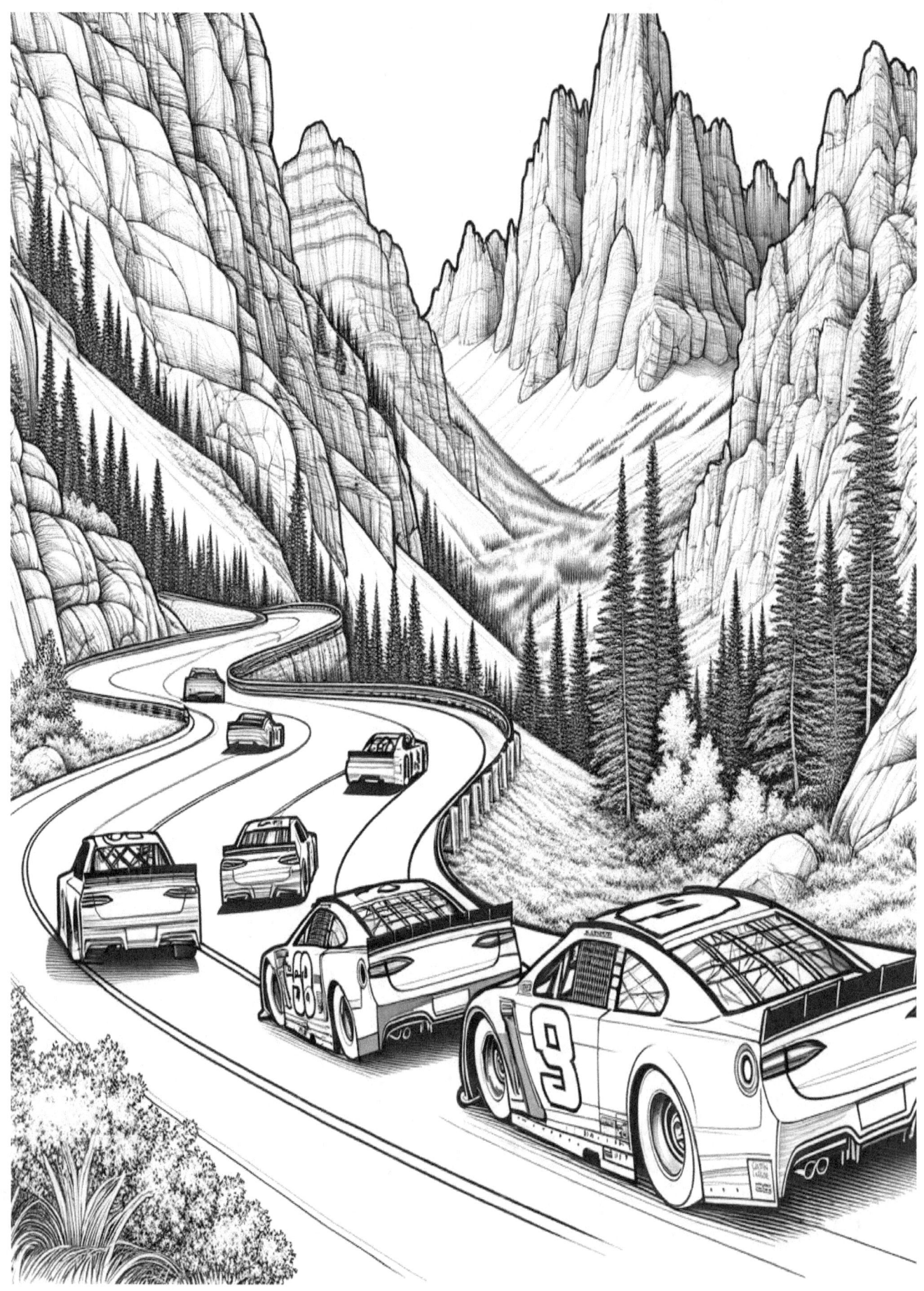

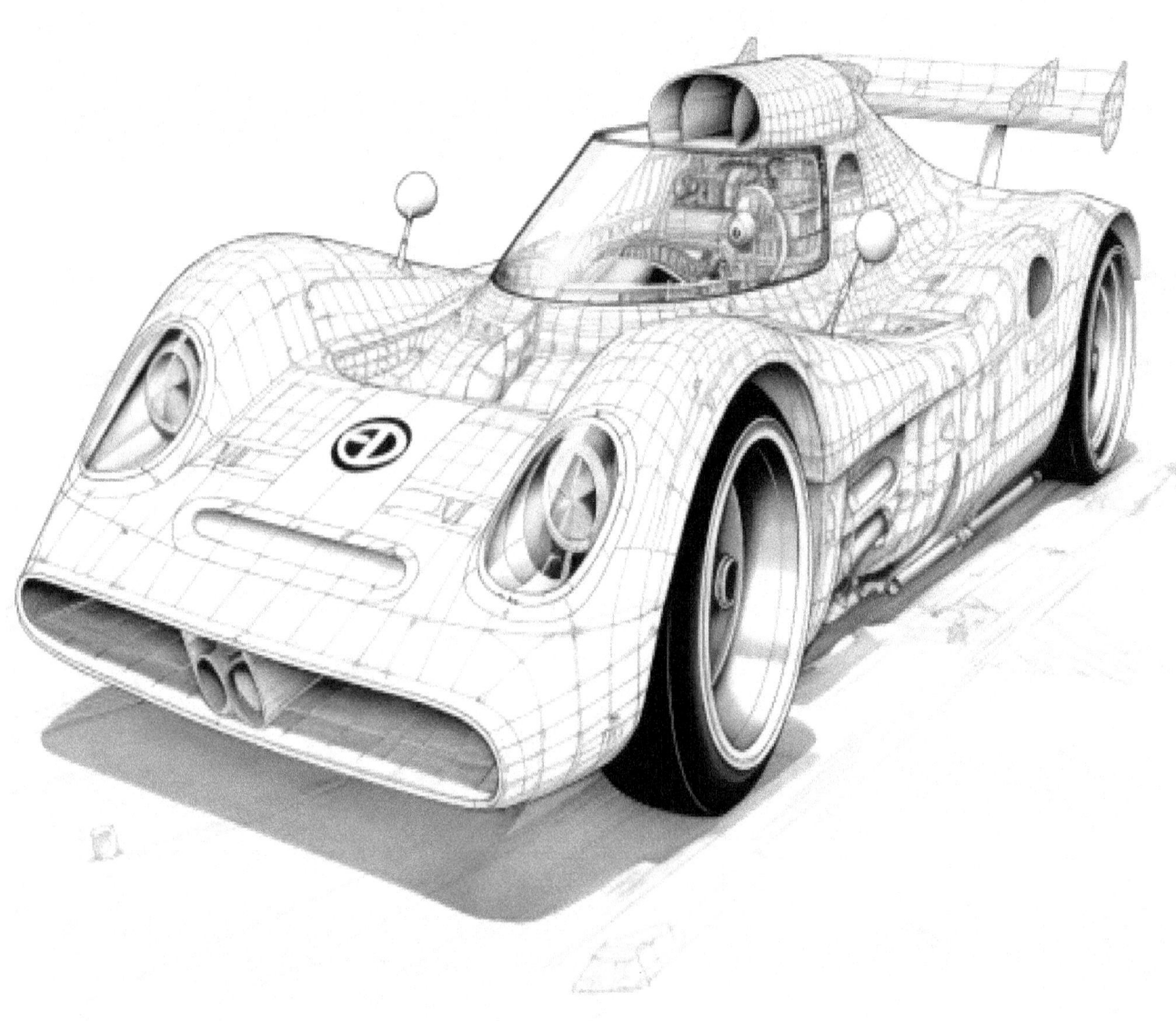

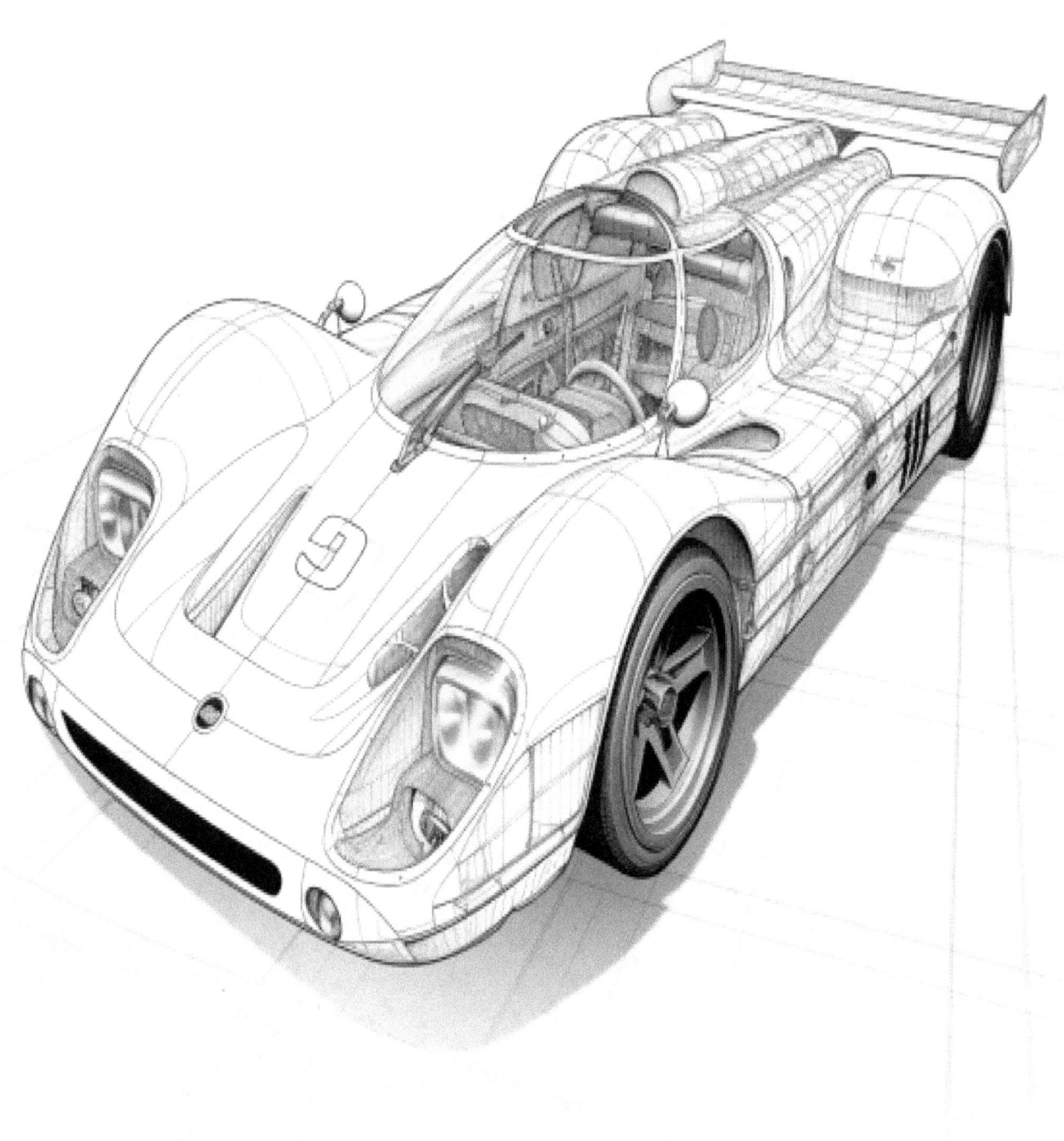

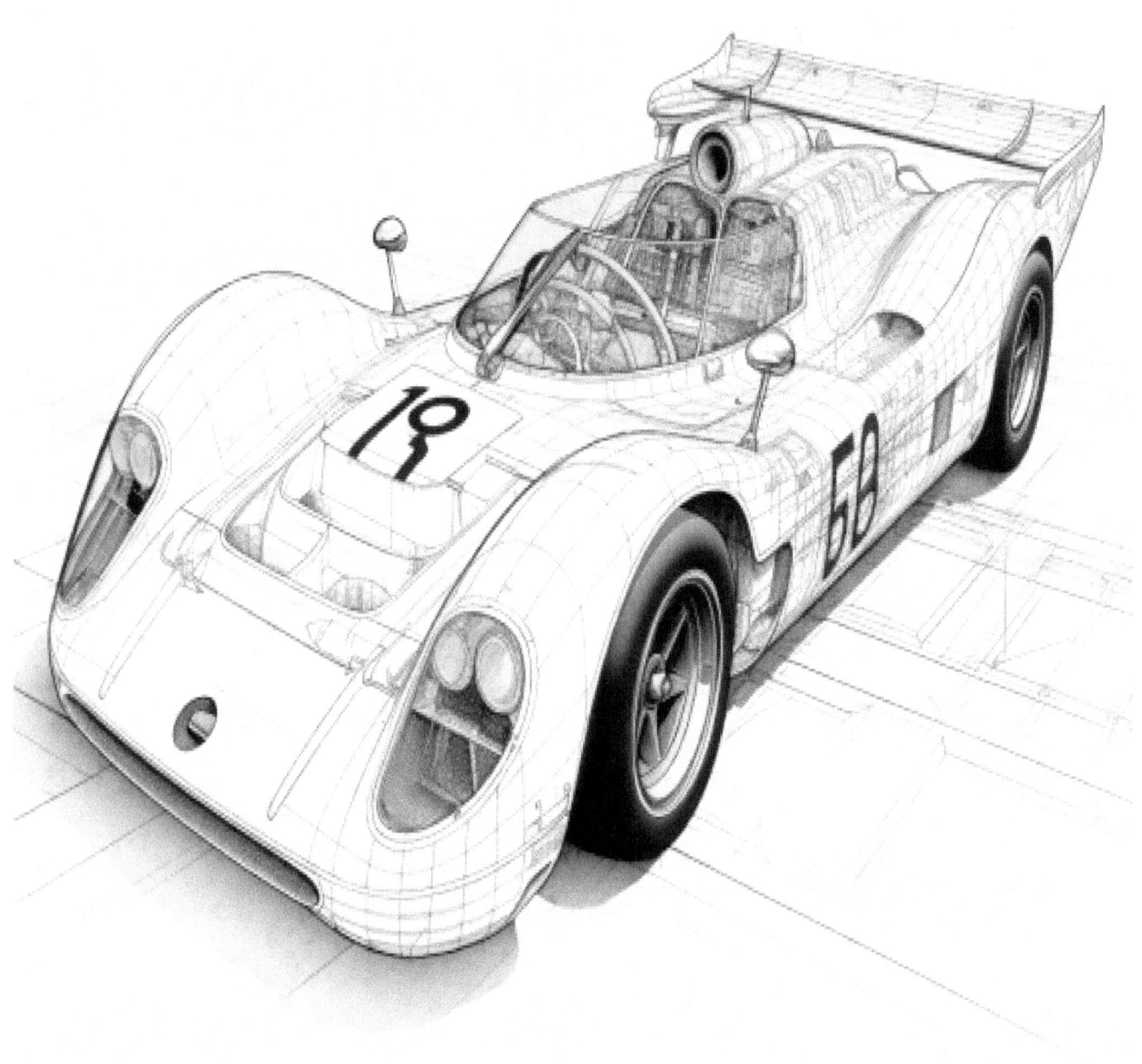

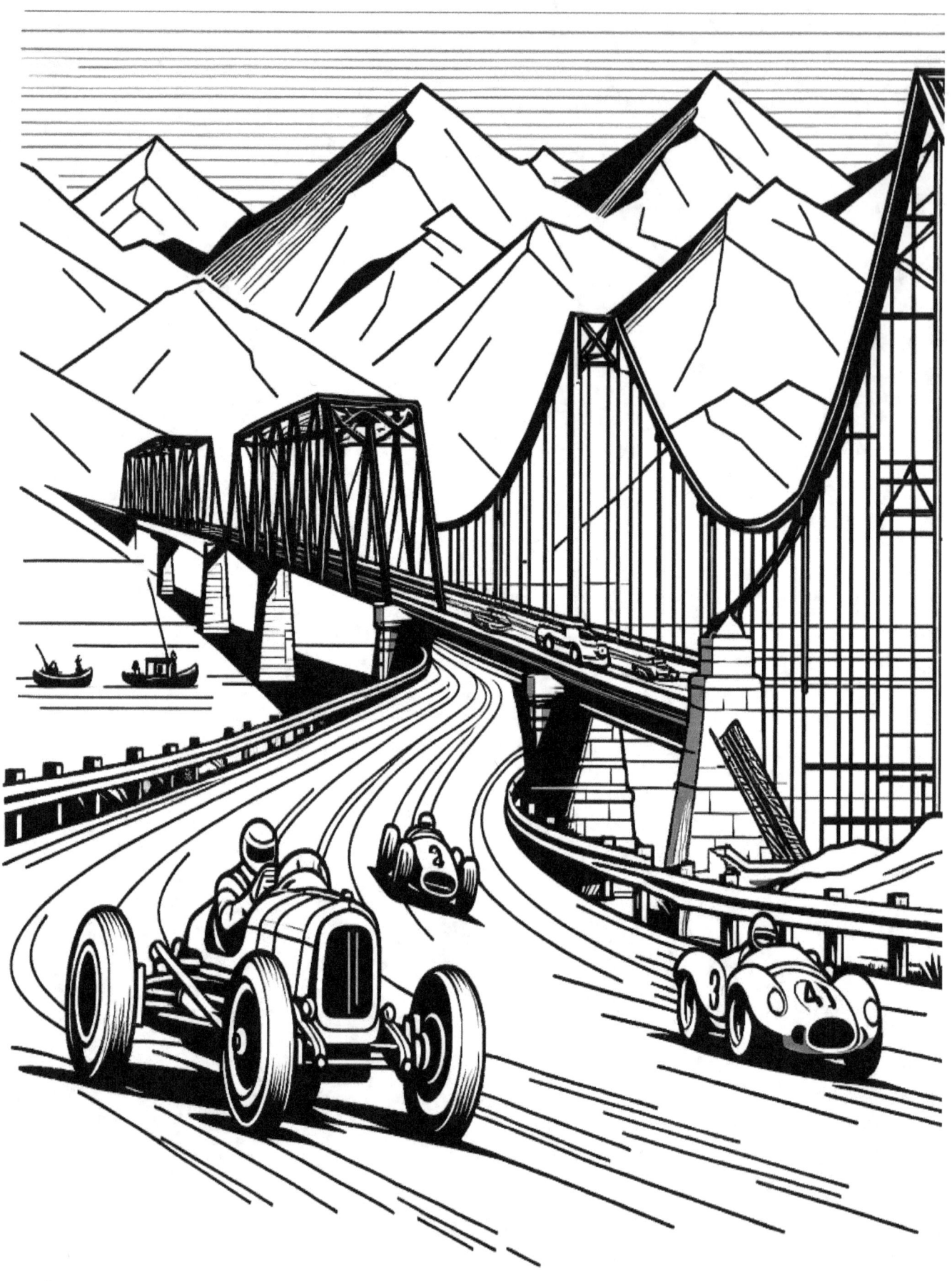

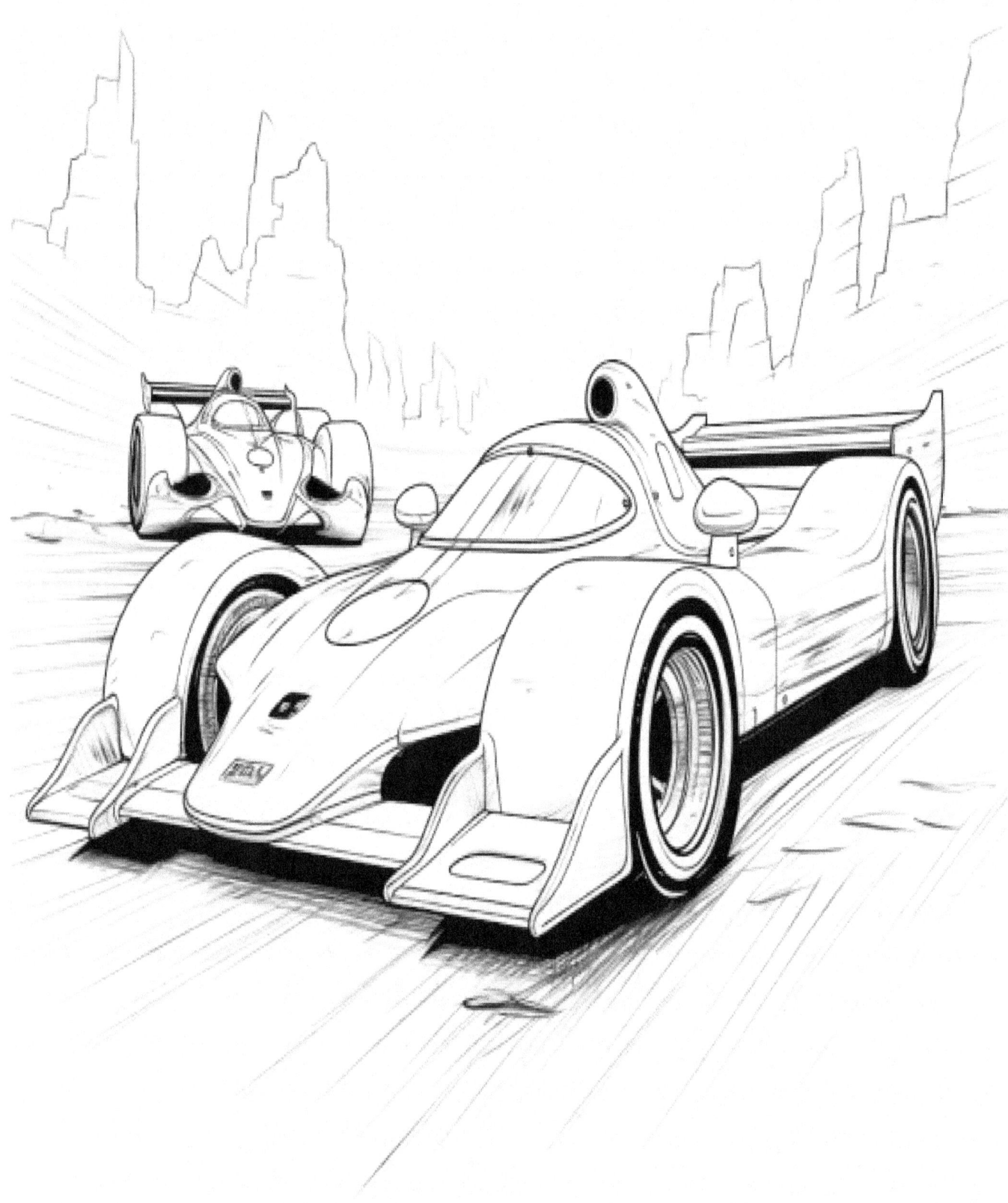

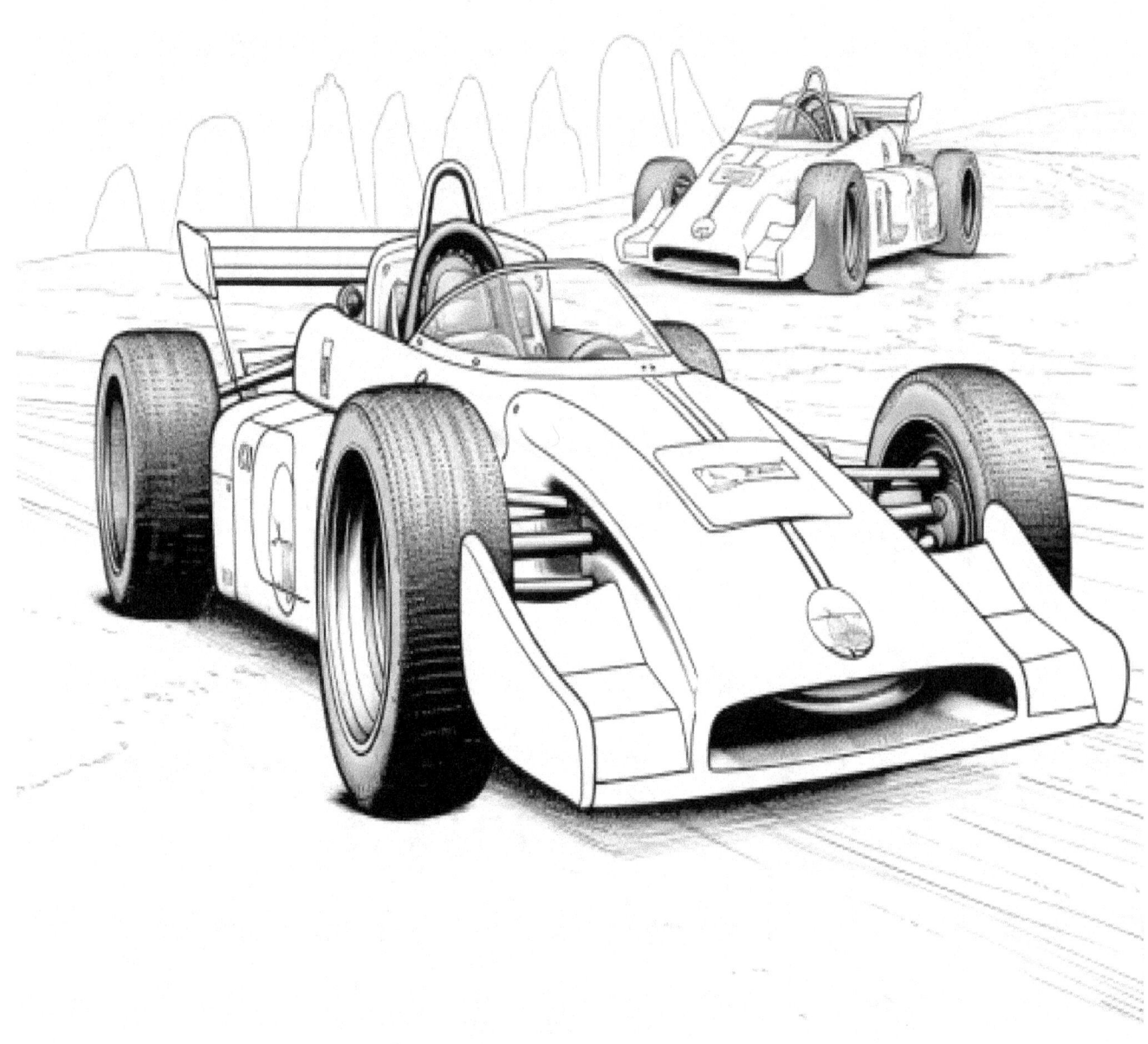

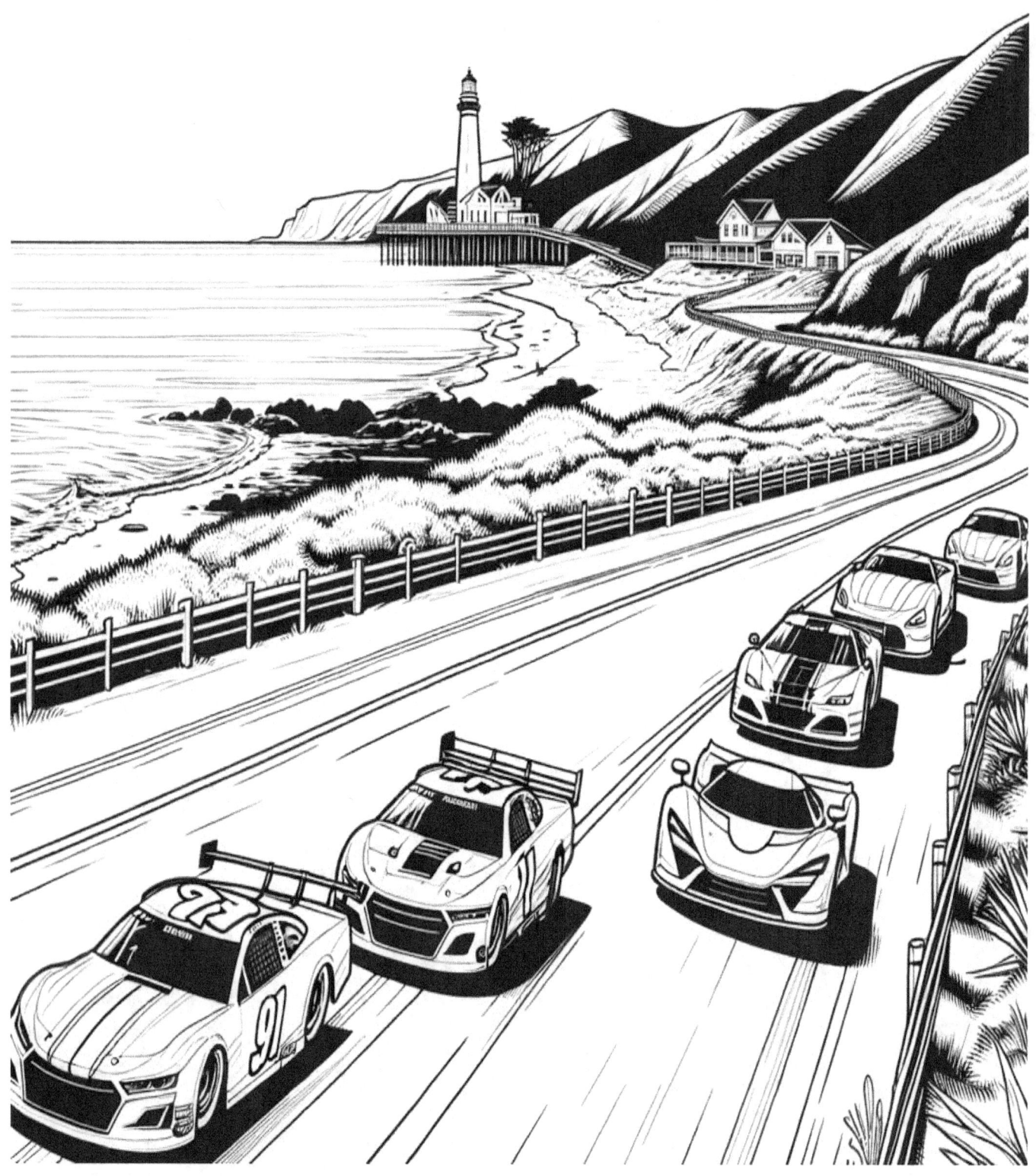

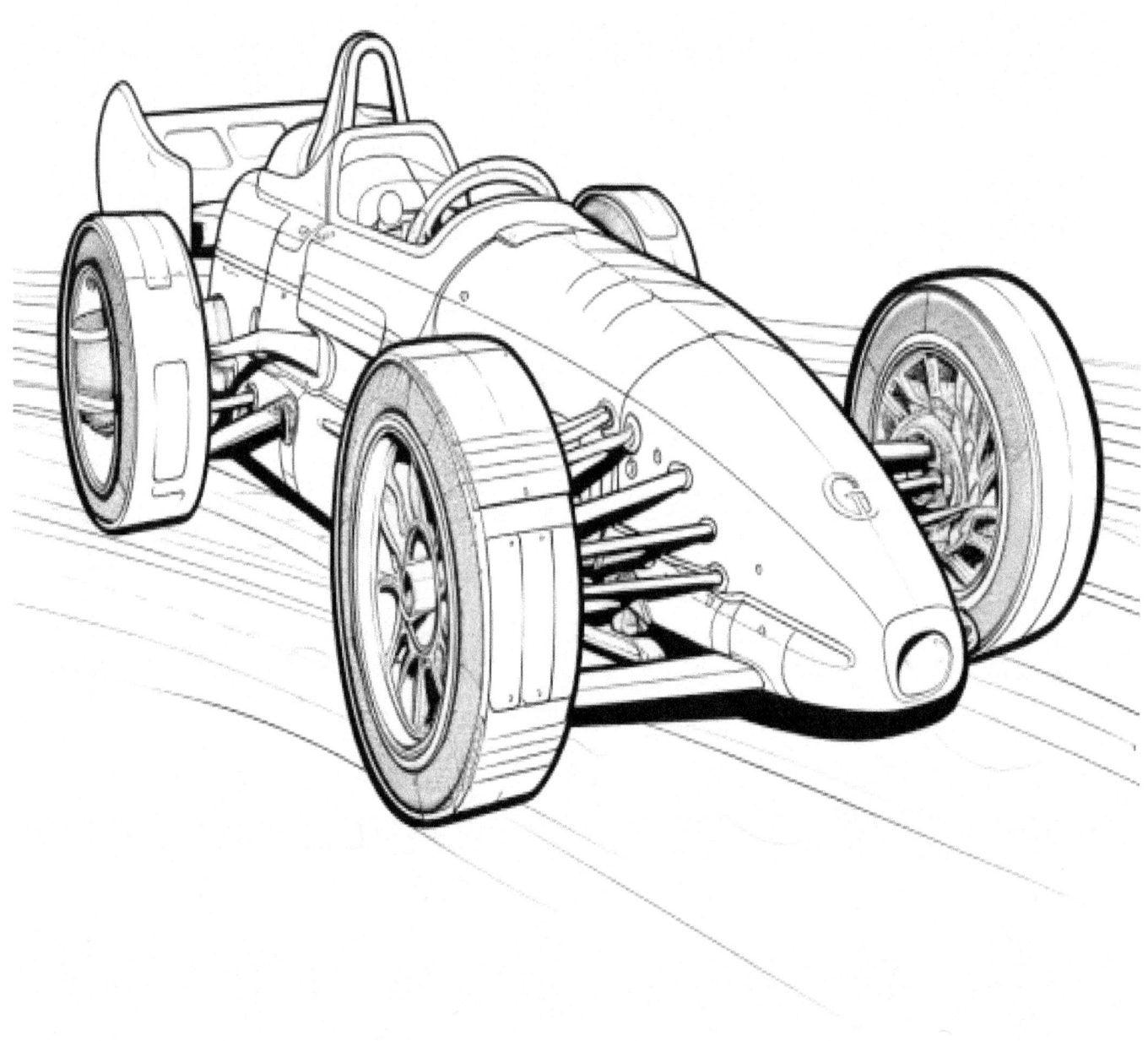

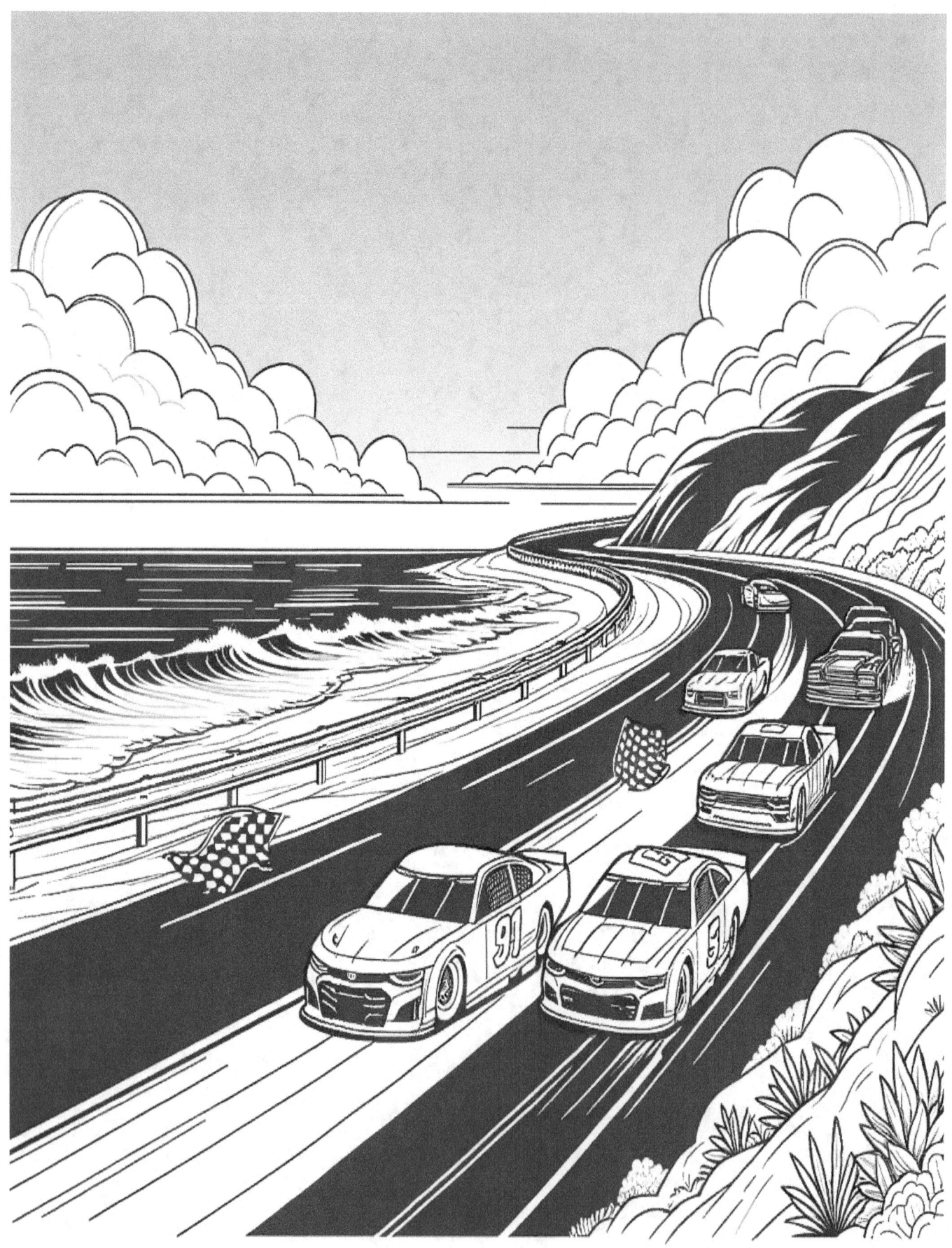

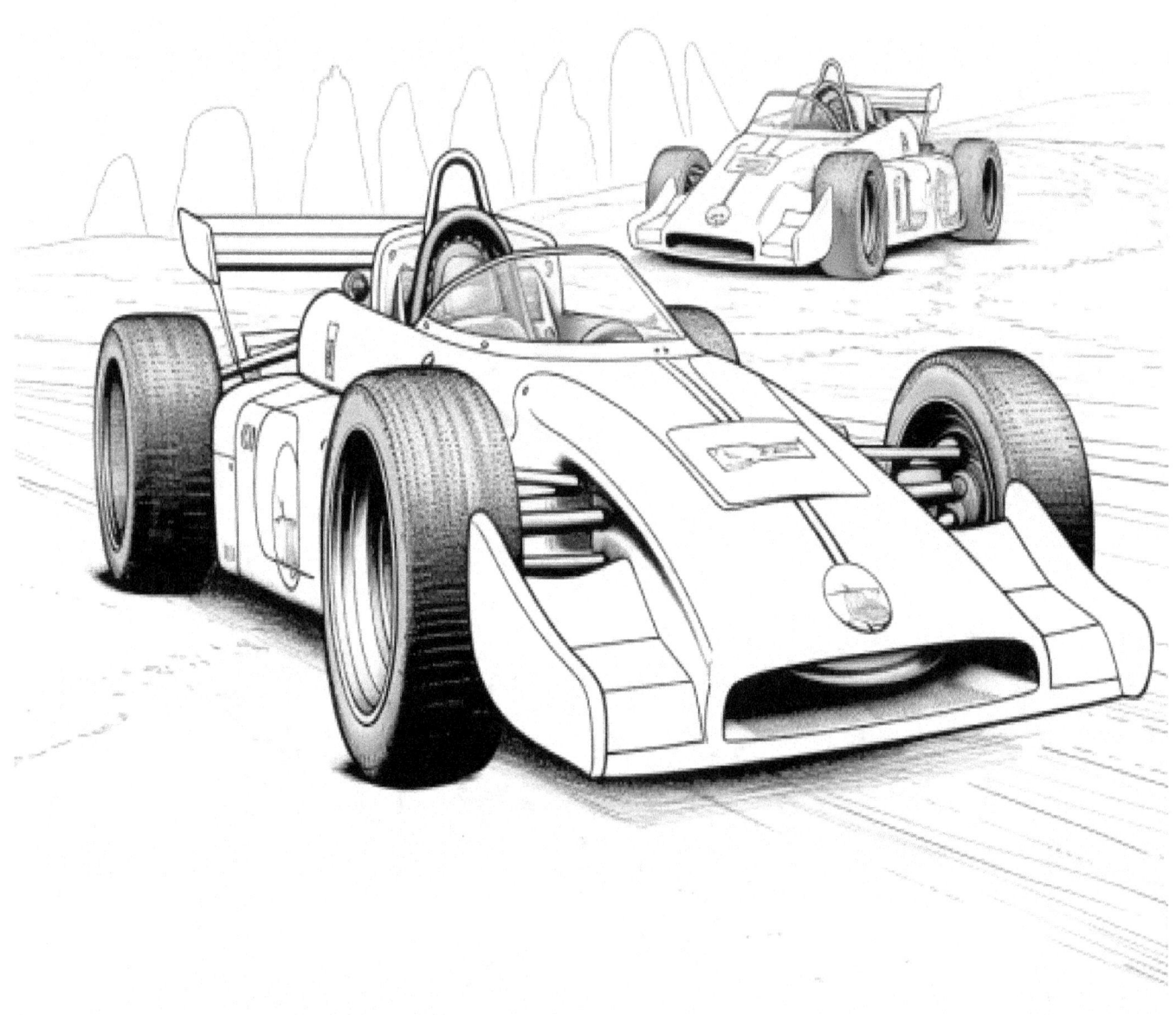

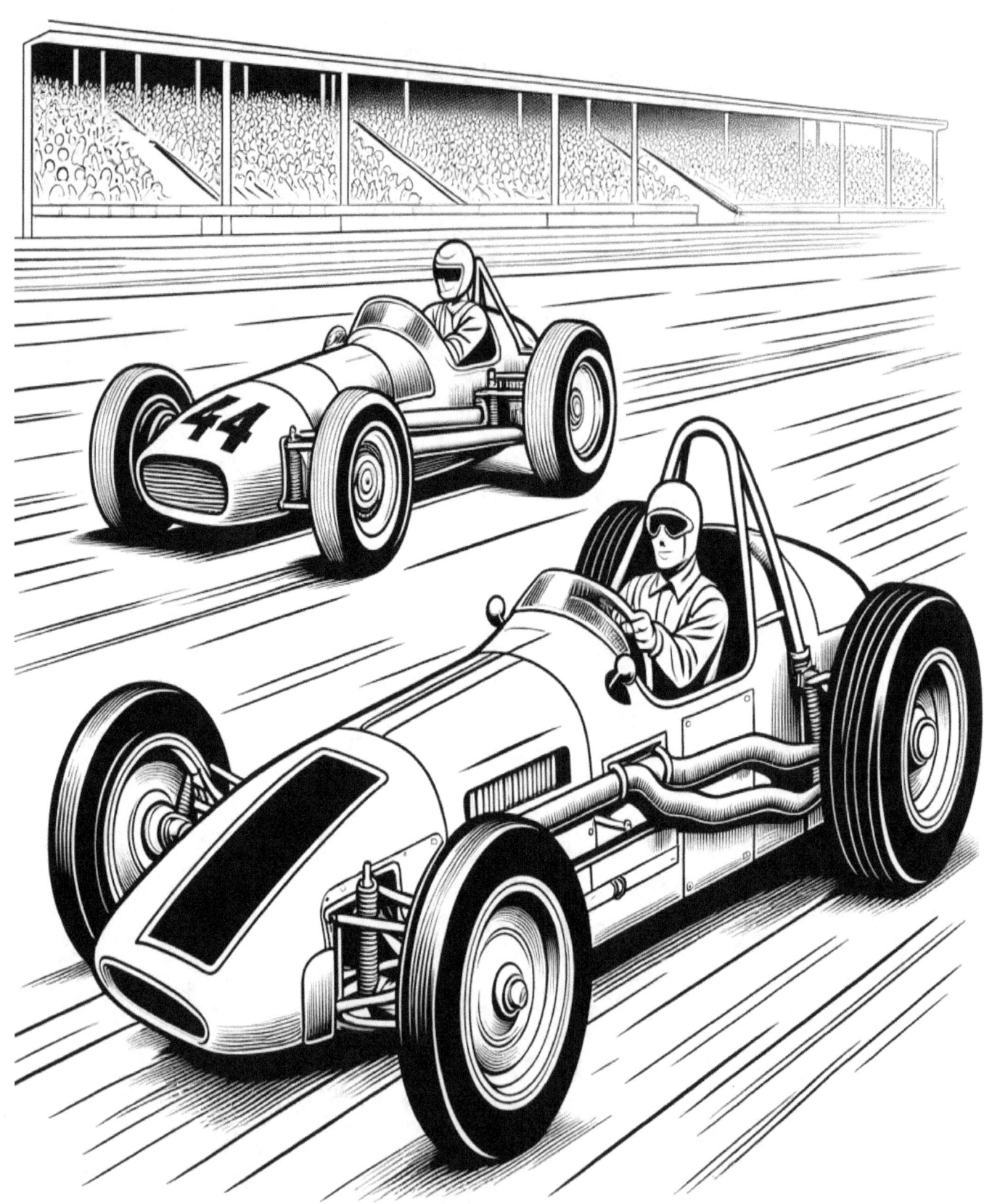

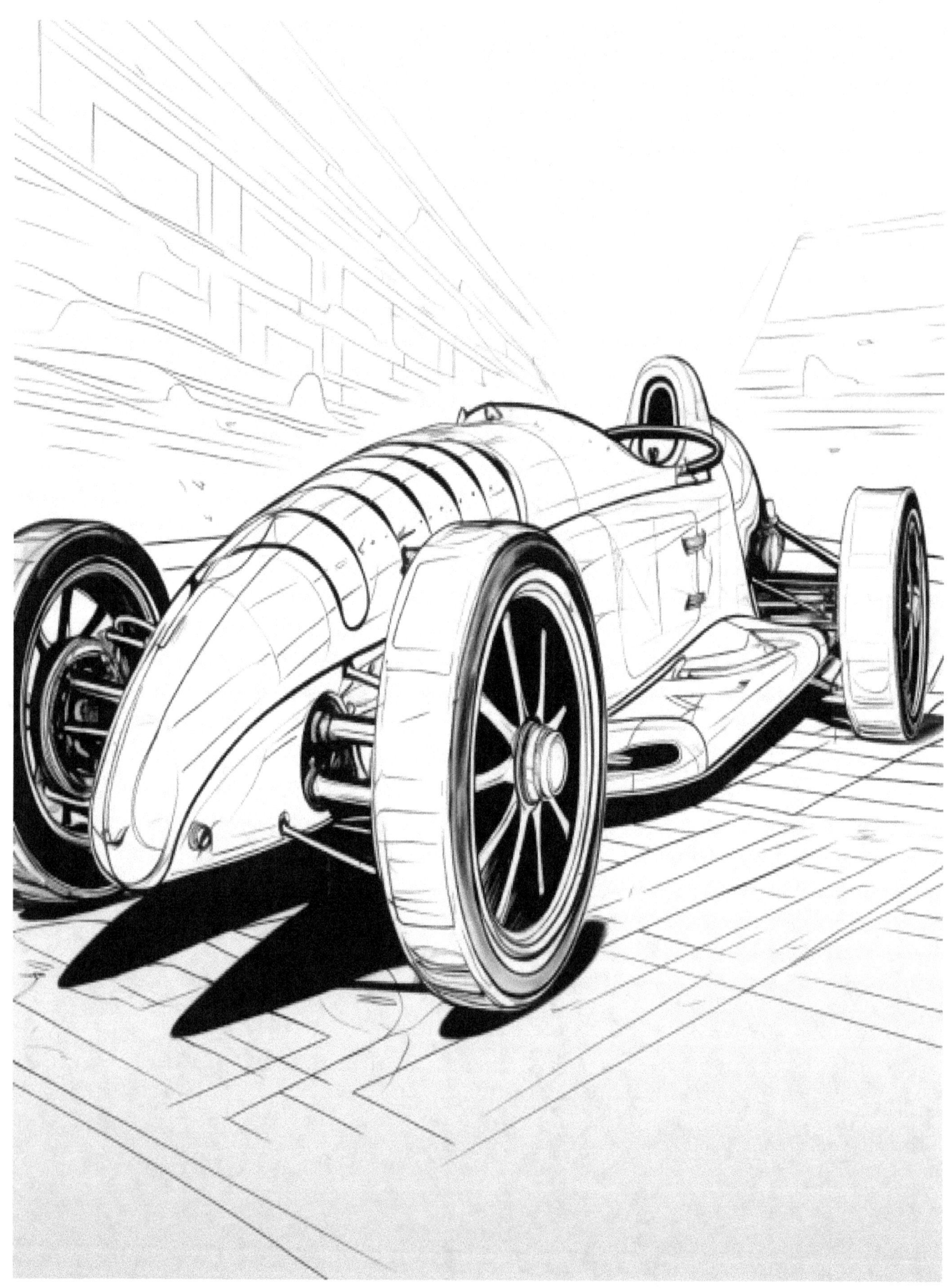

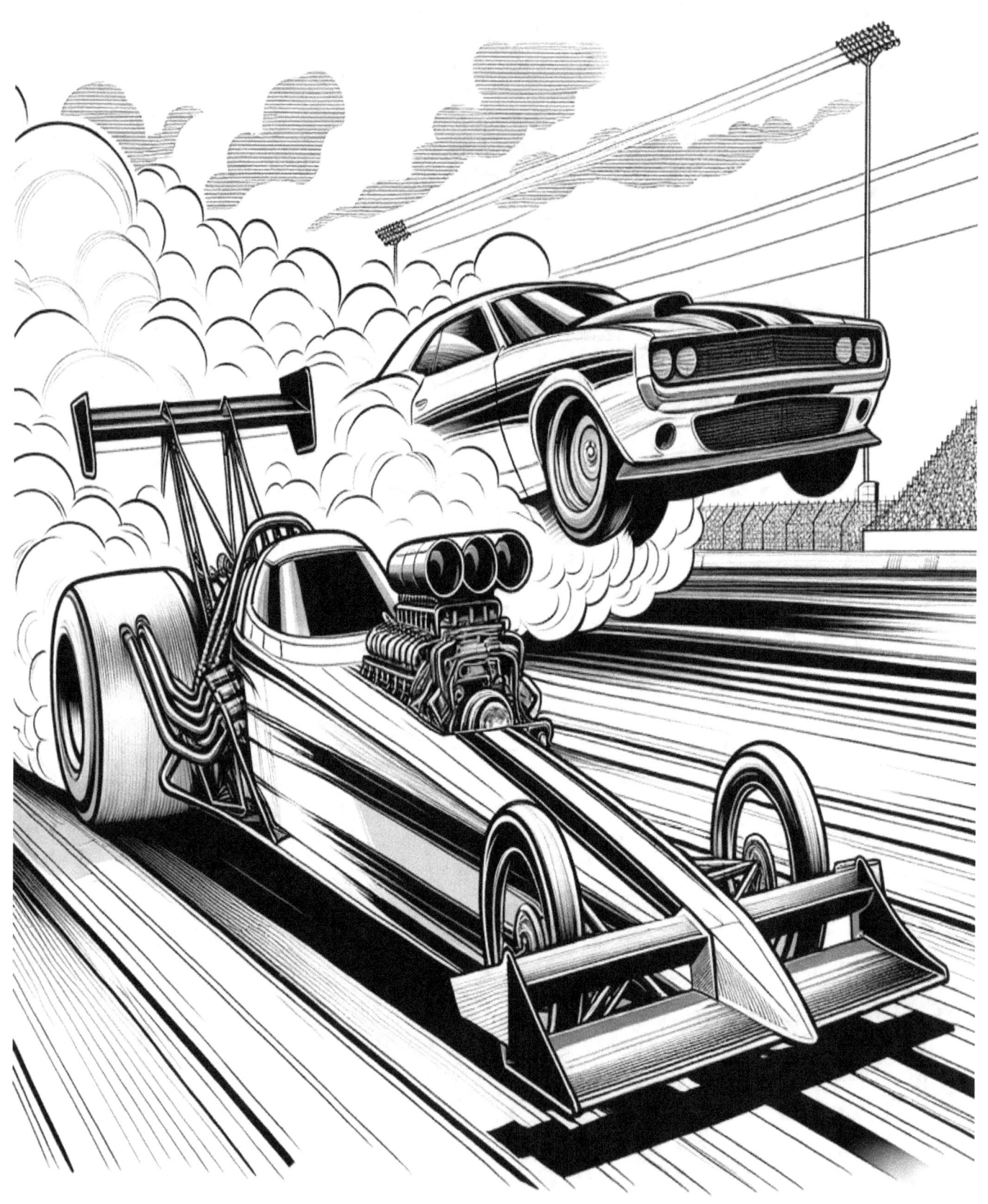

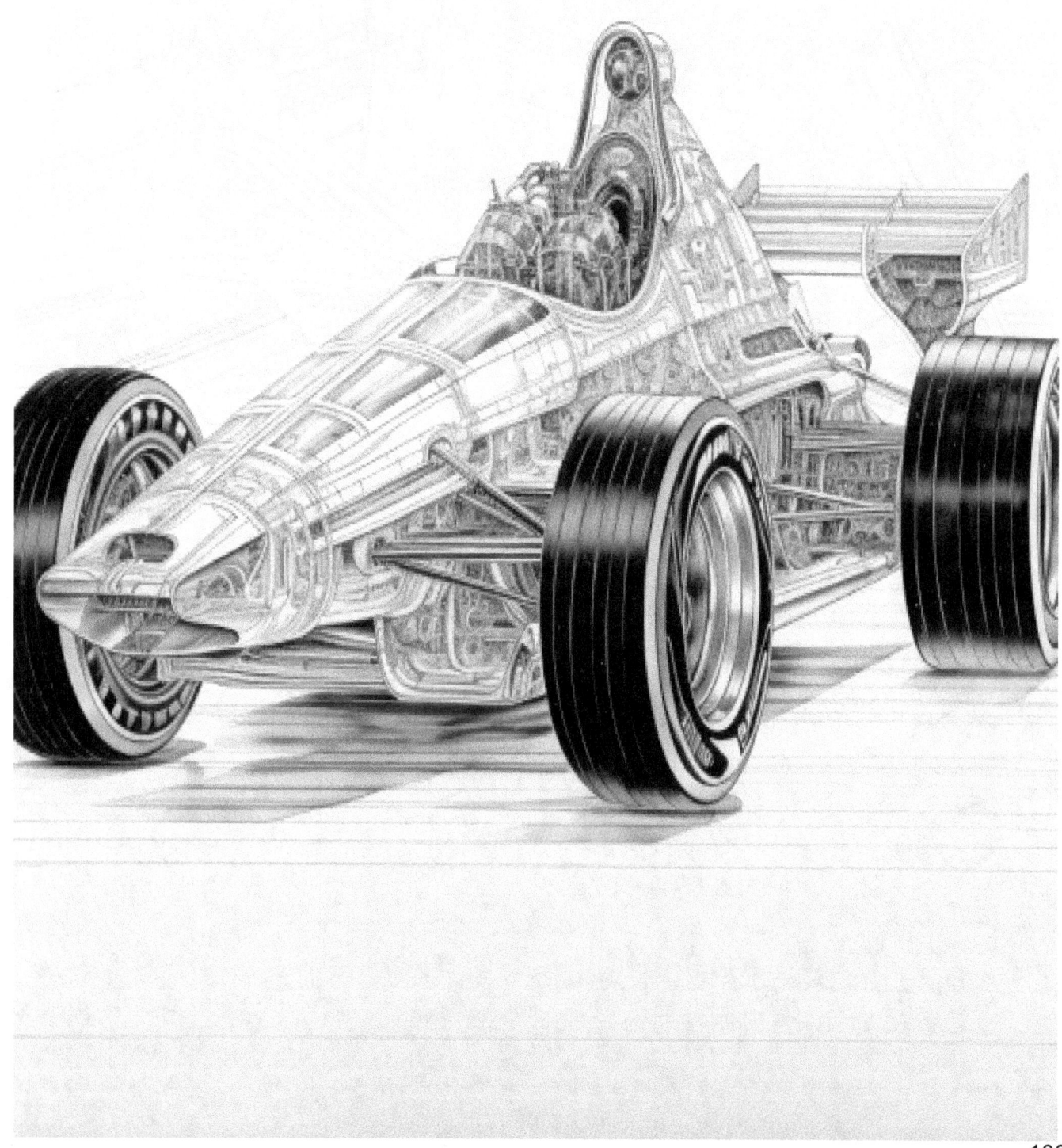

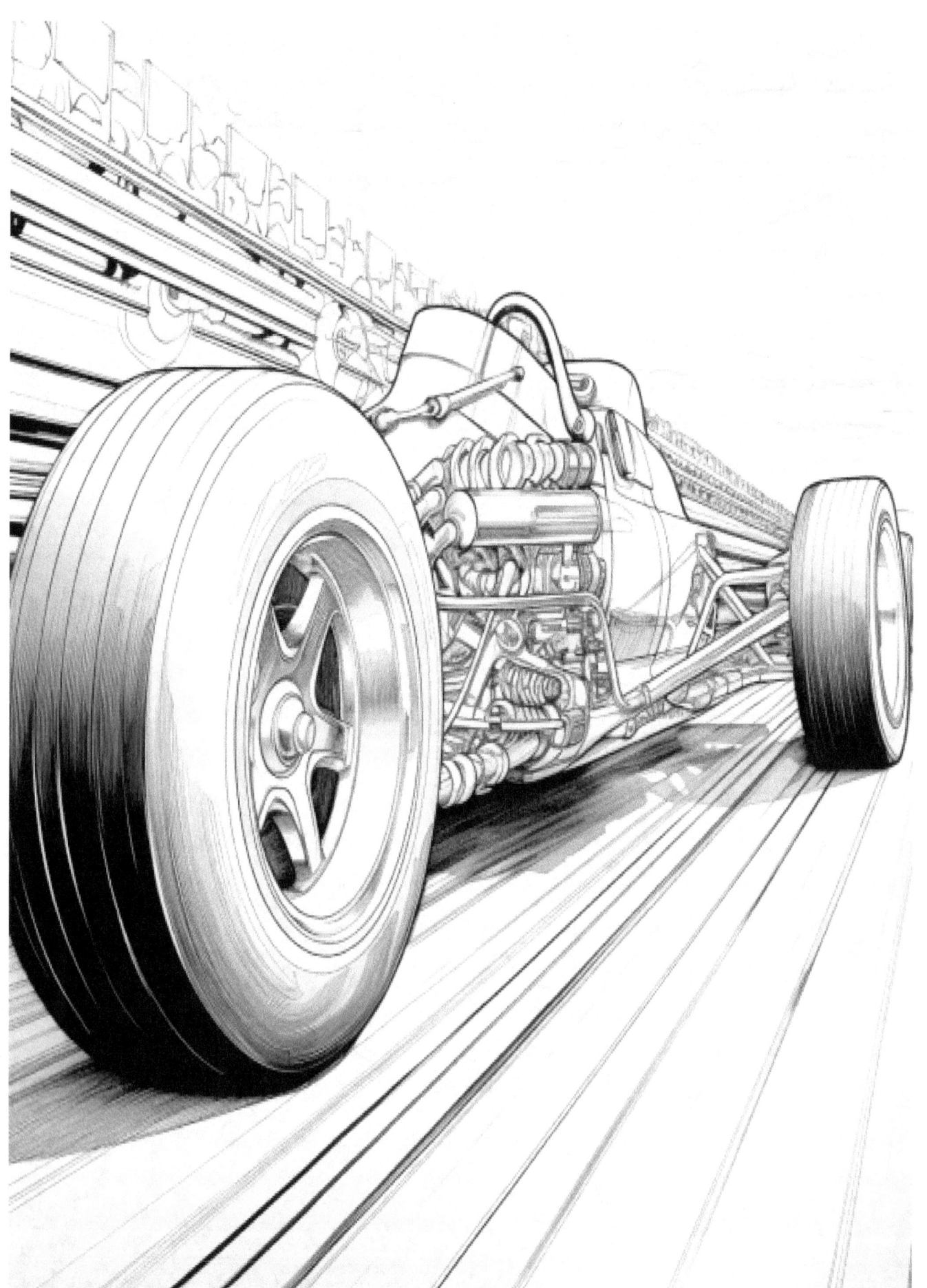

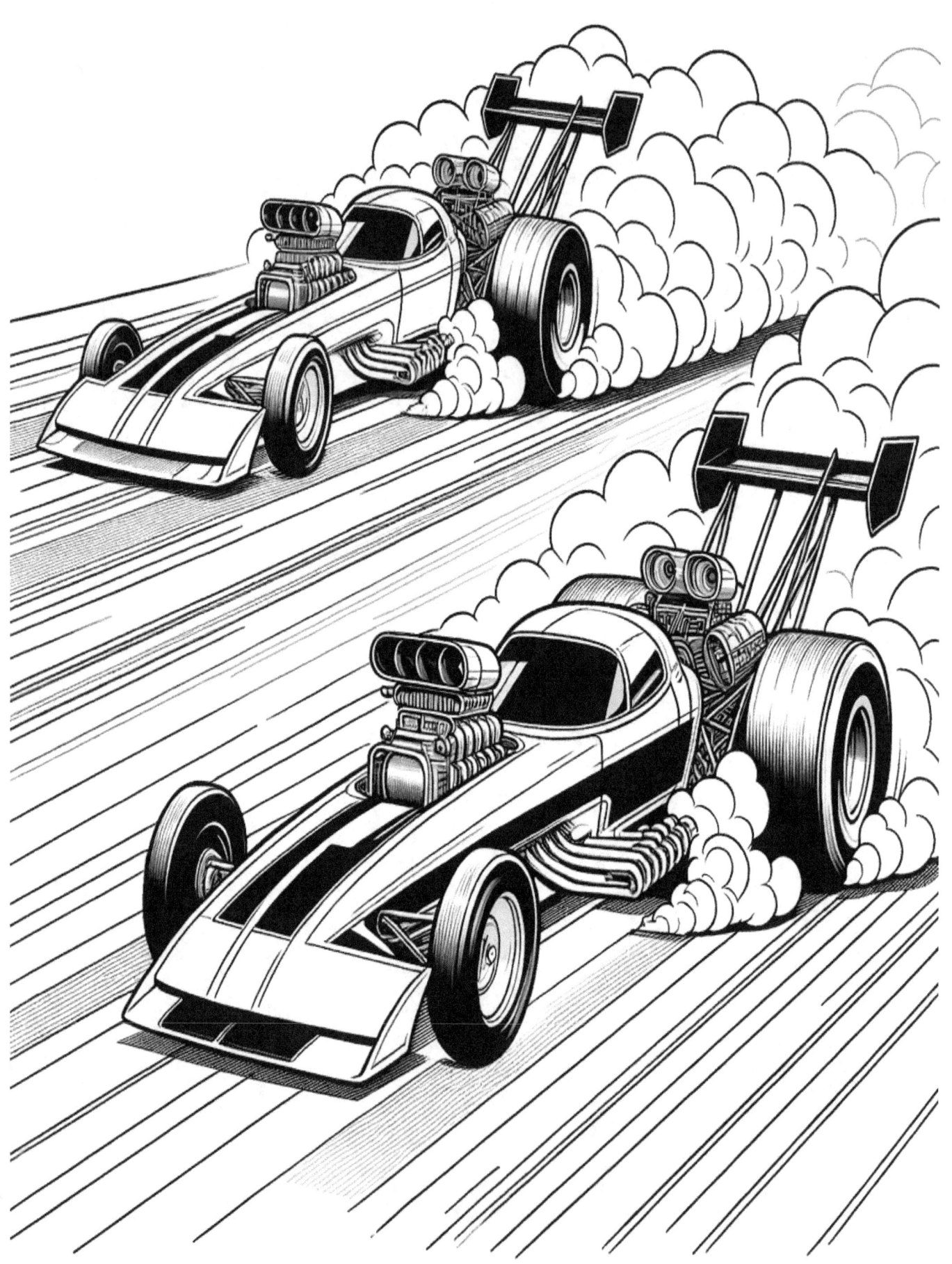

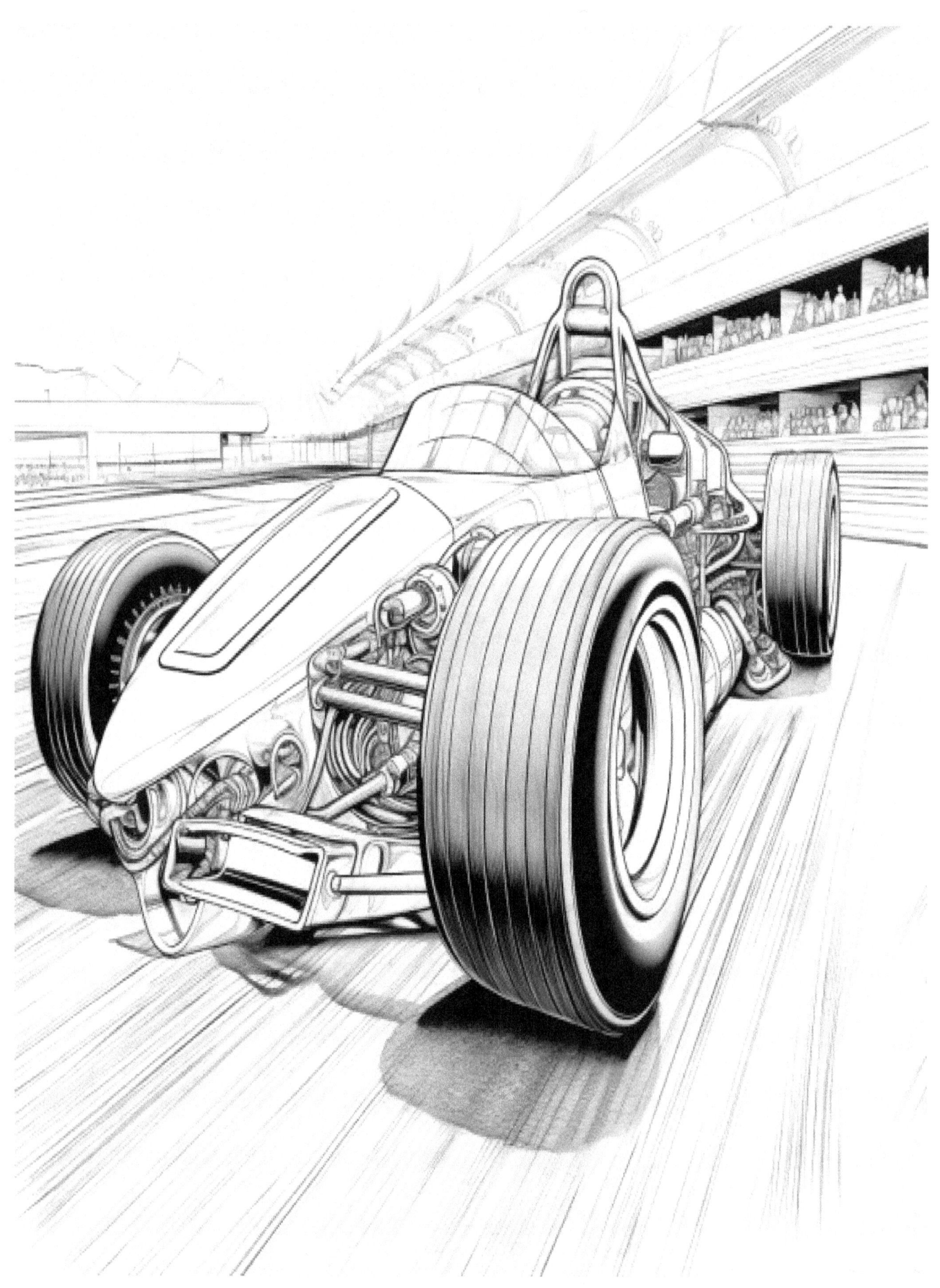

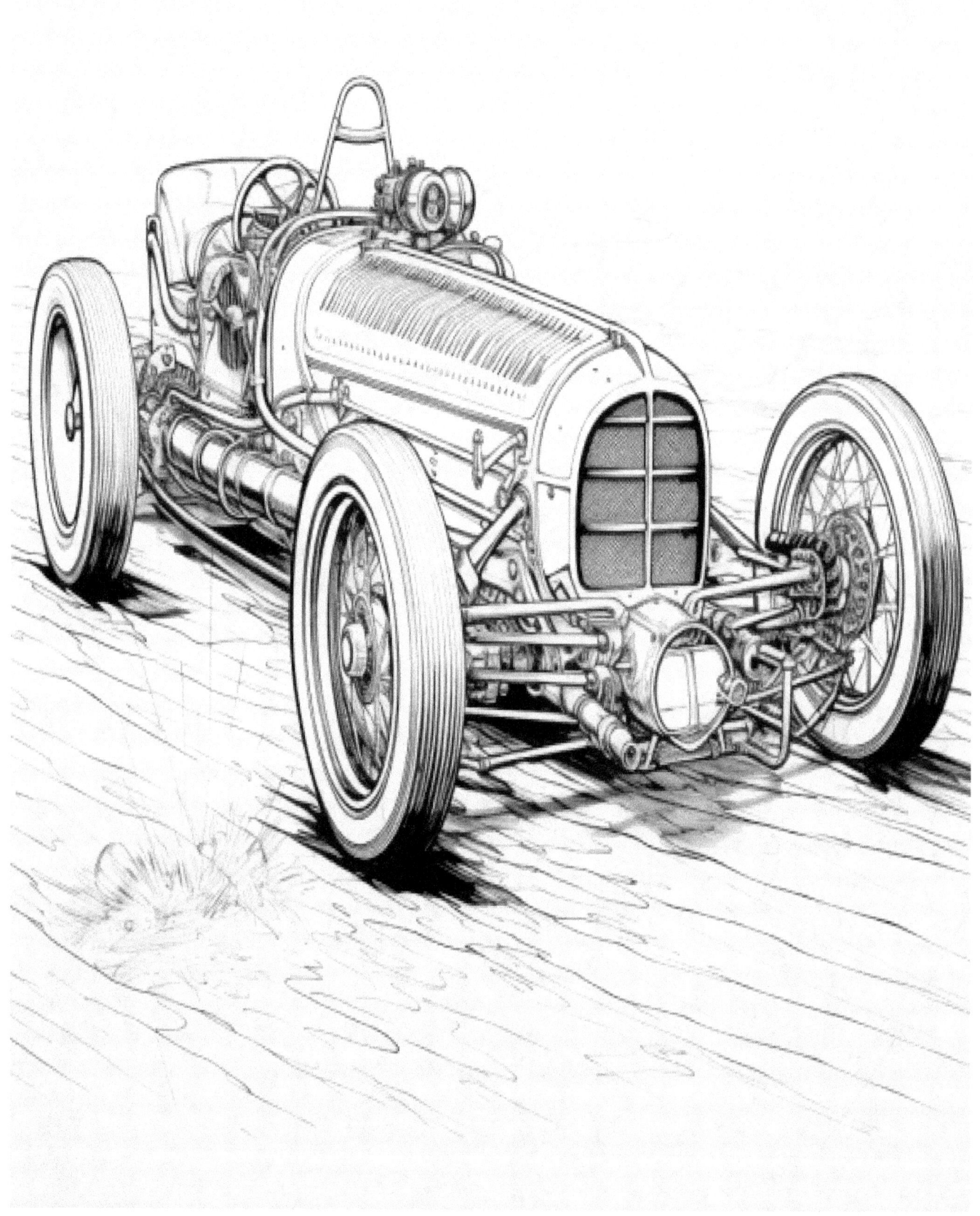

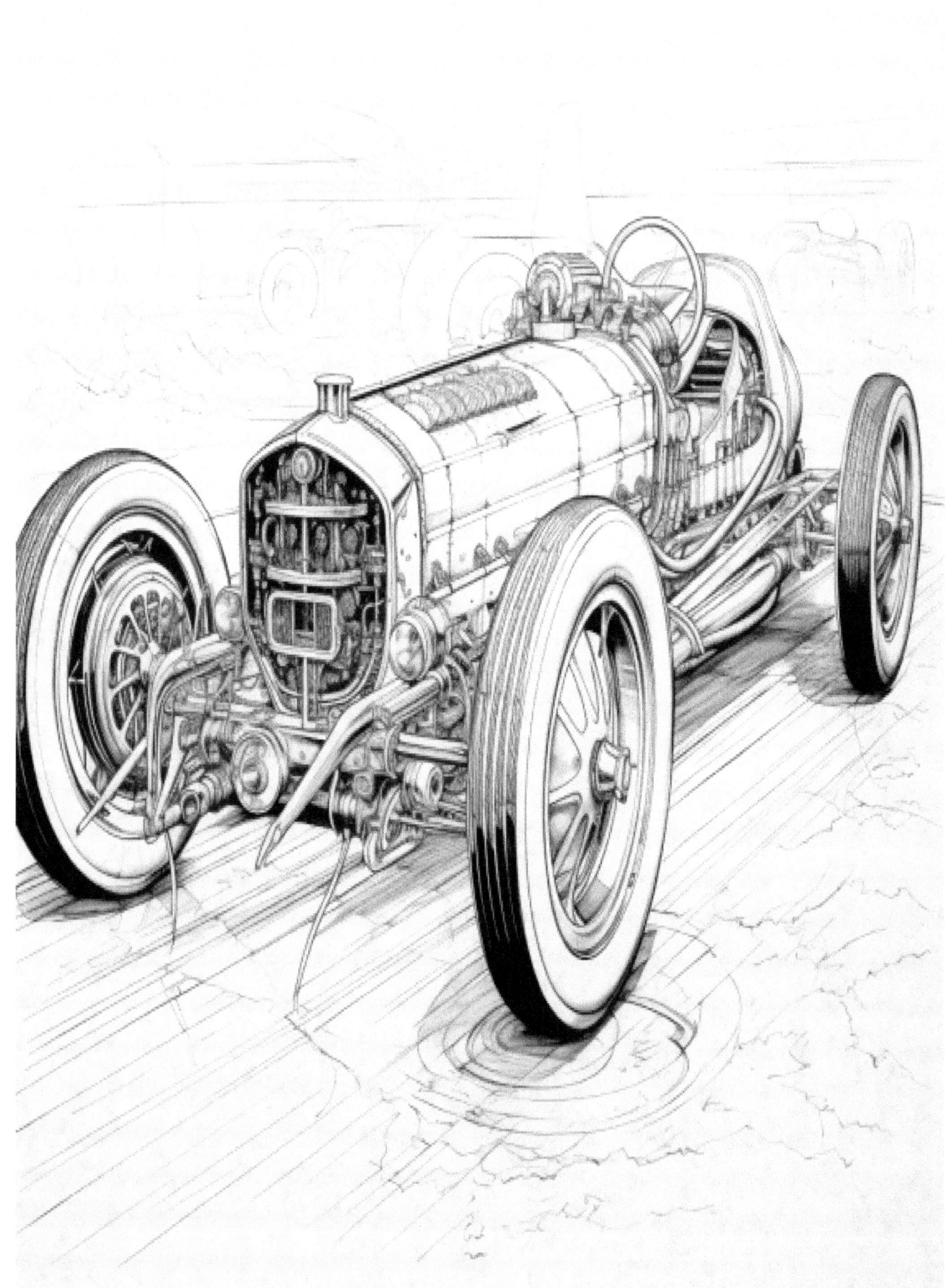

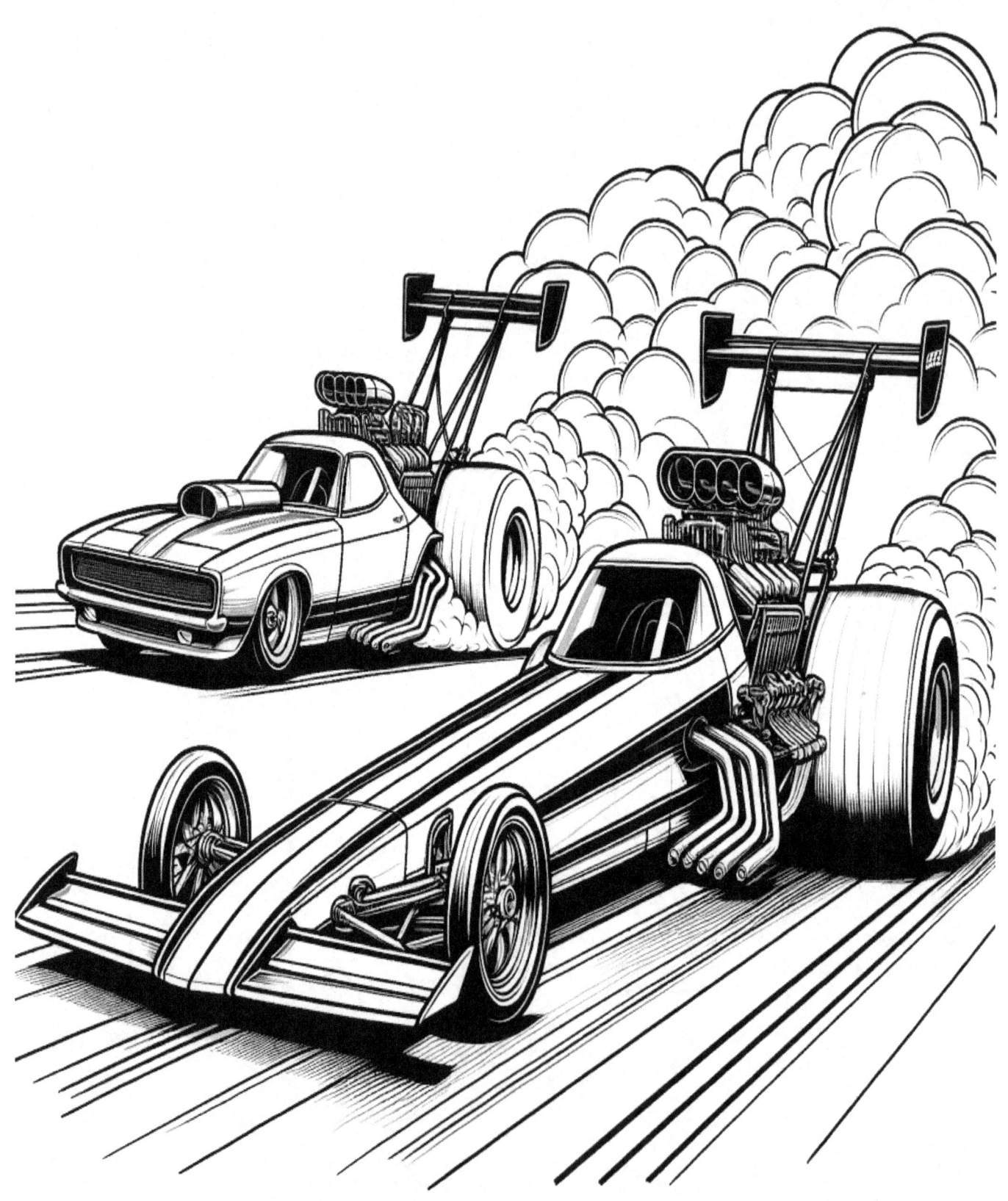

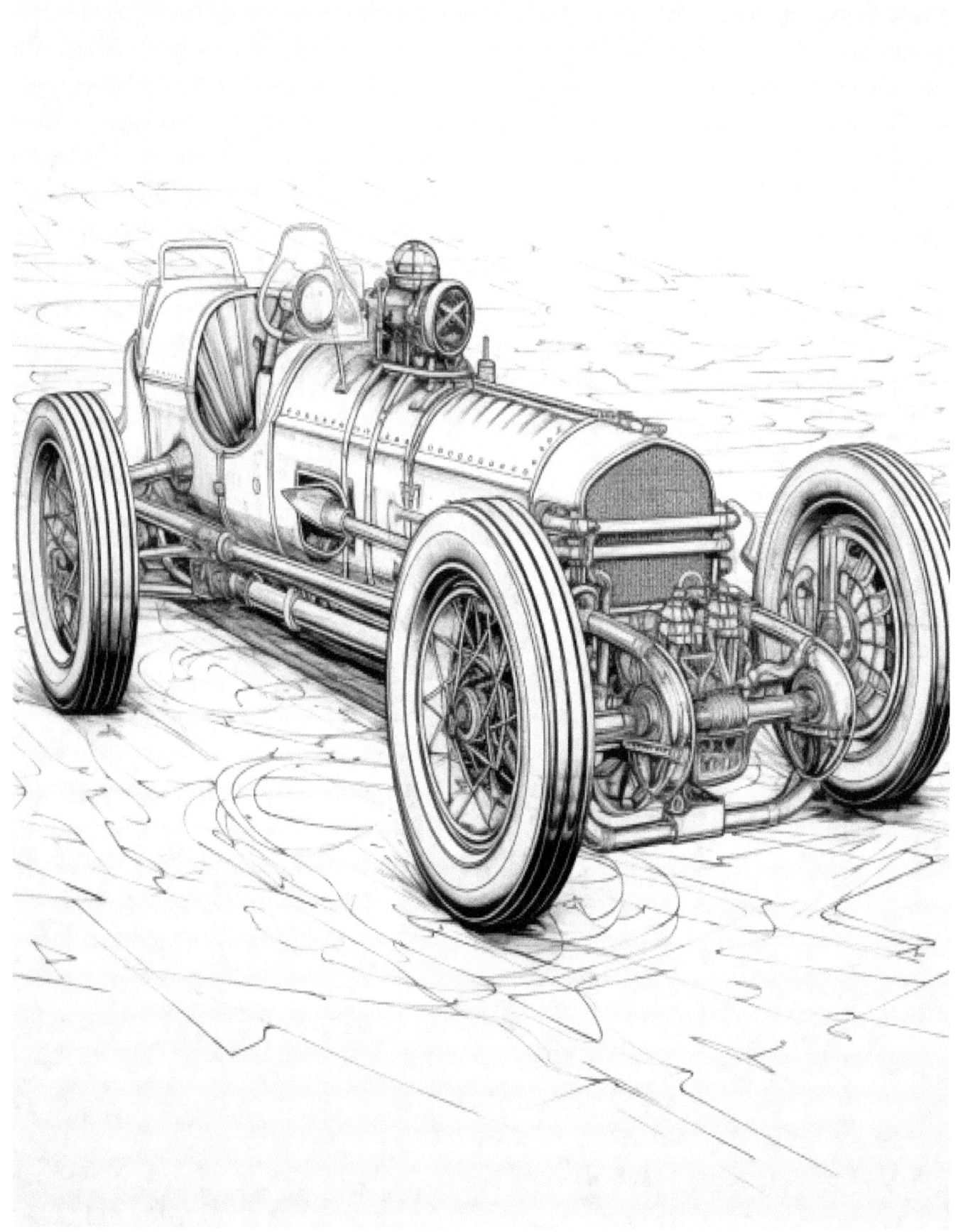

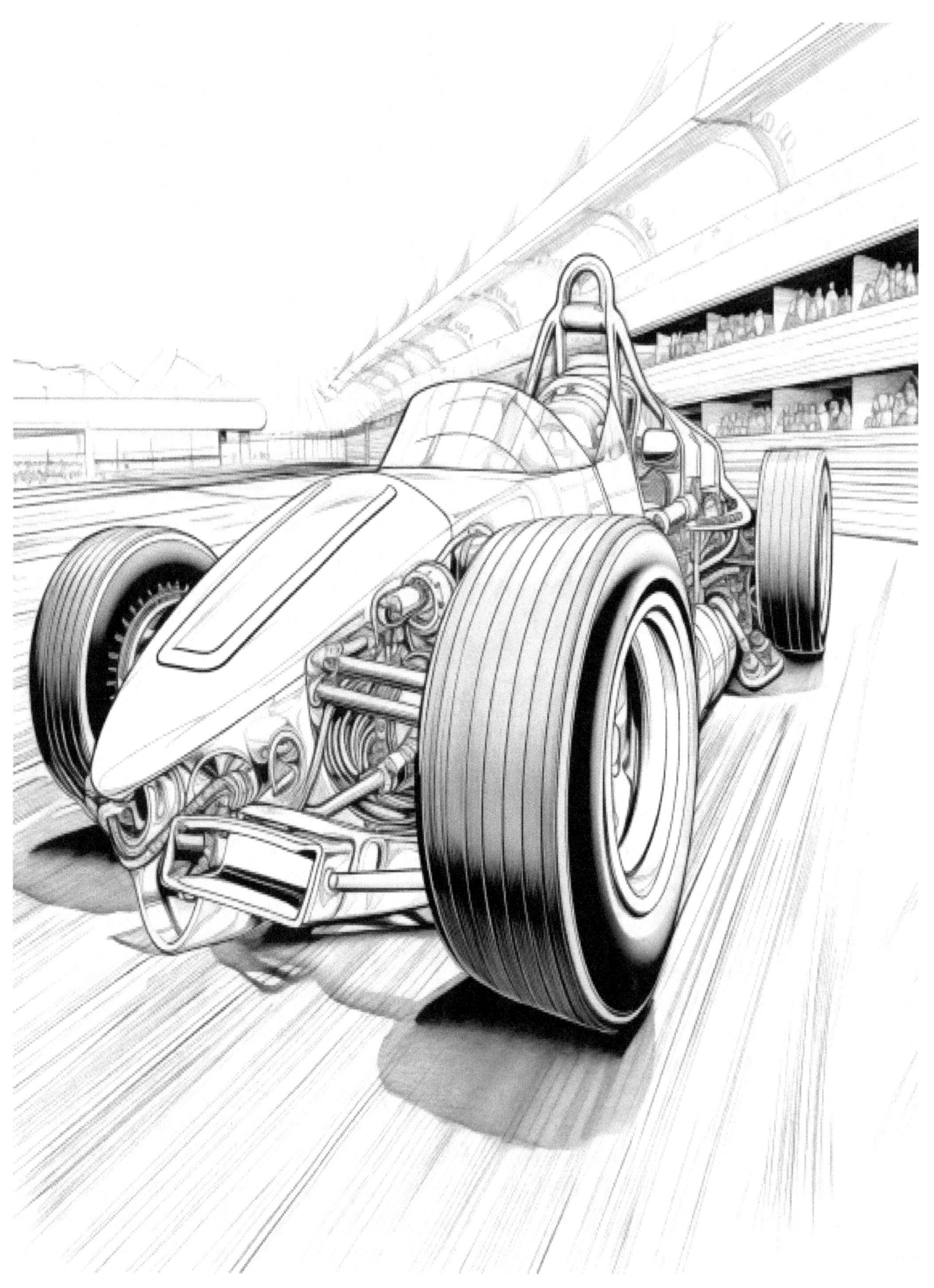

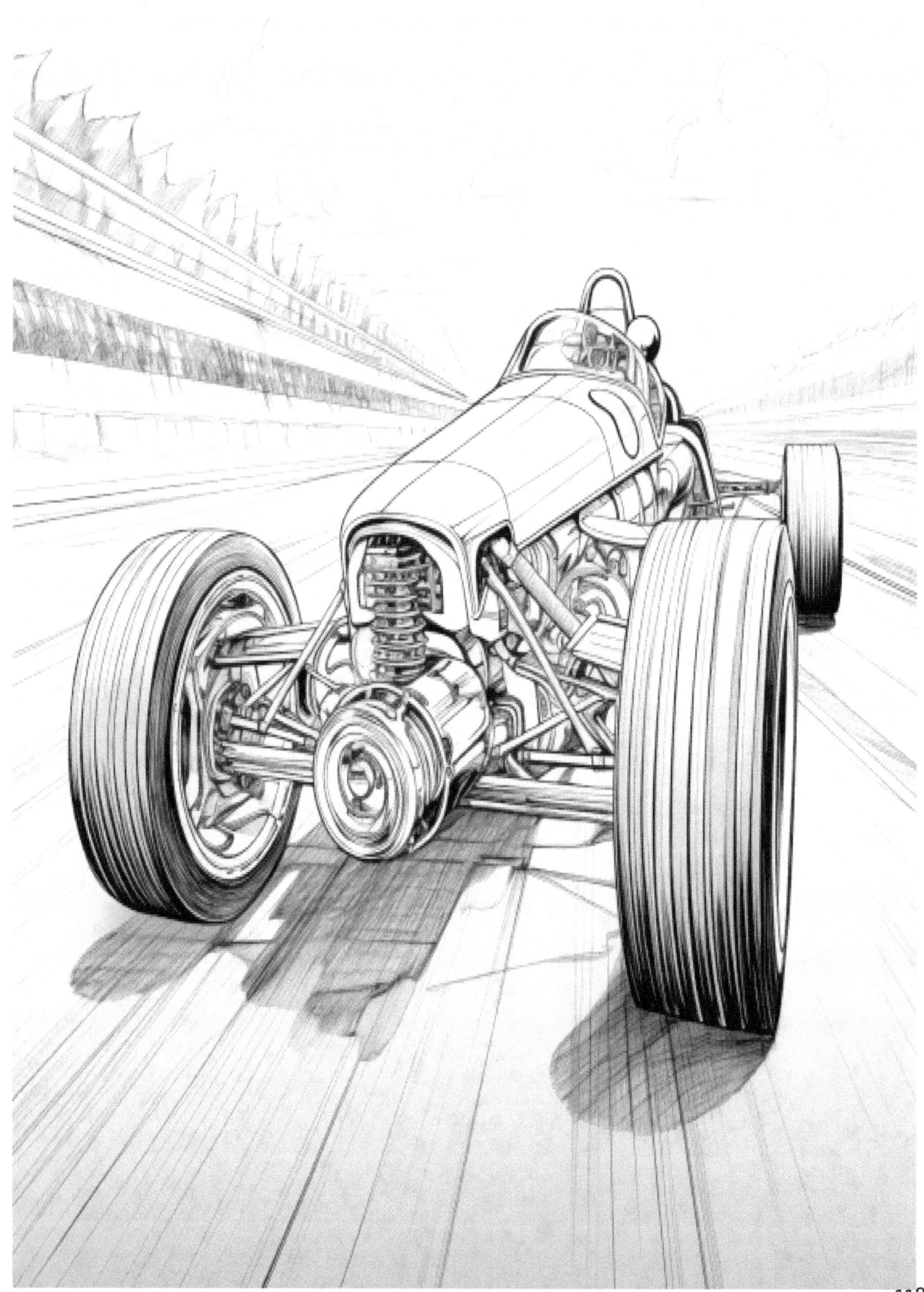

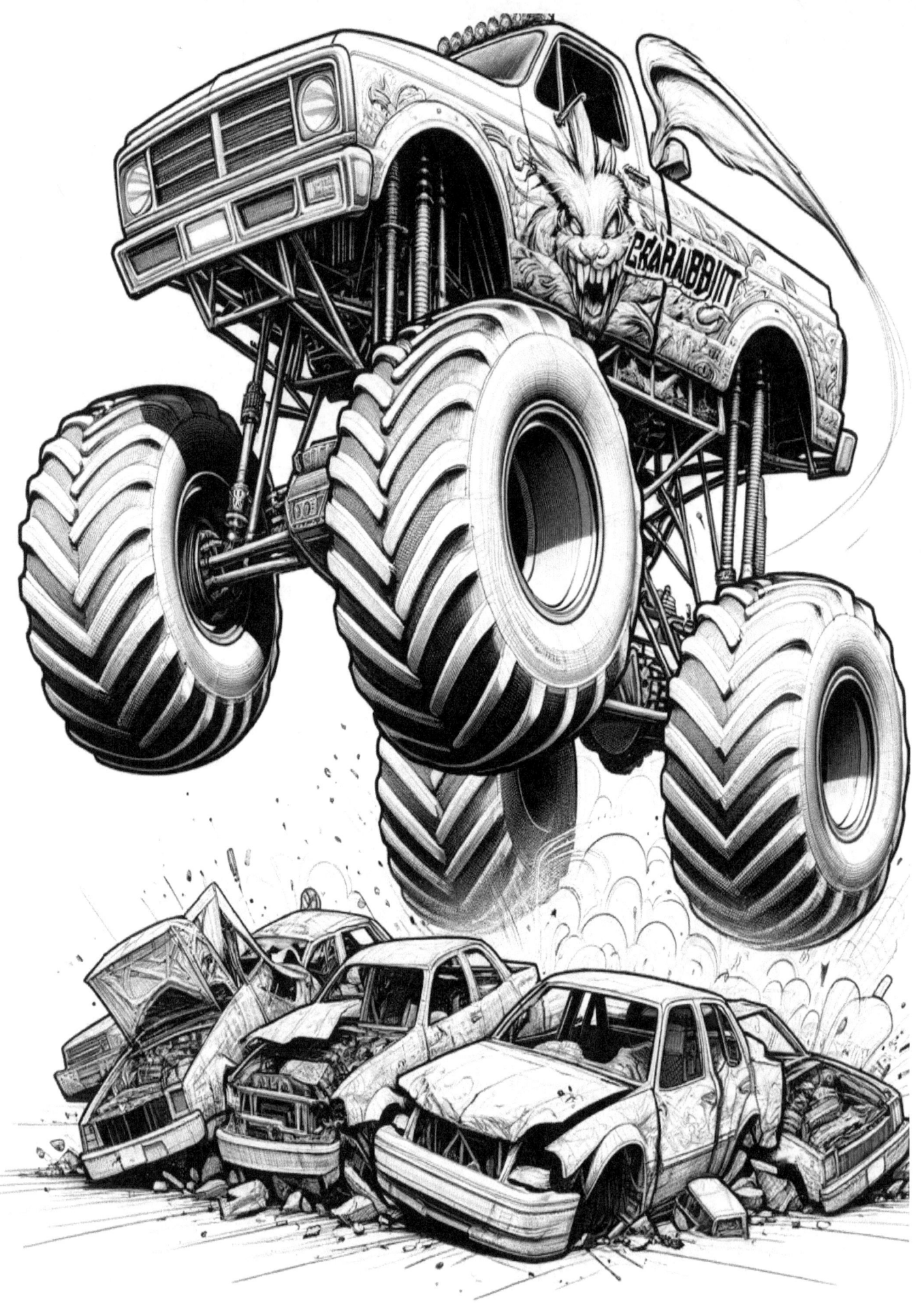

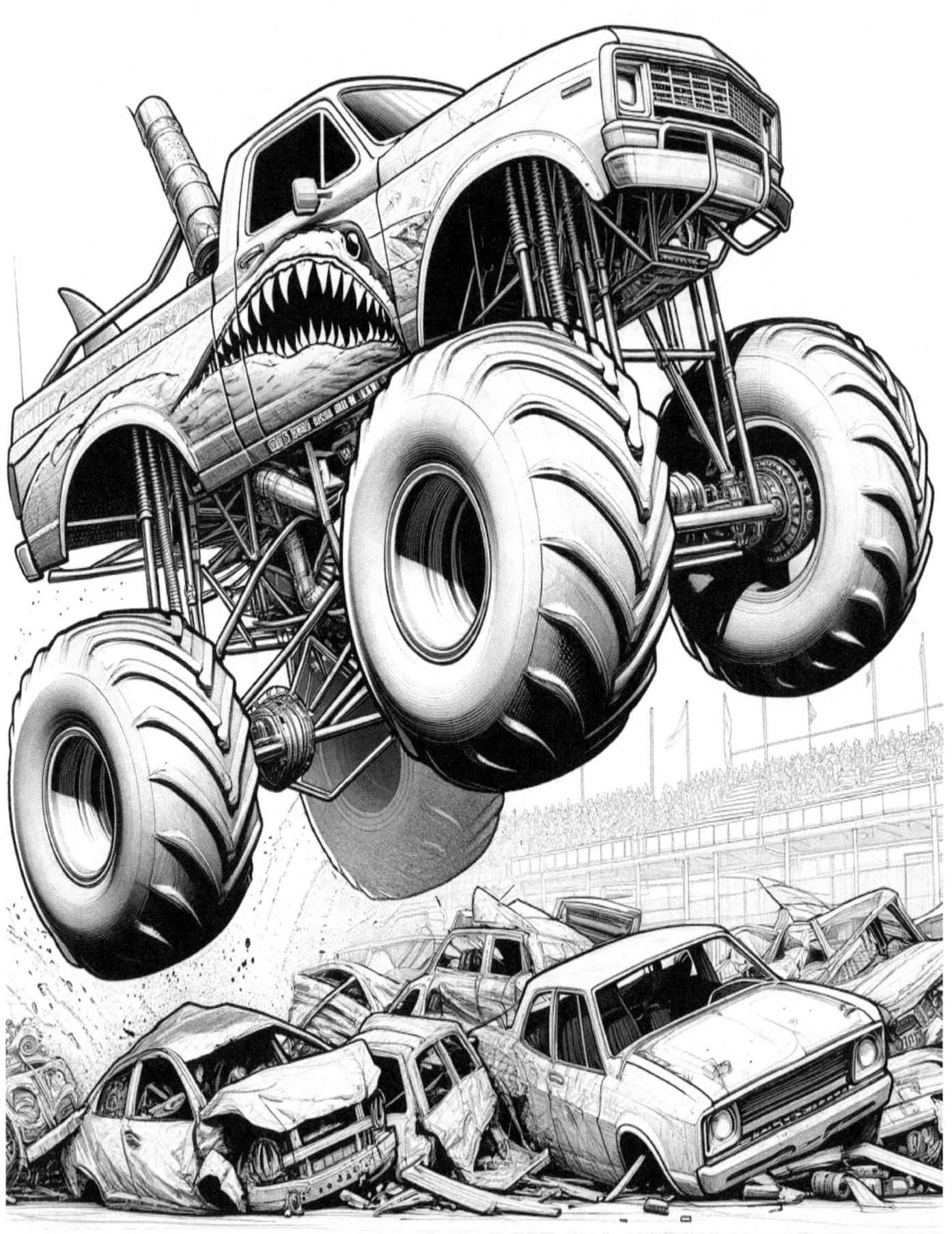

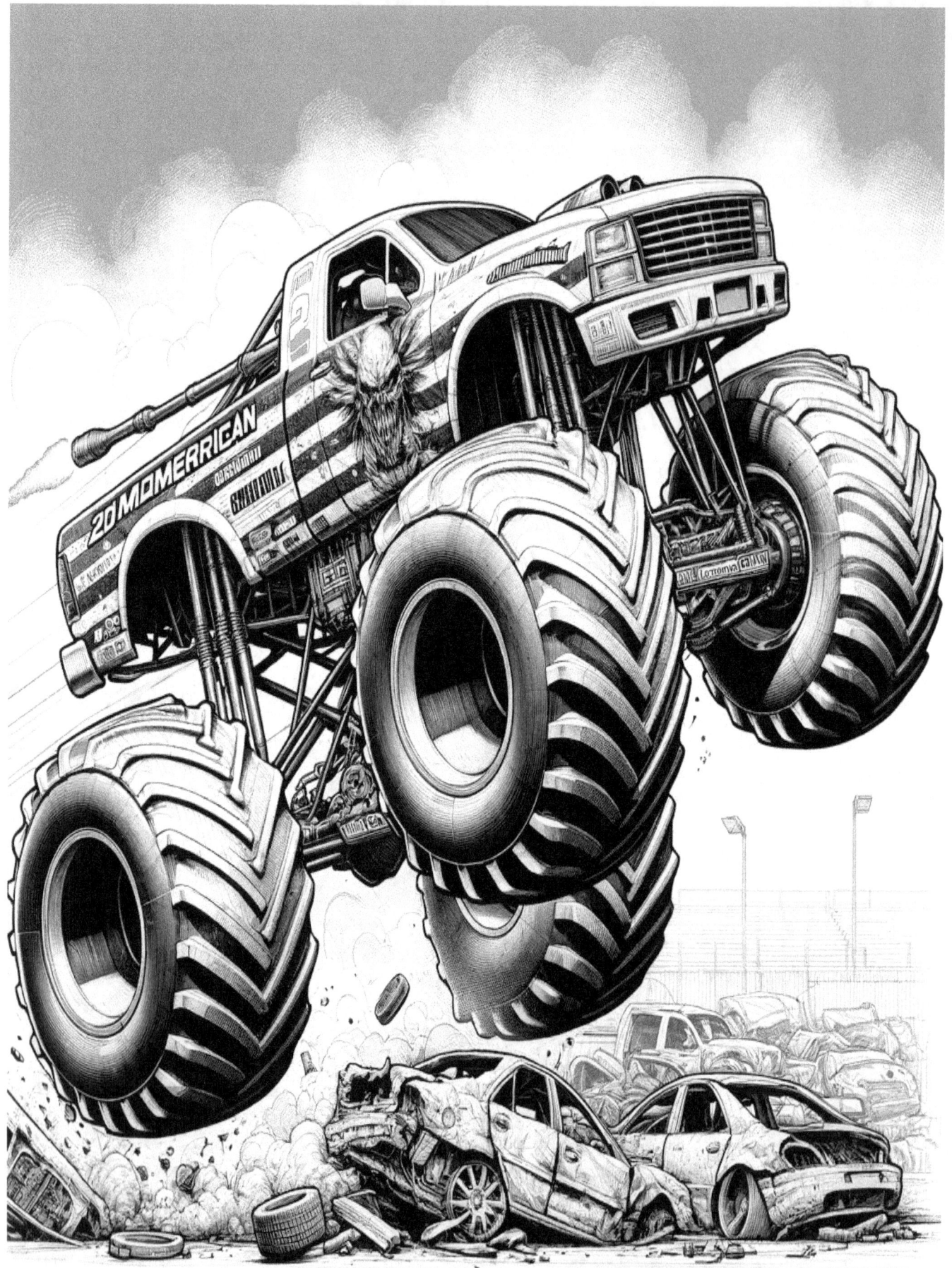

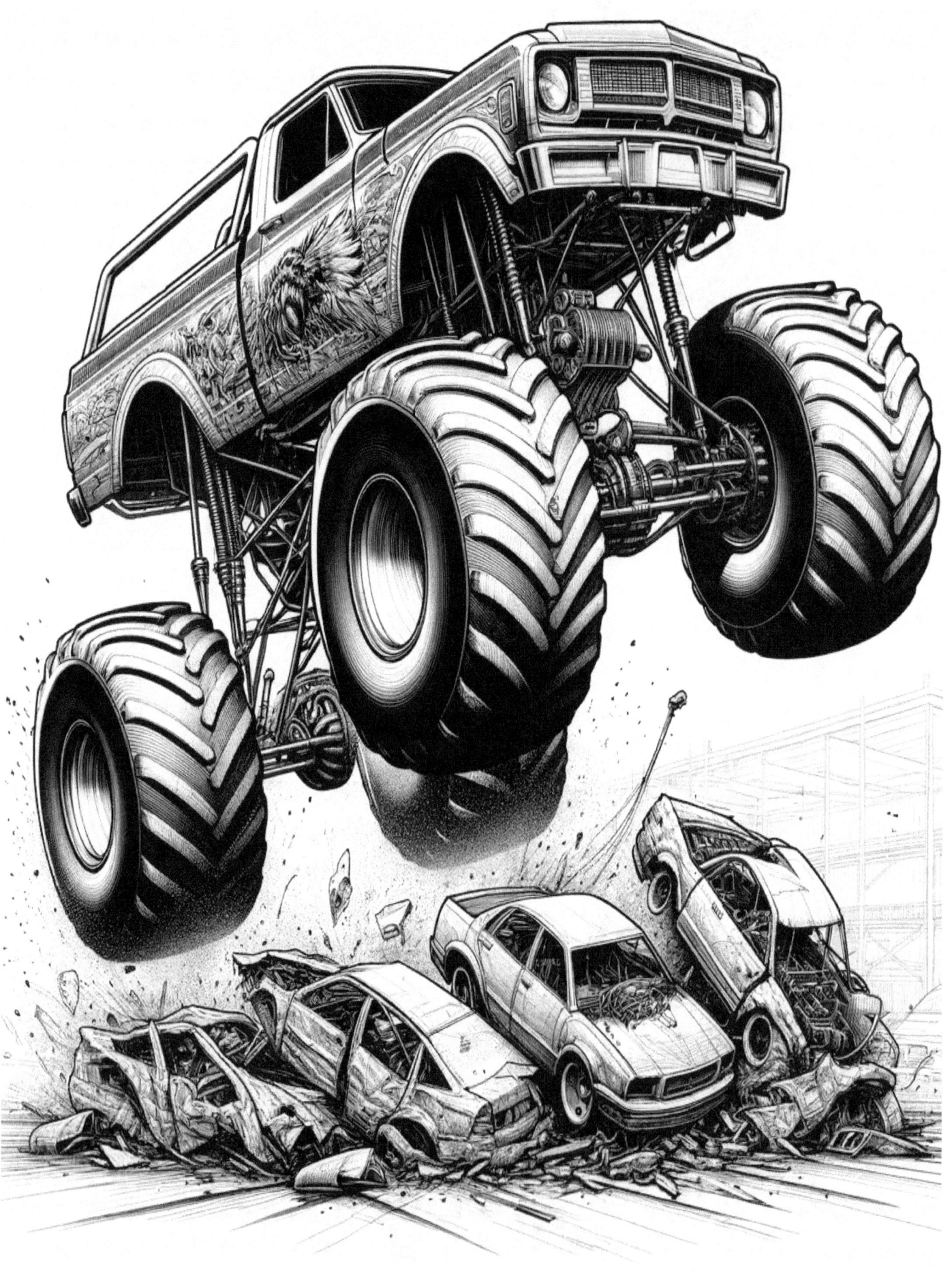

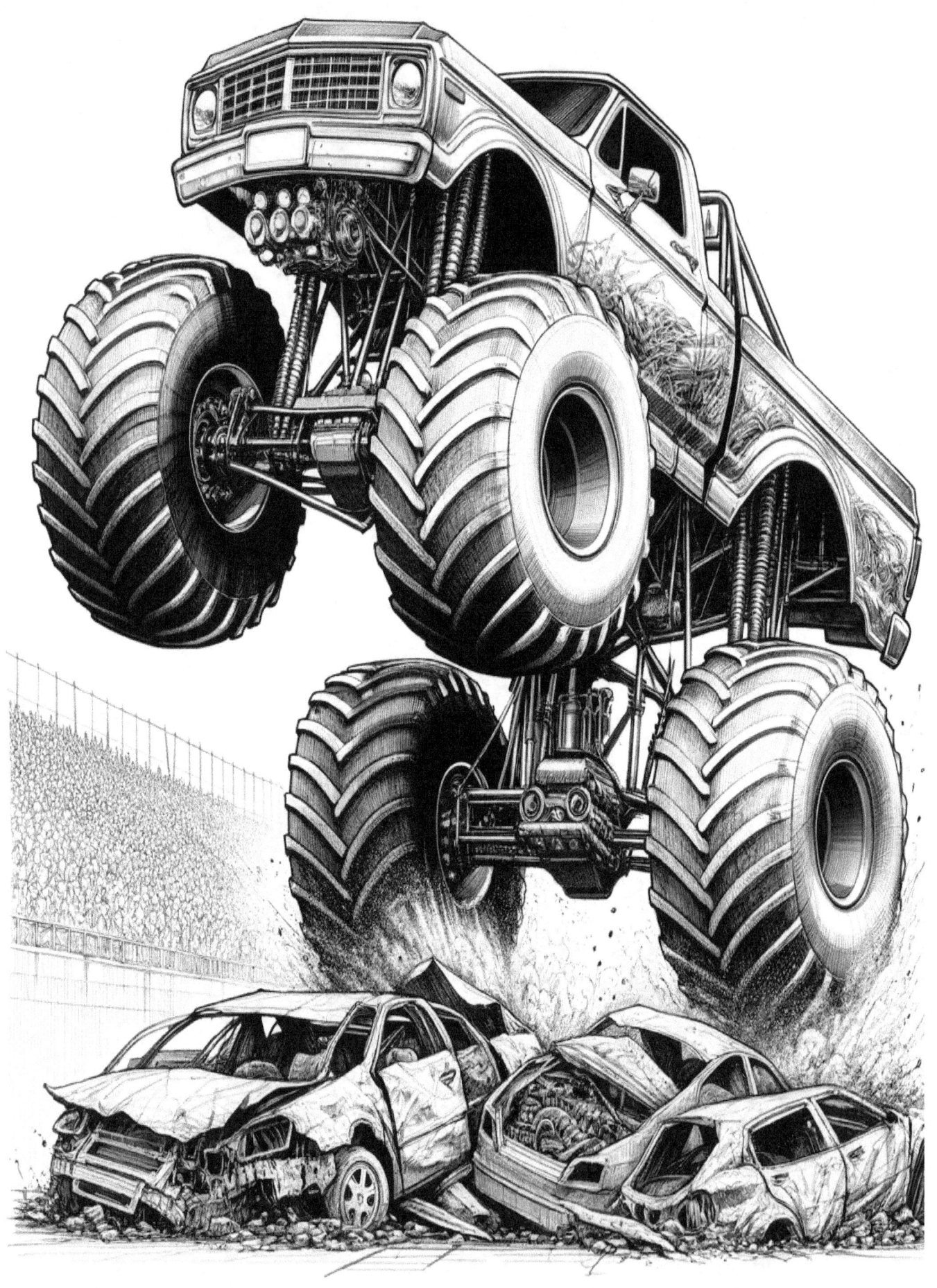

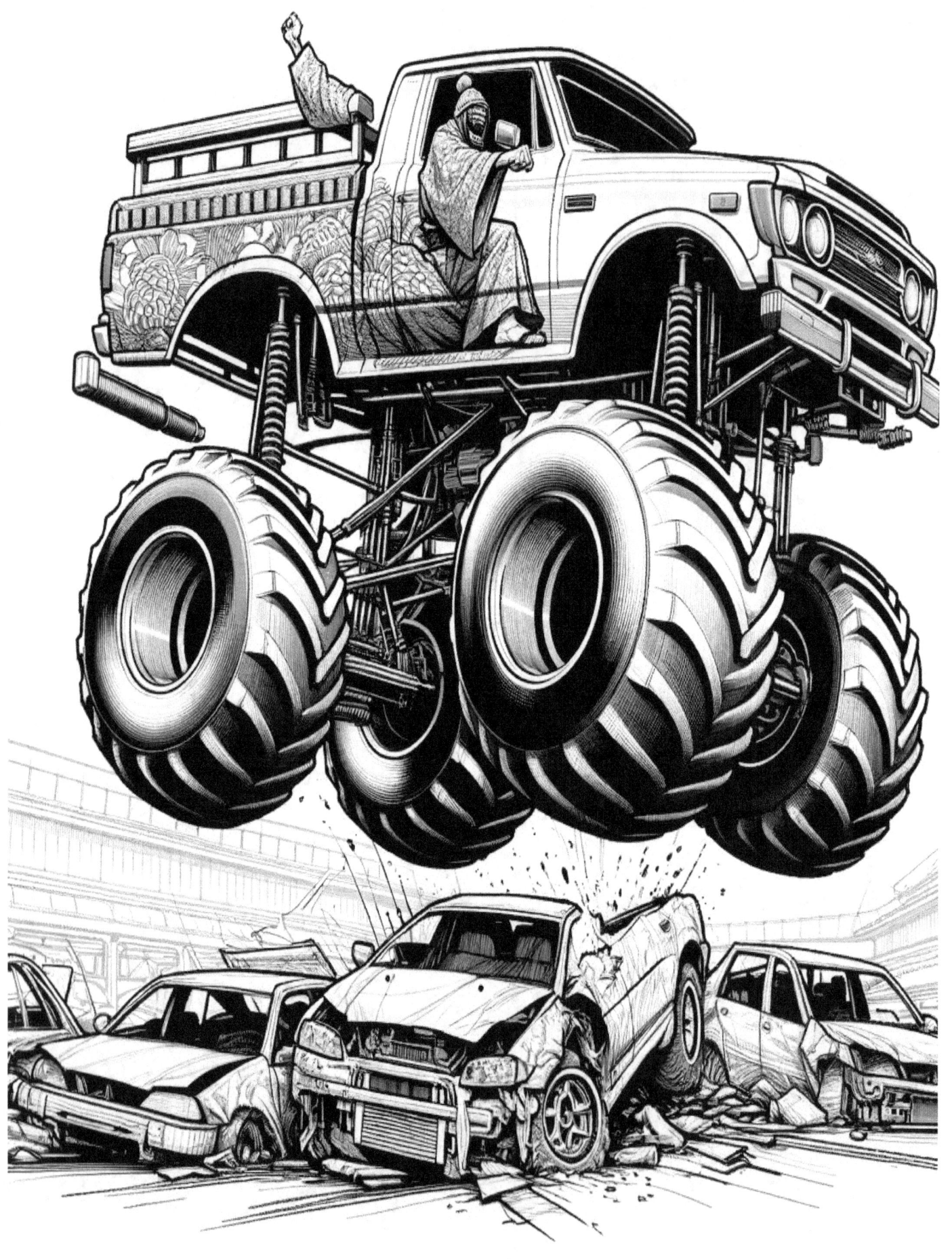

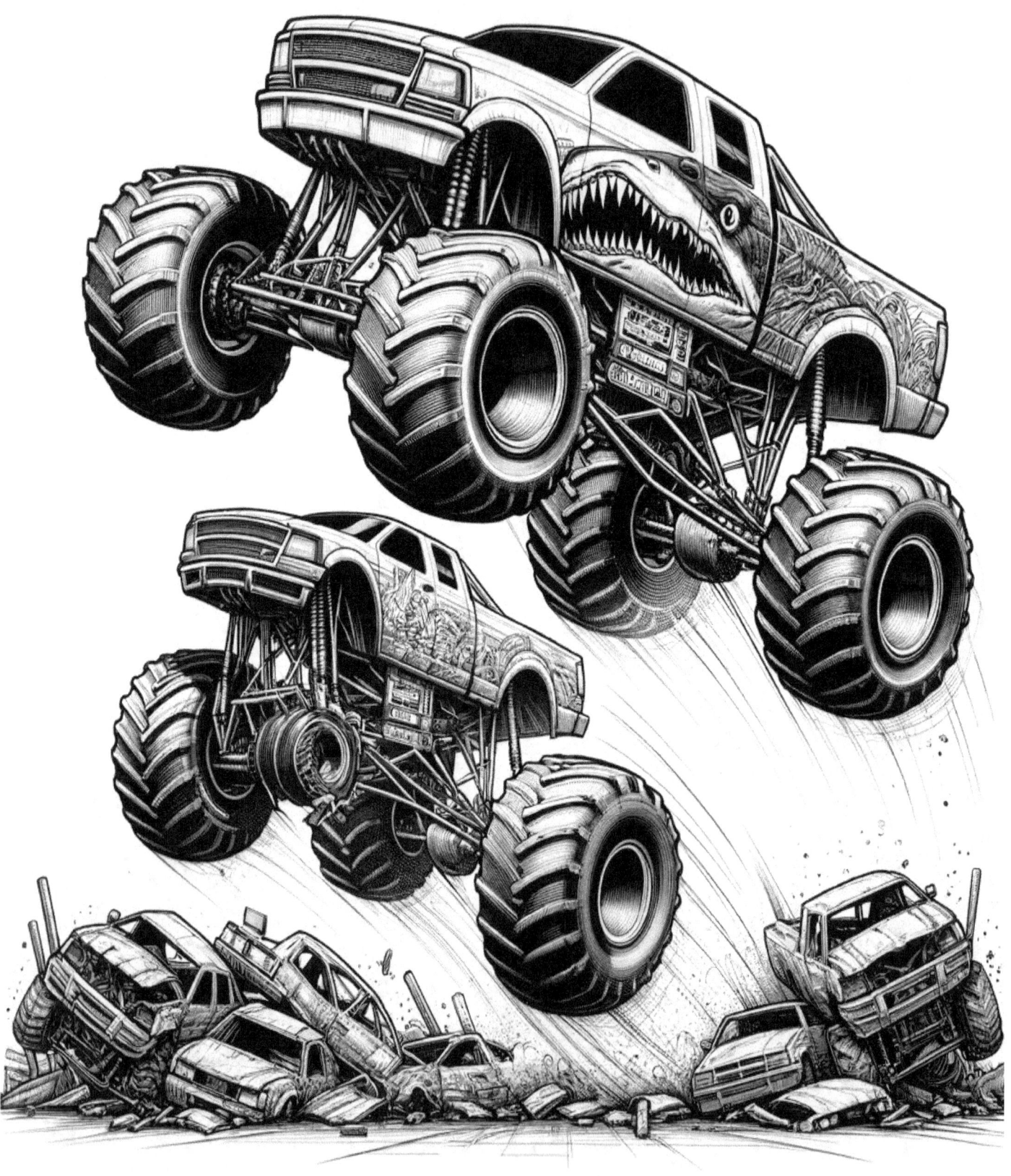

13

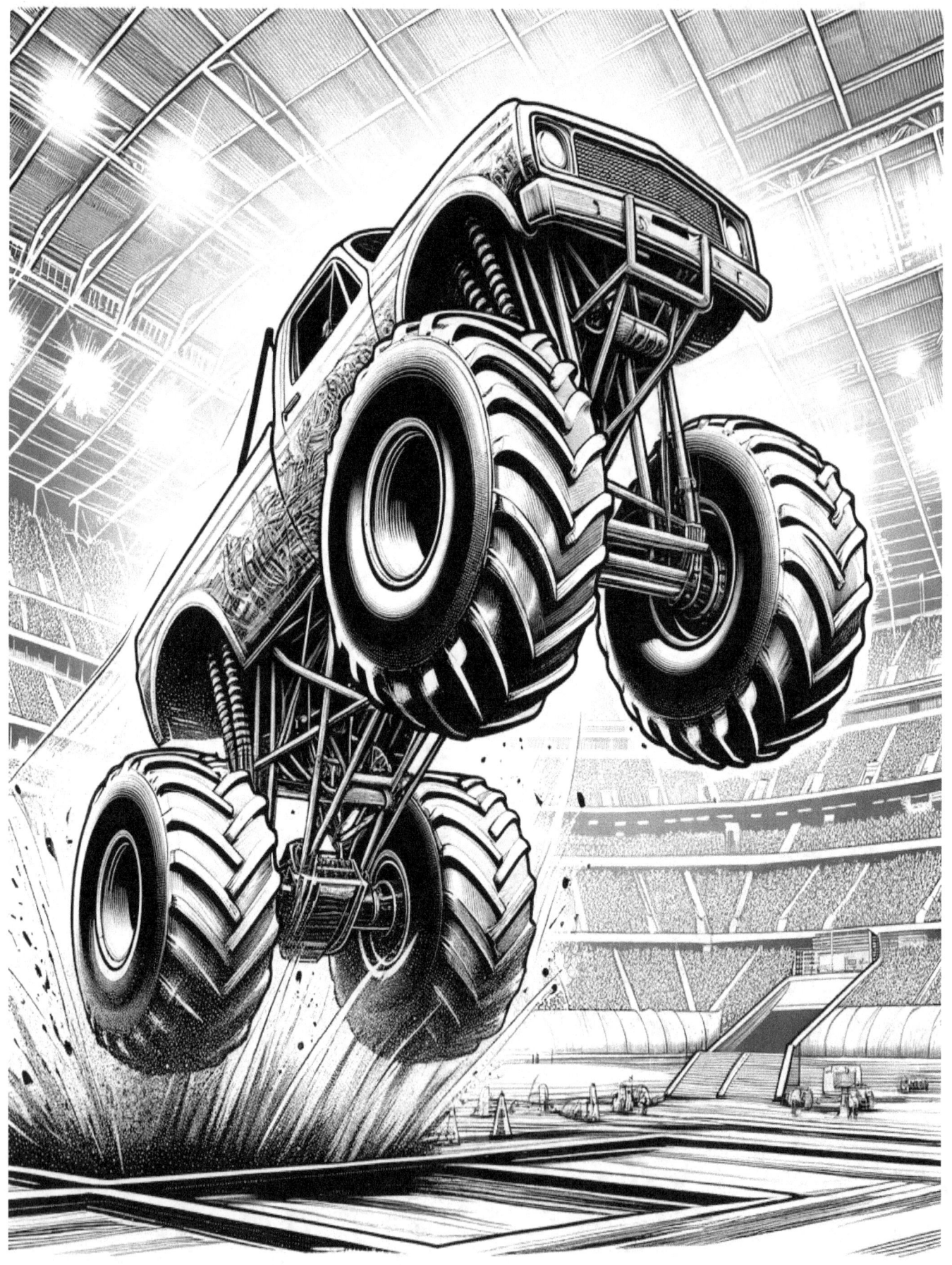

15

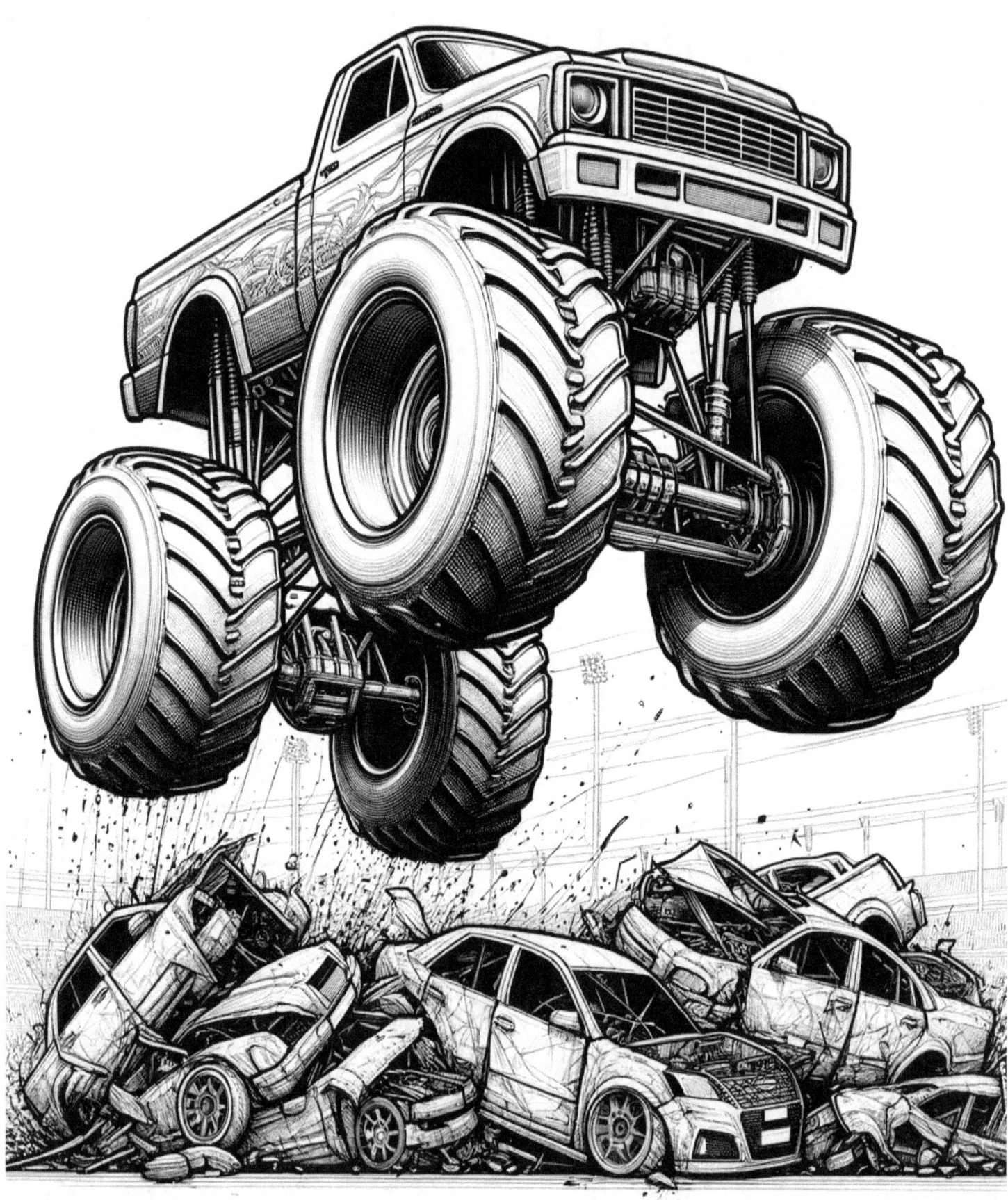

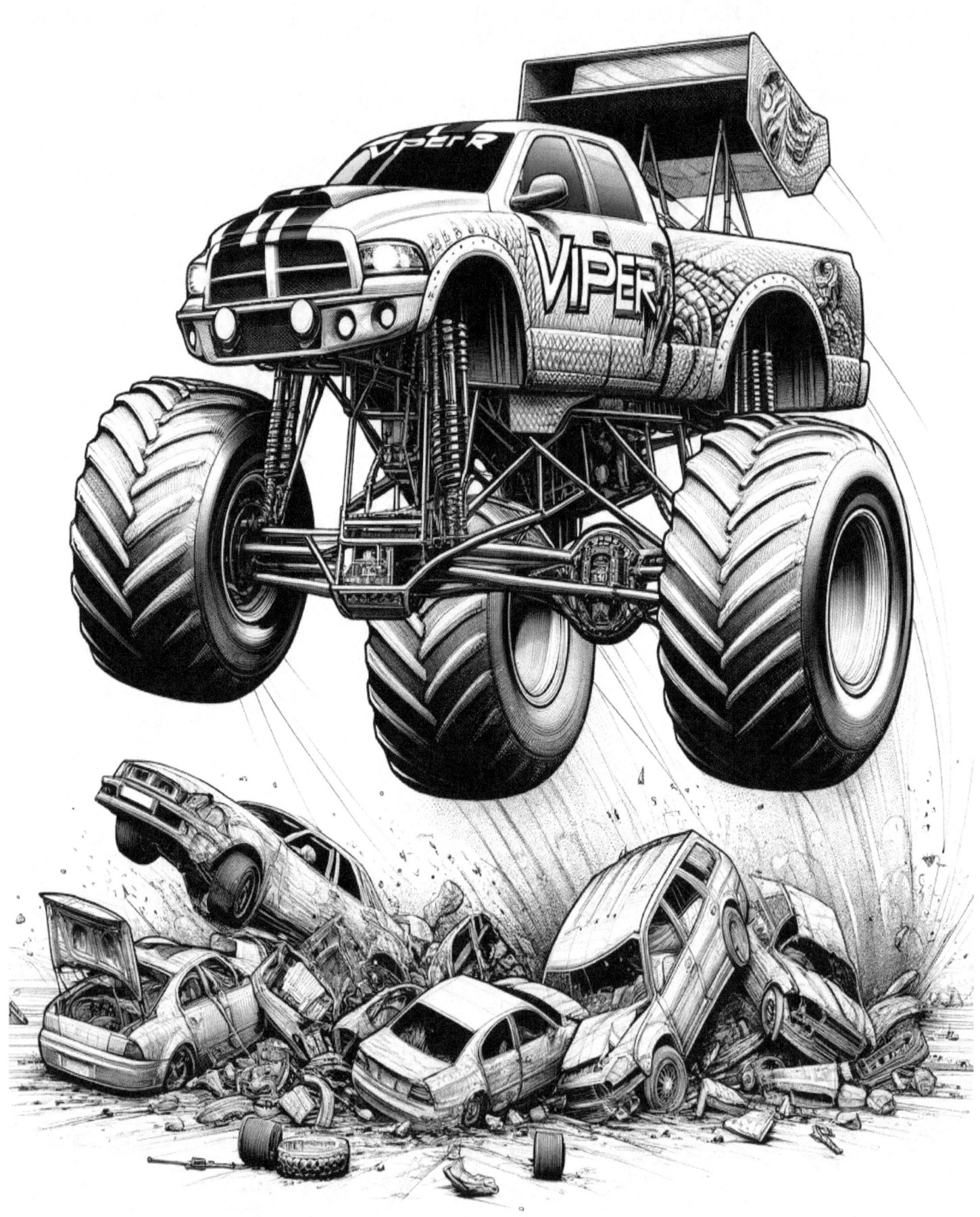

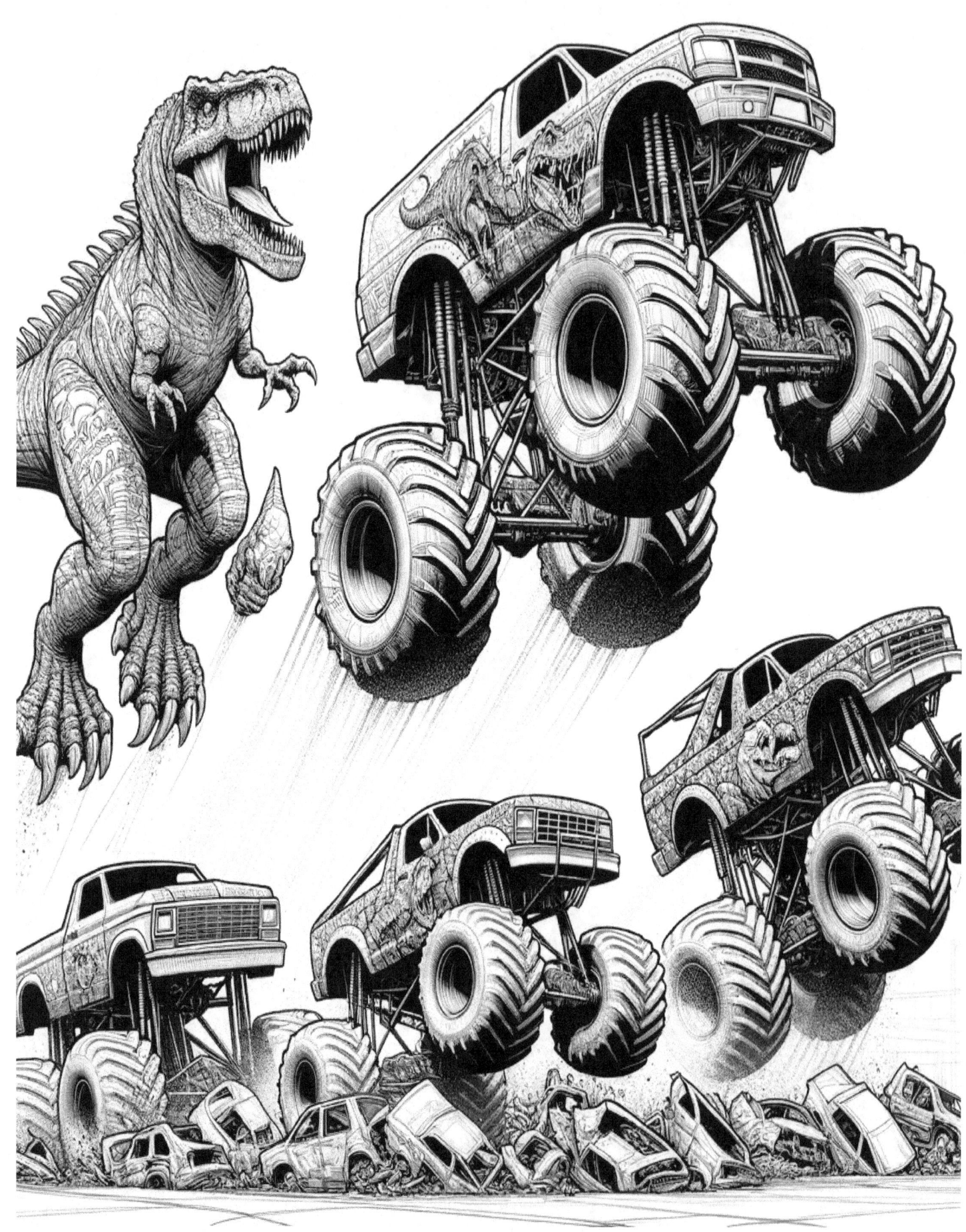

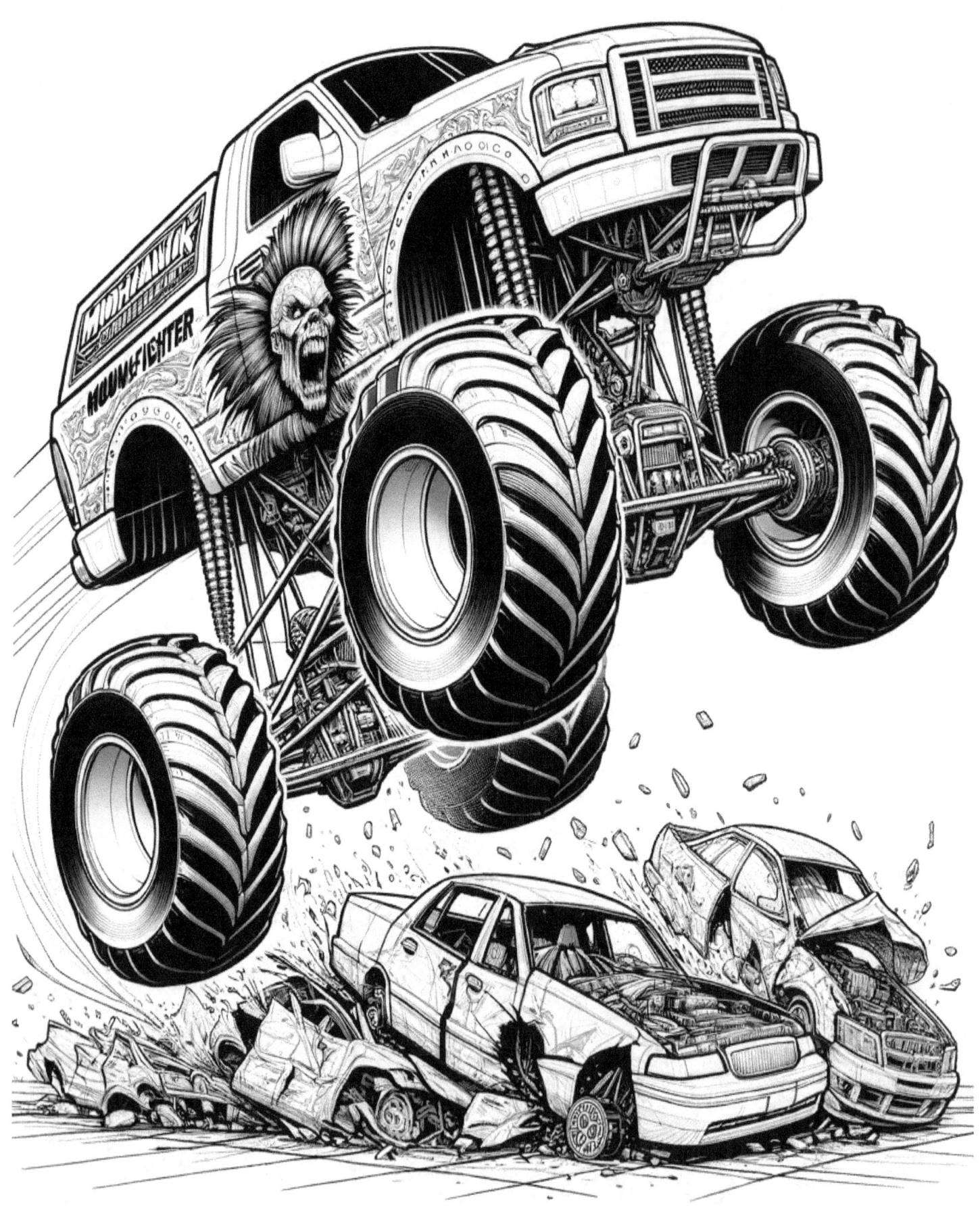

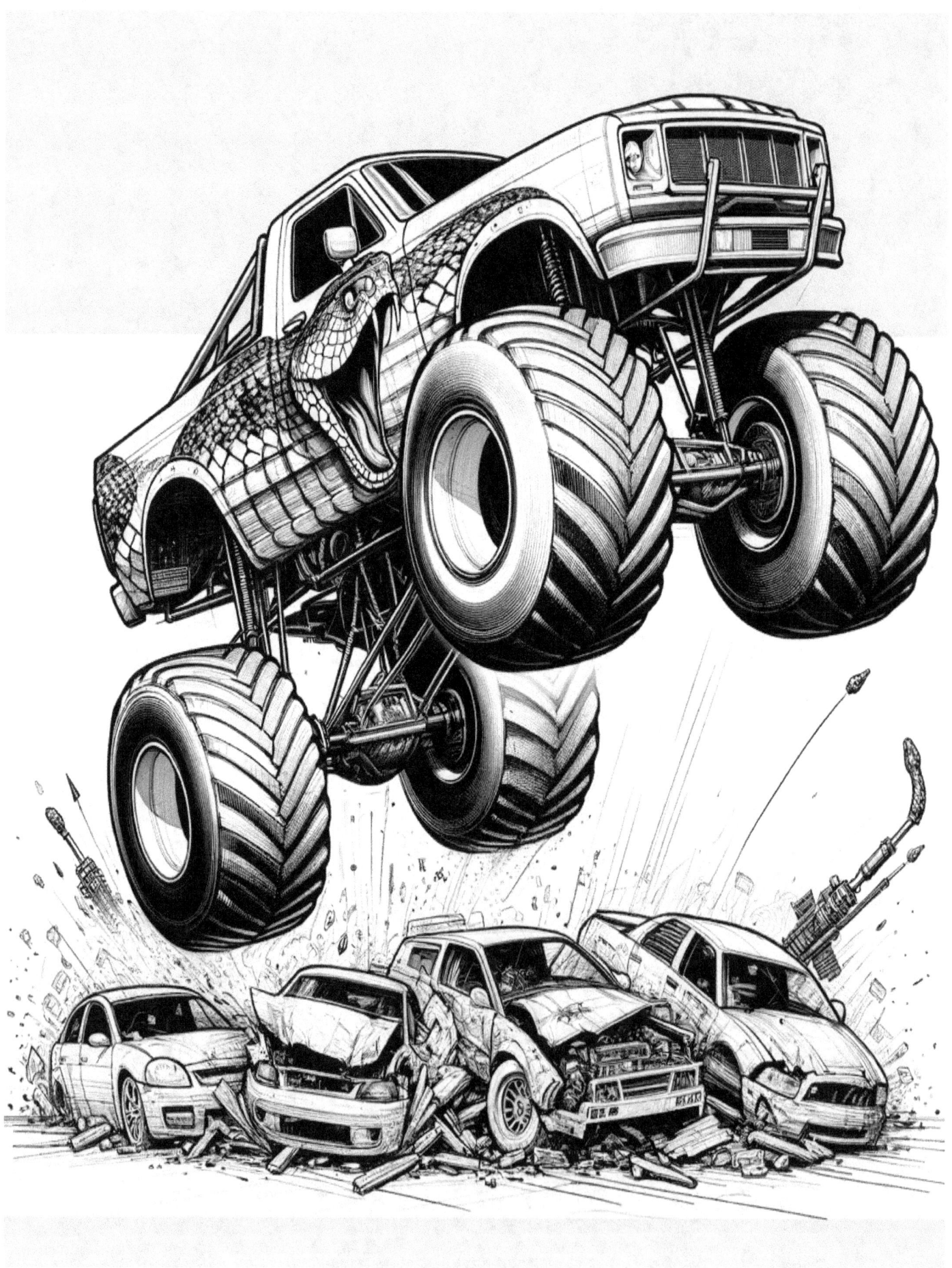

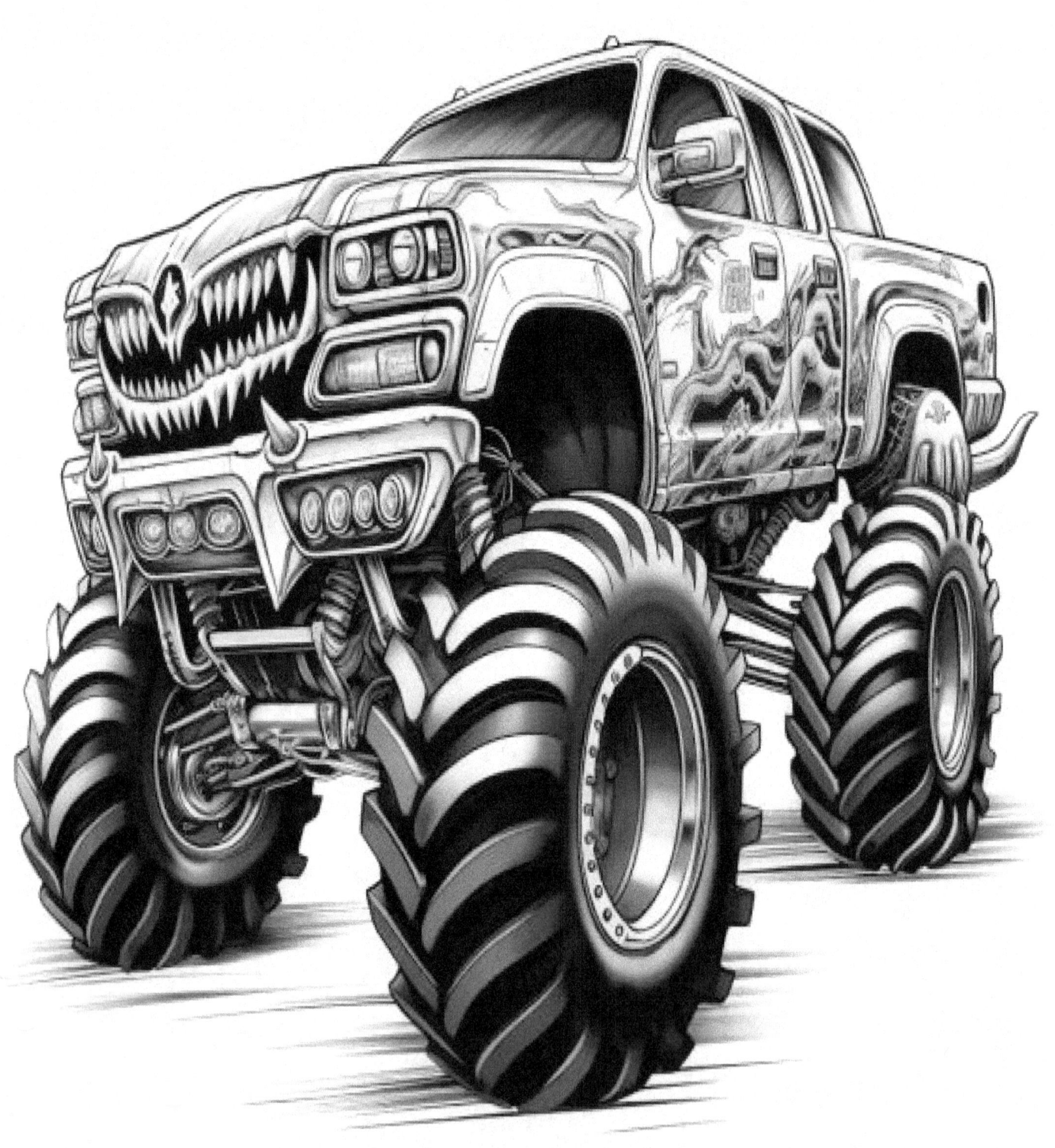

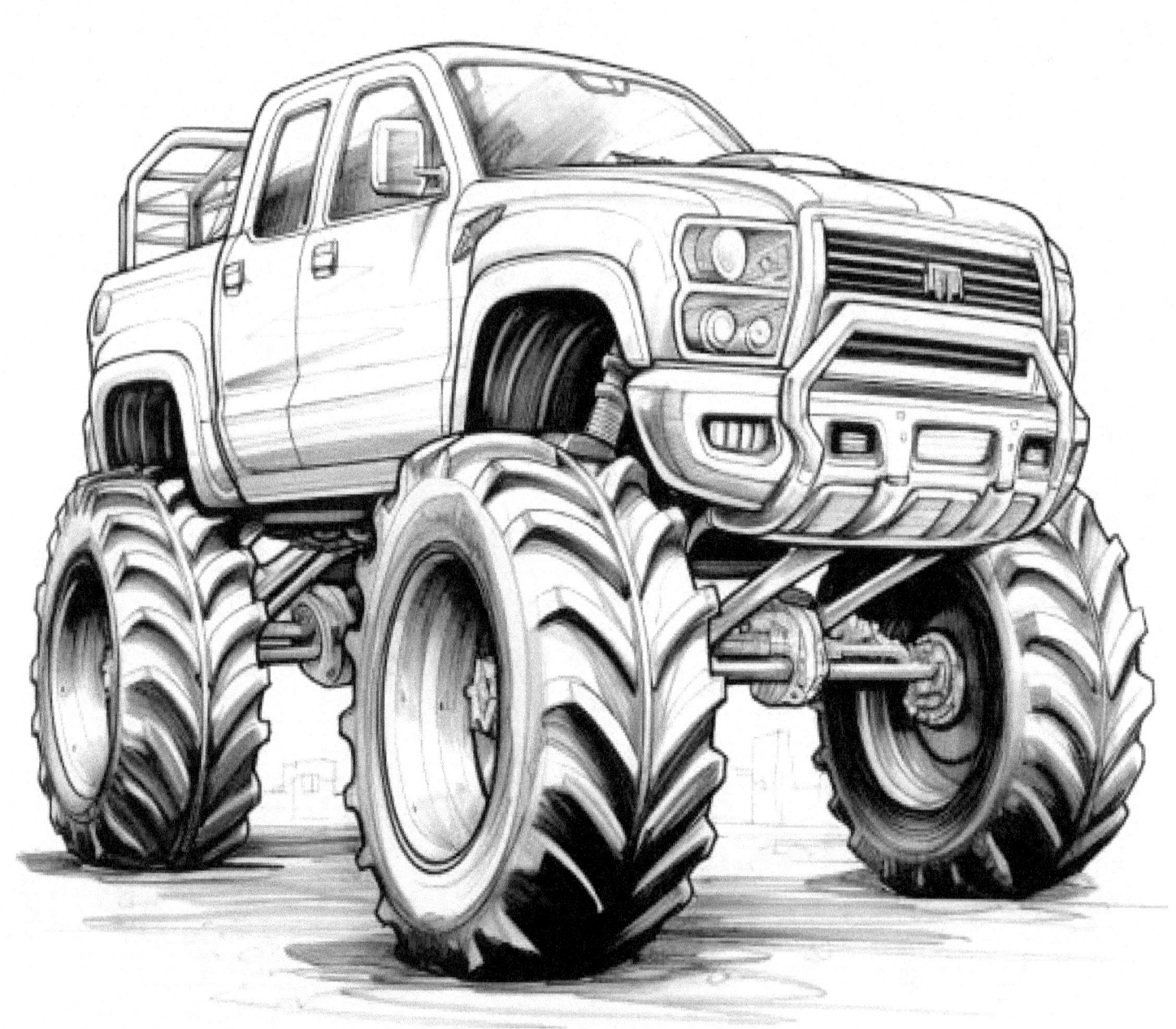

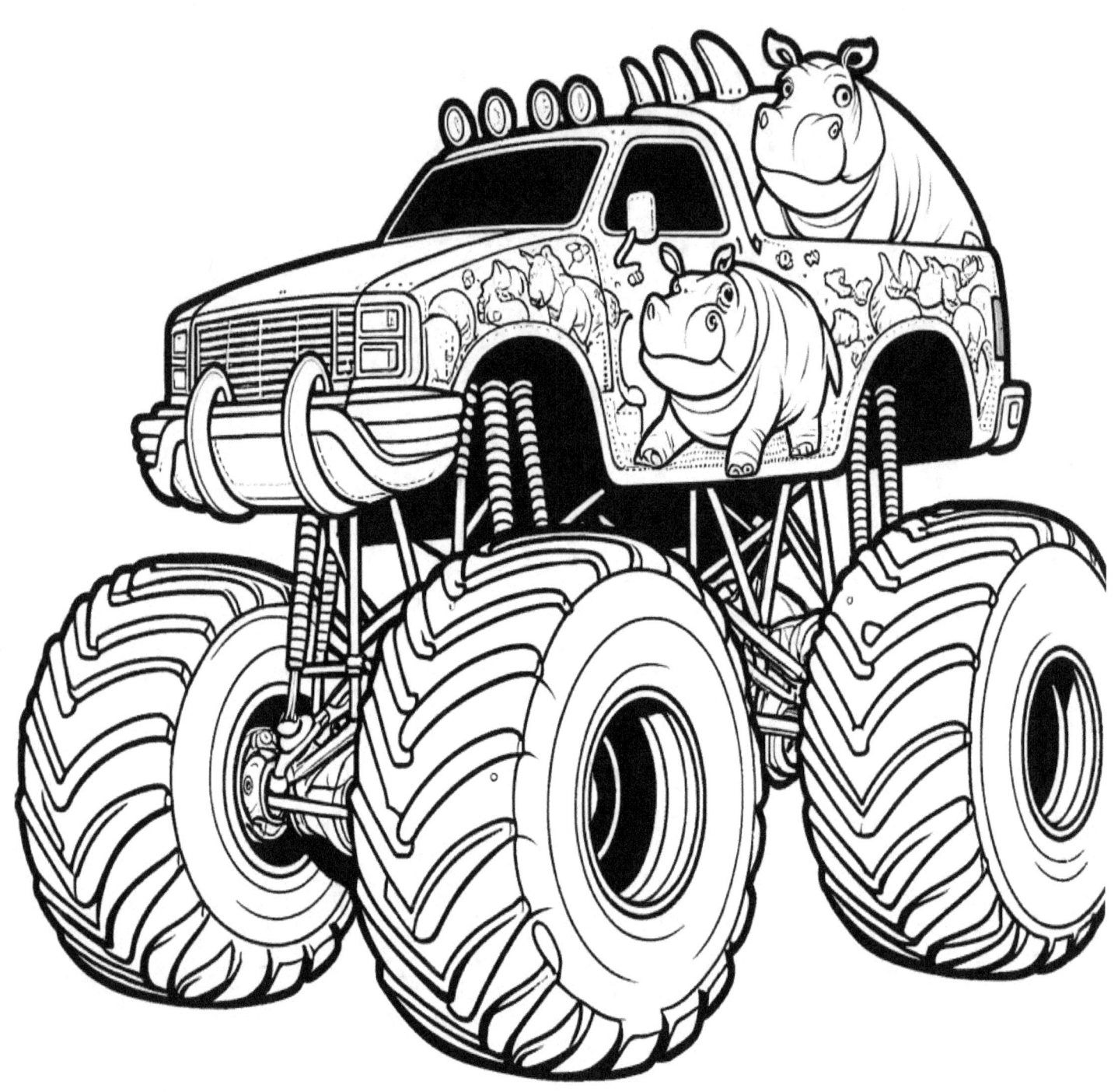

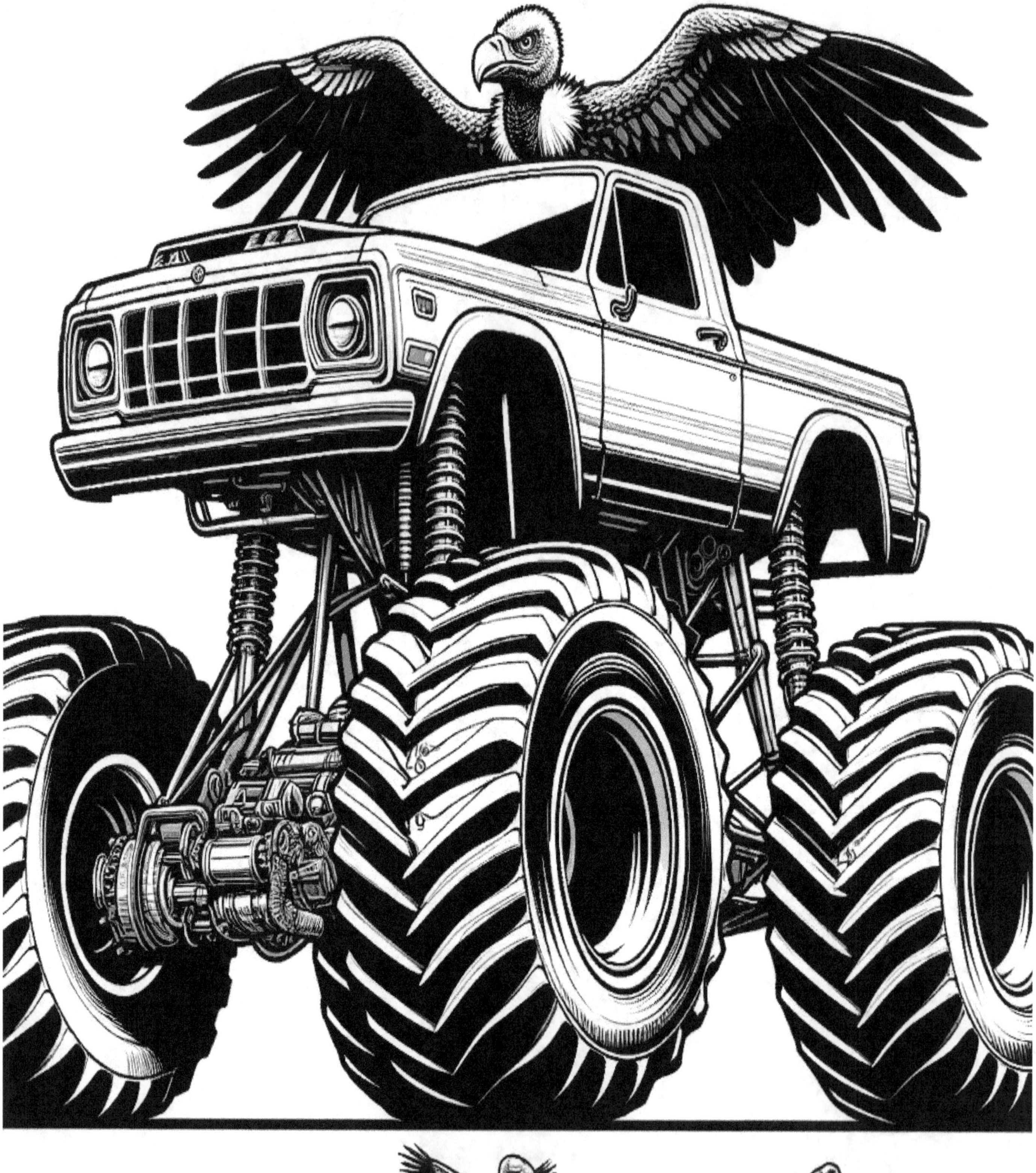

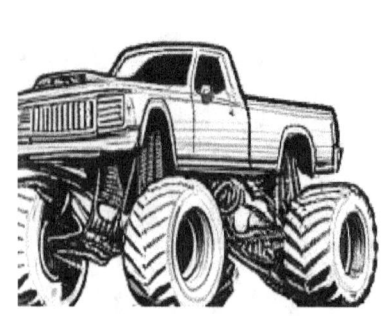
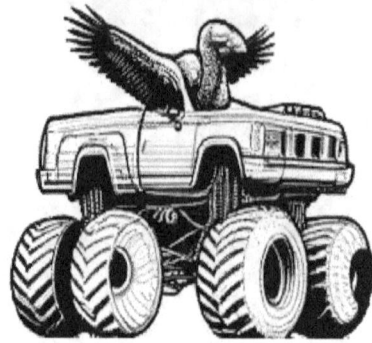
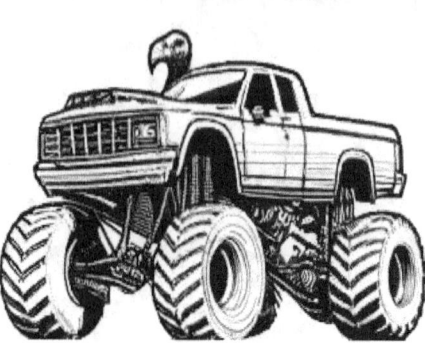

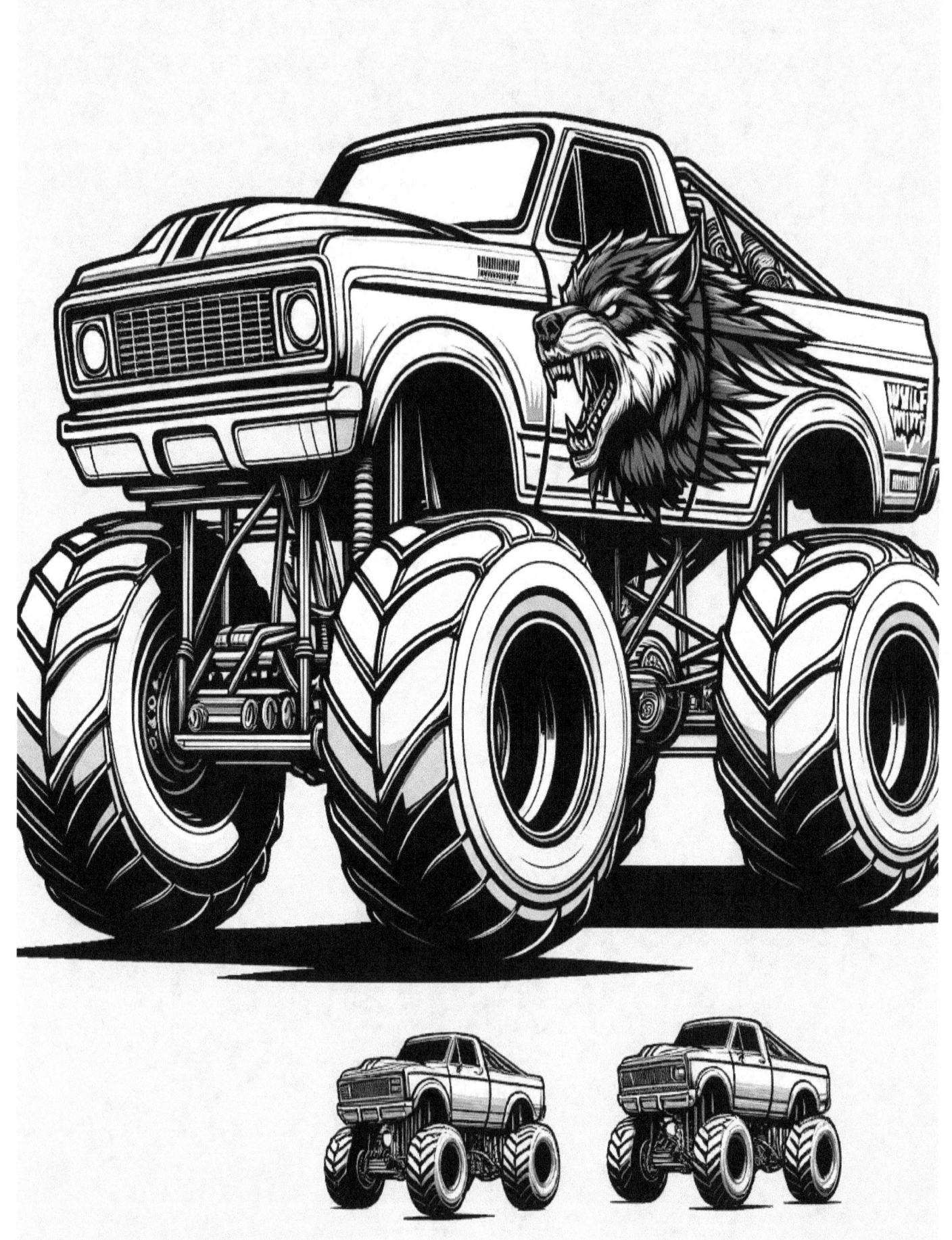

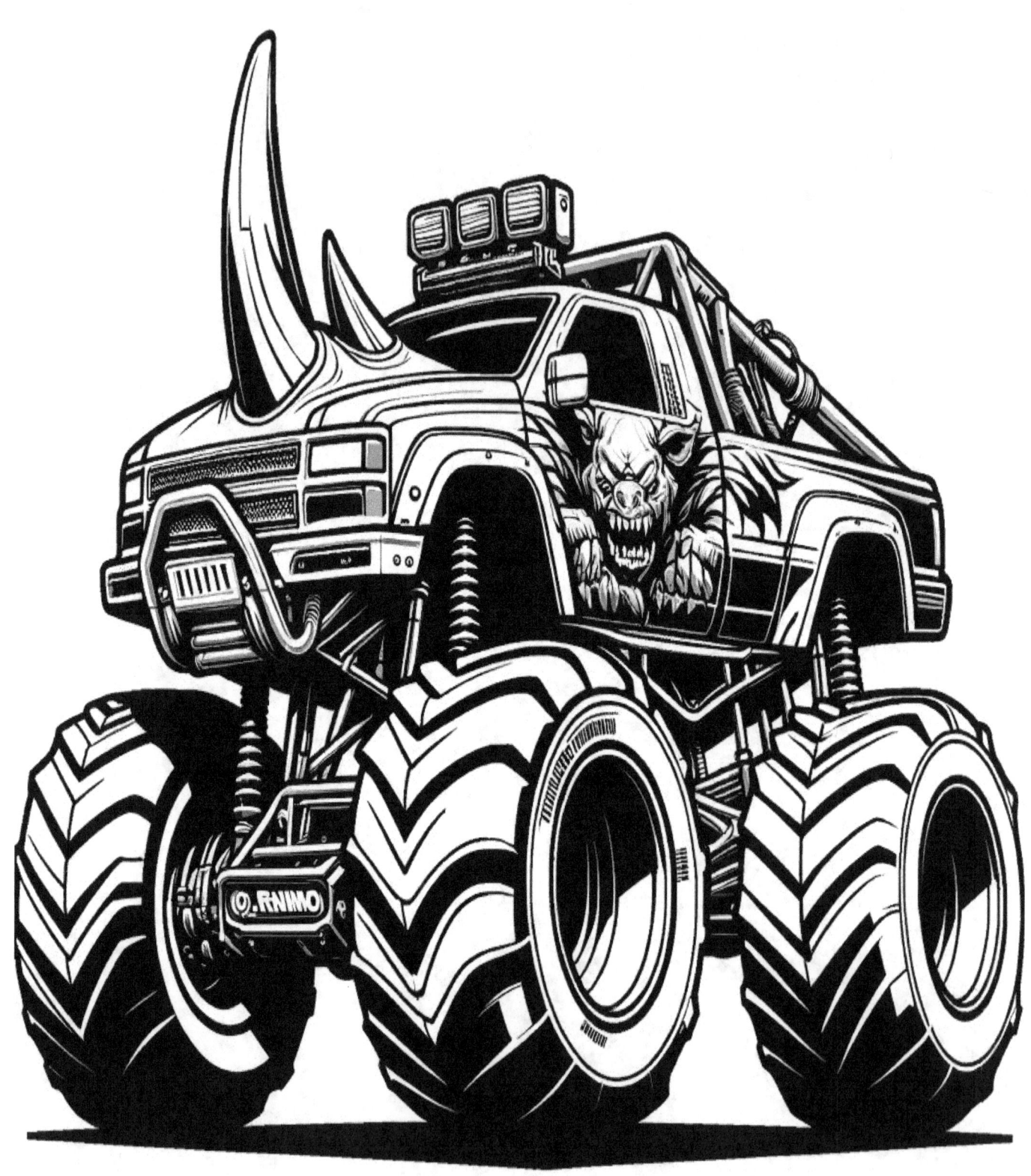

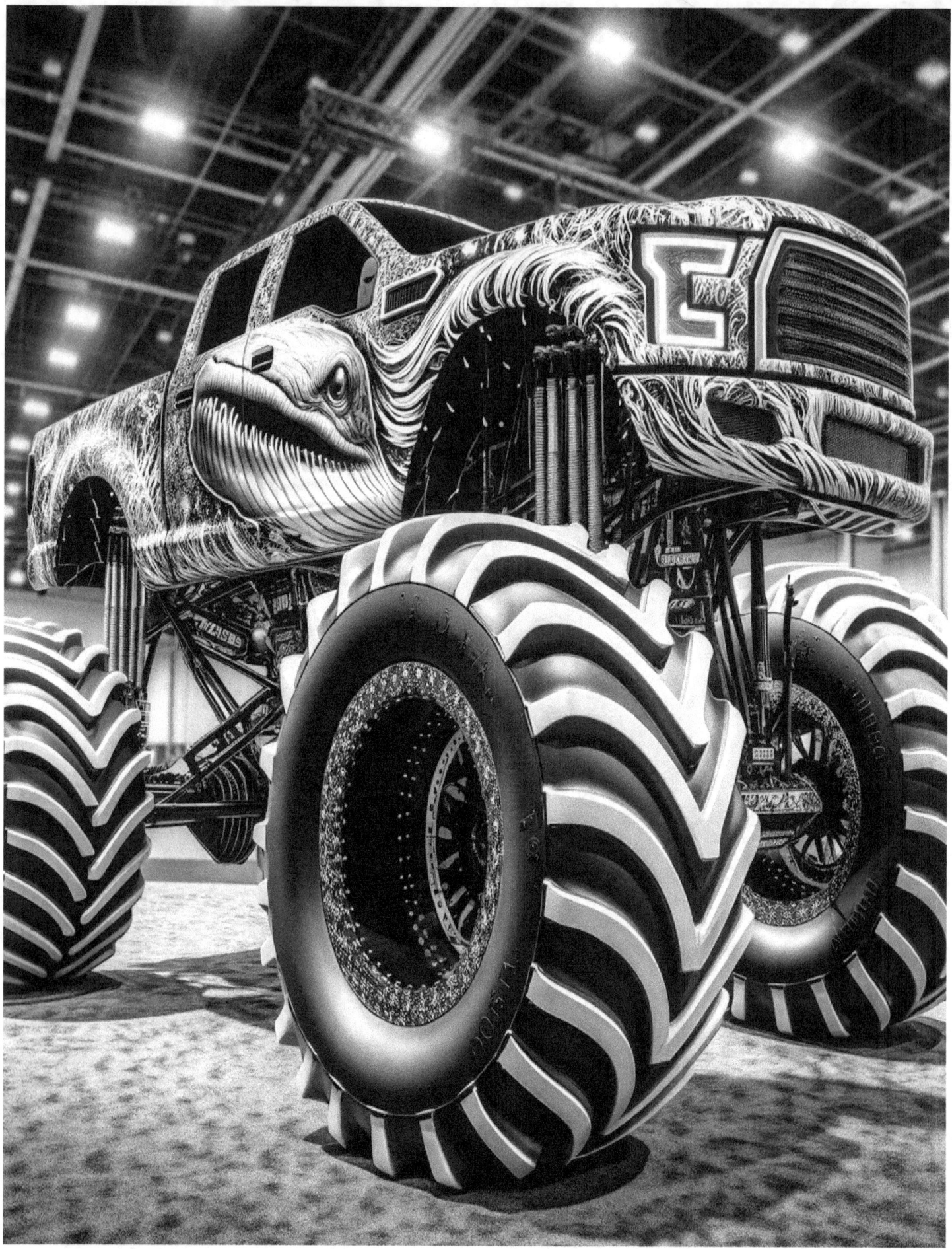

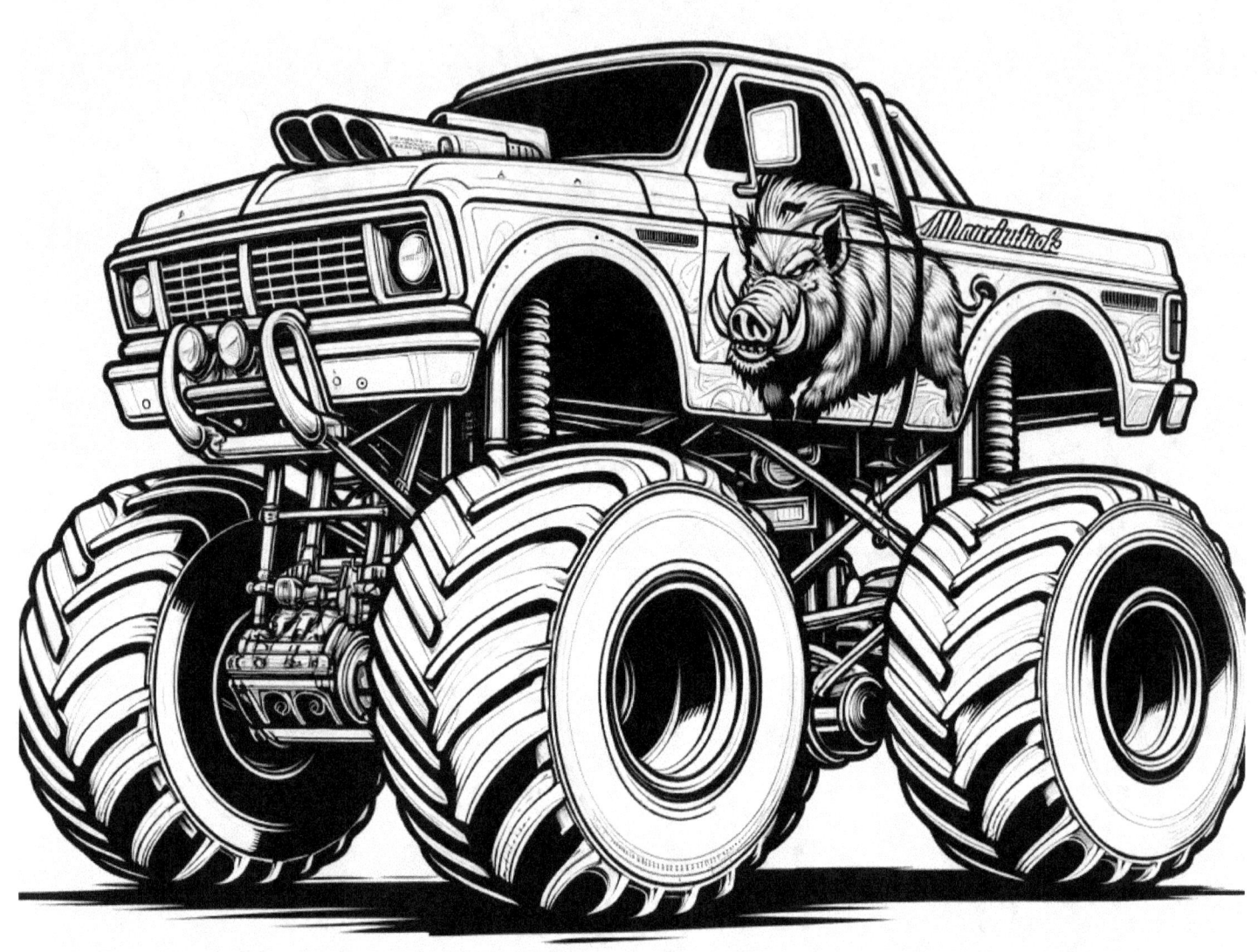

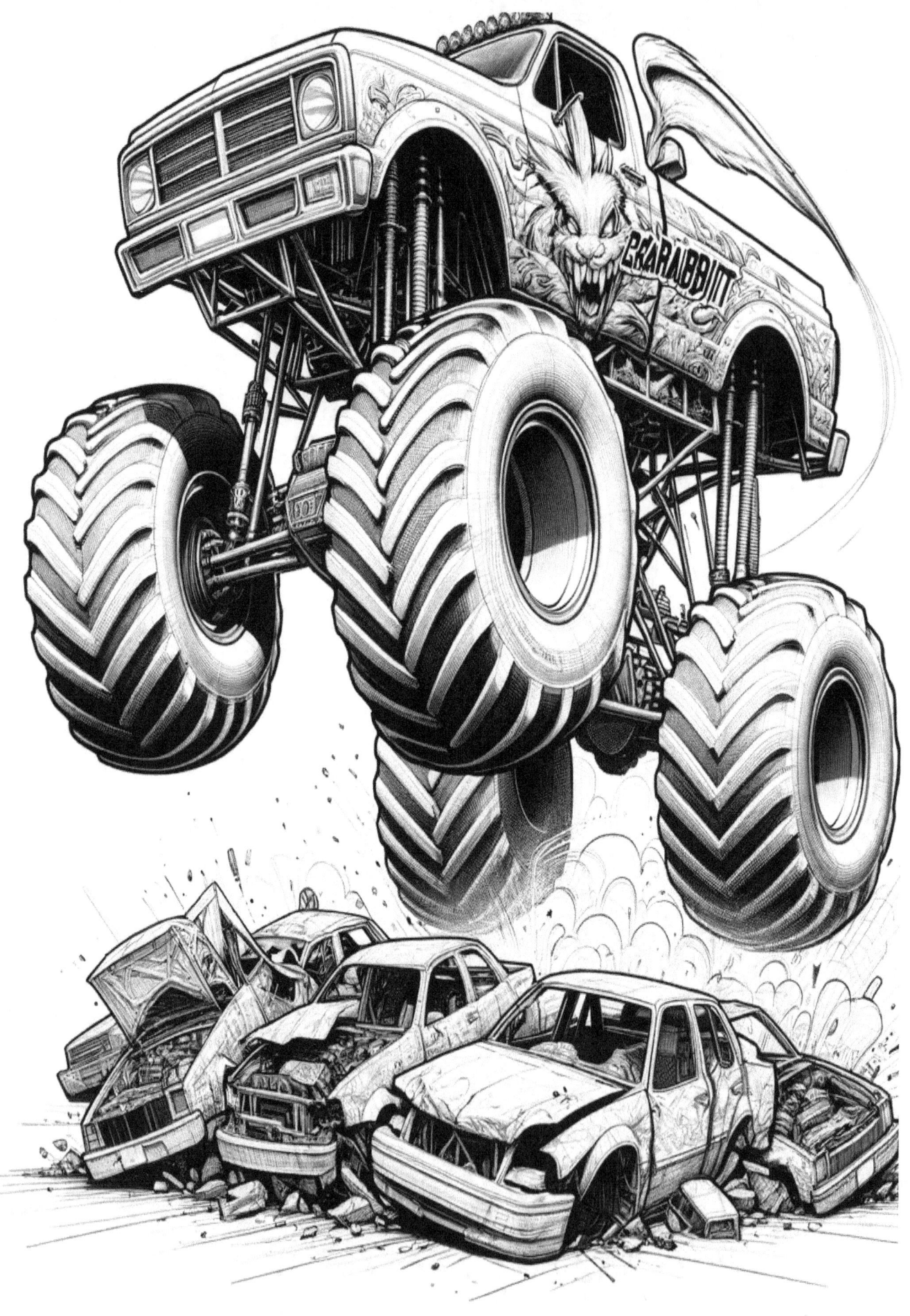

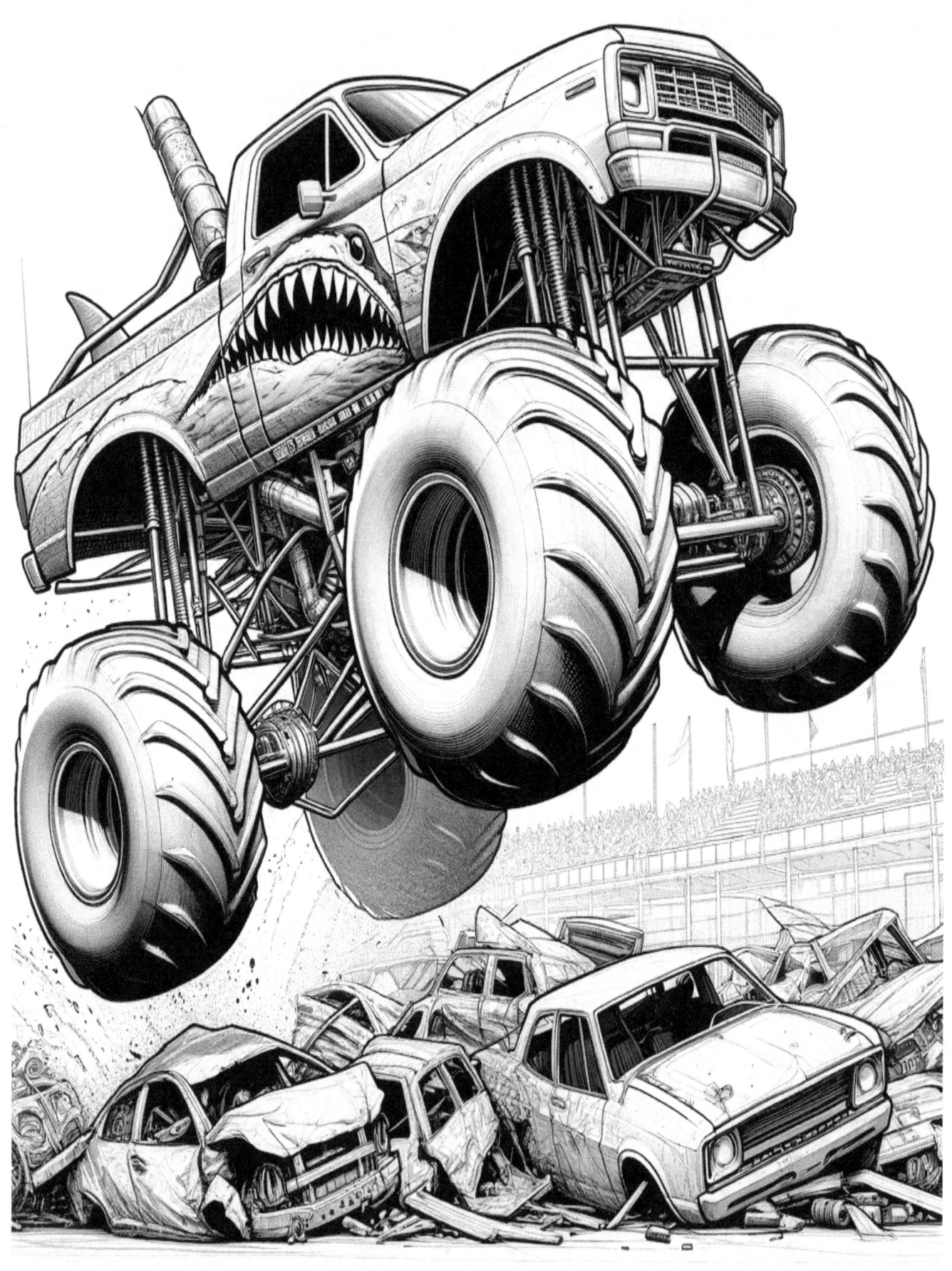

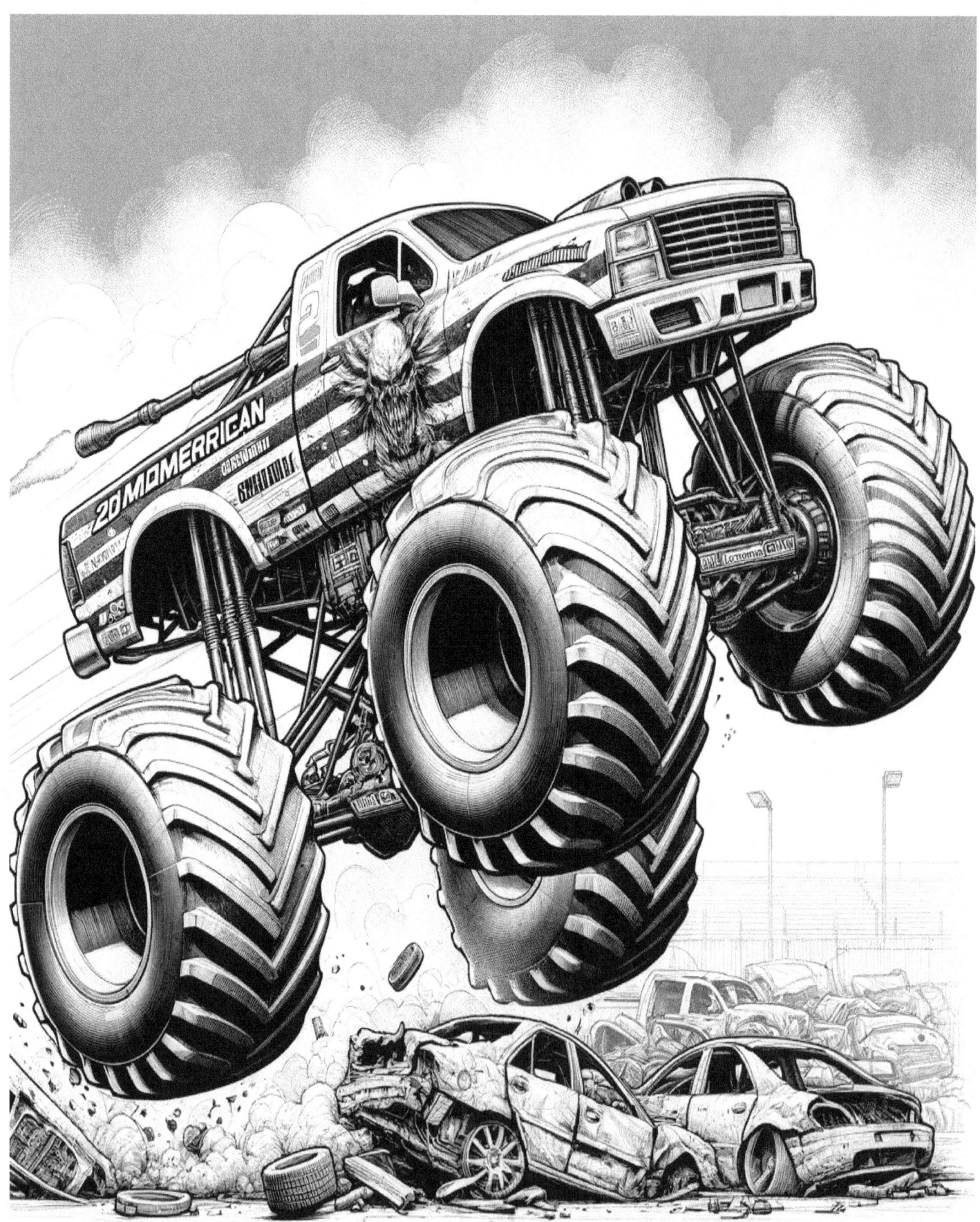

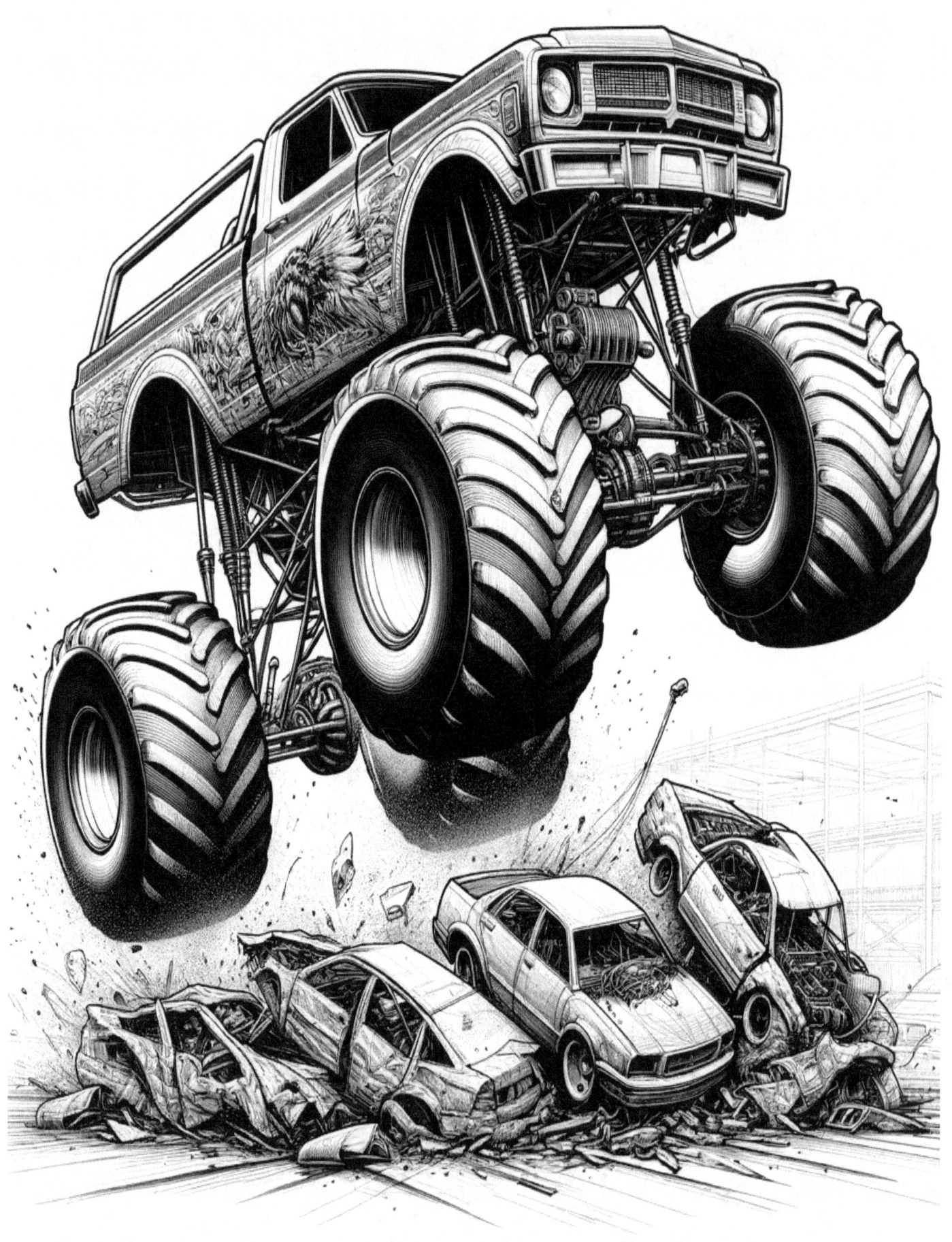

49

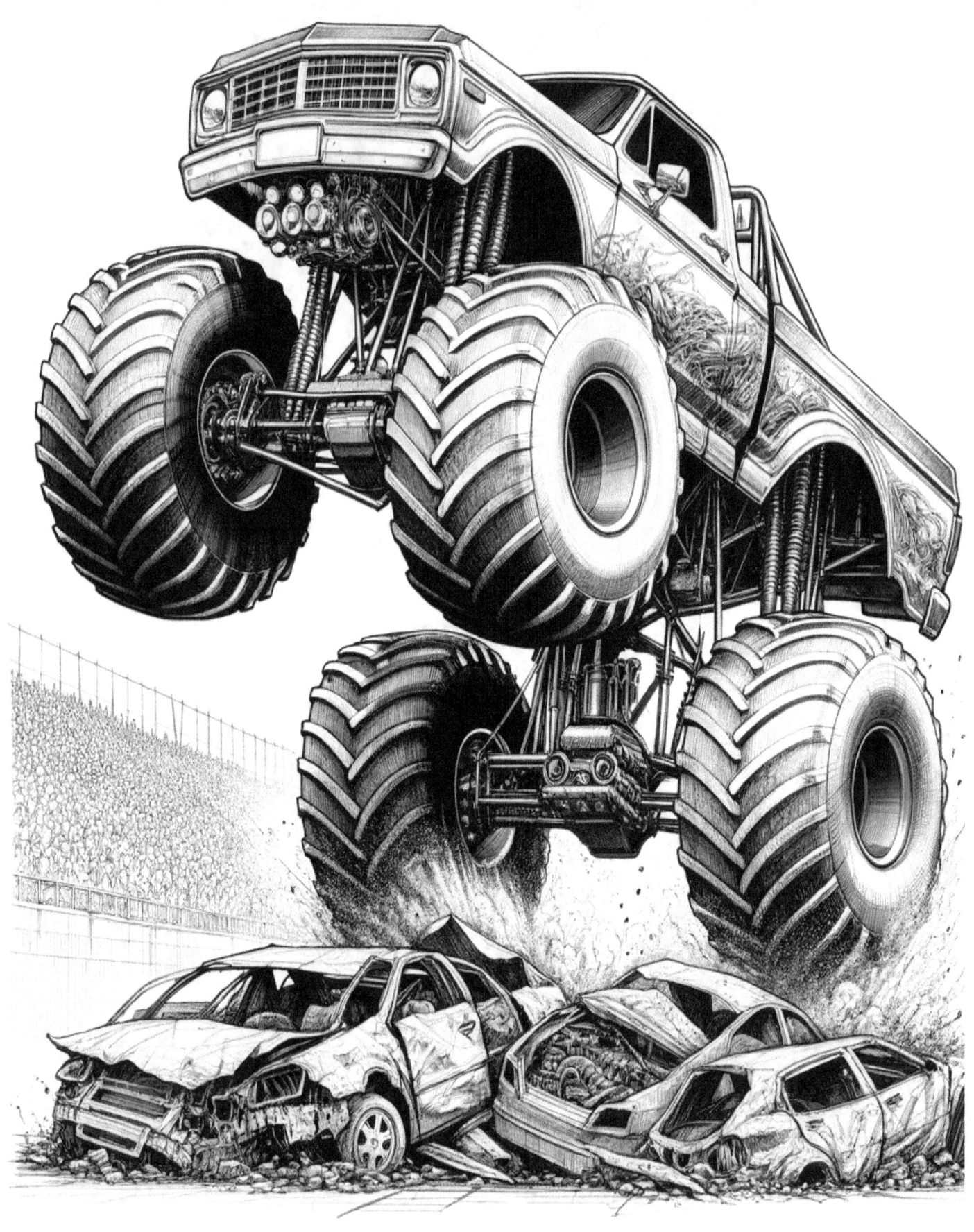

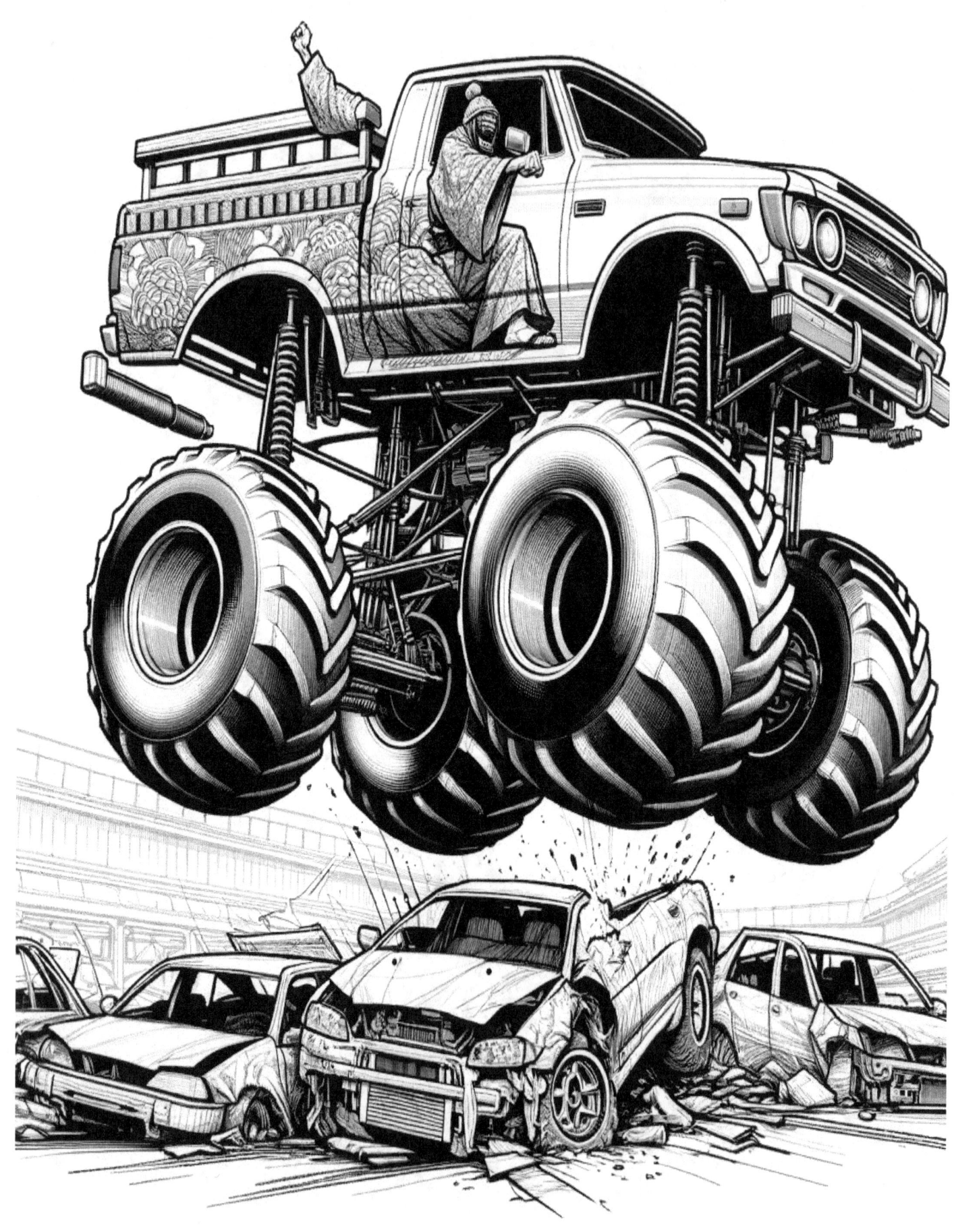

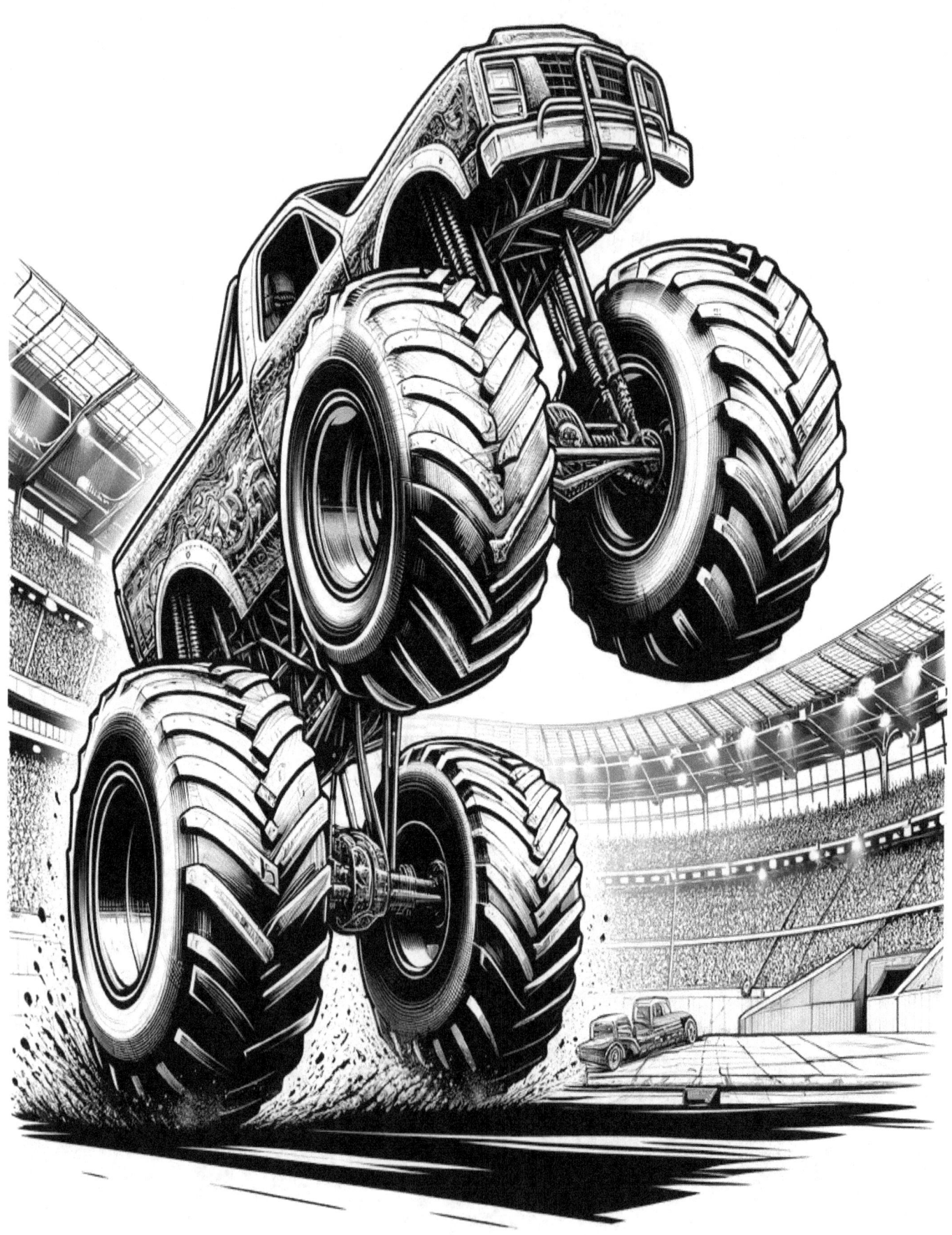

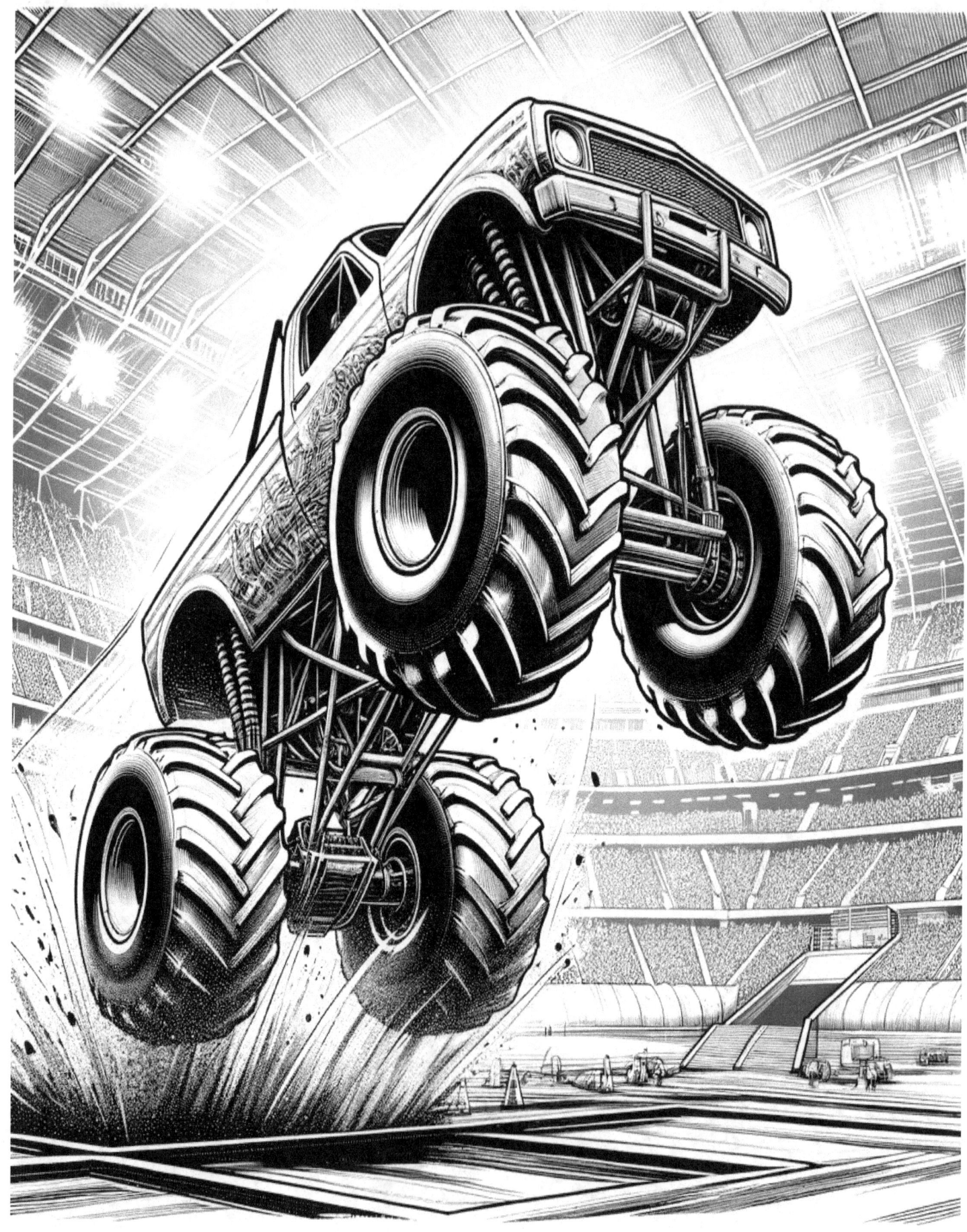

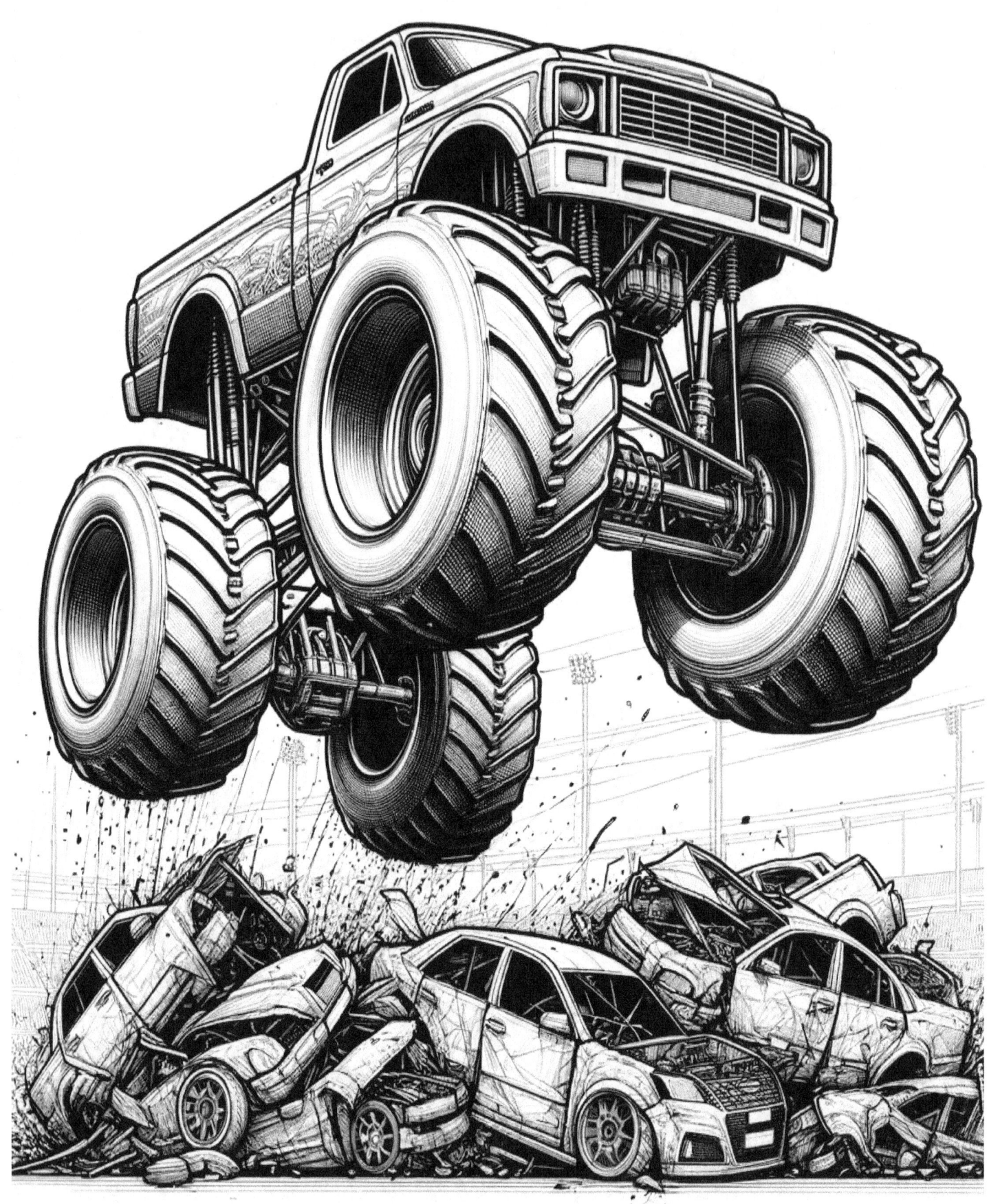

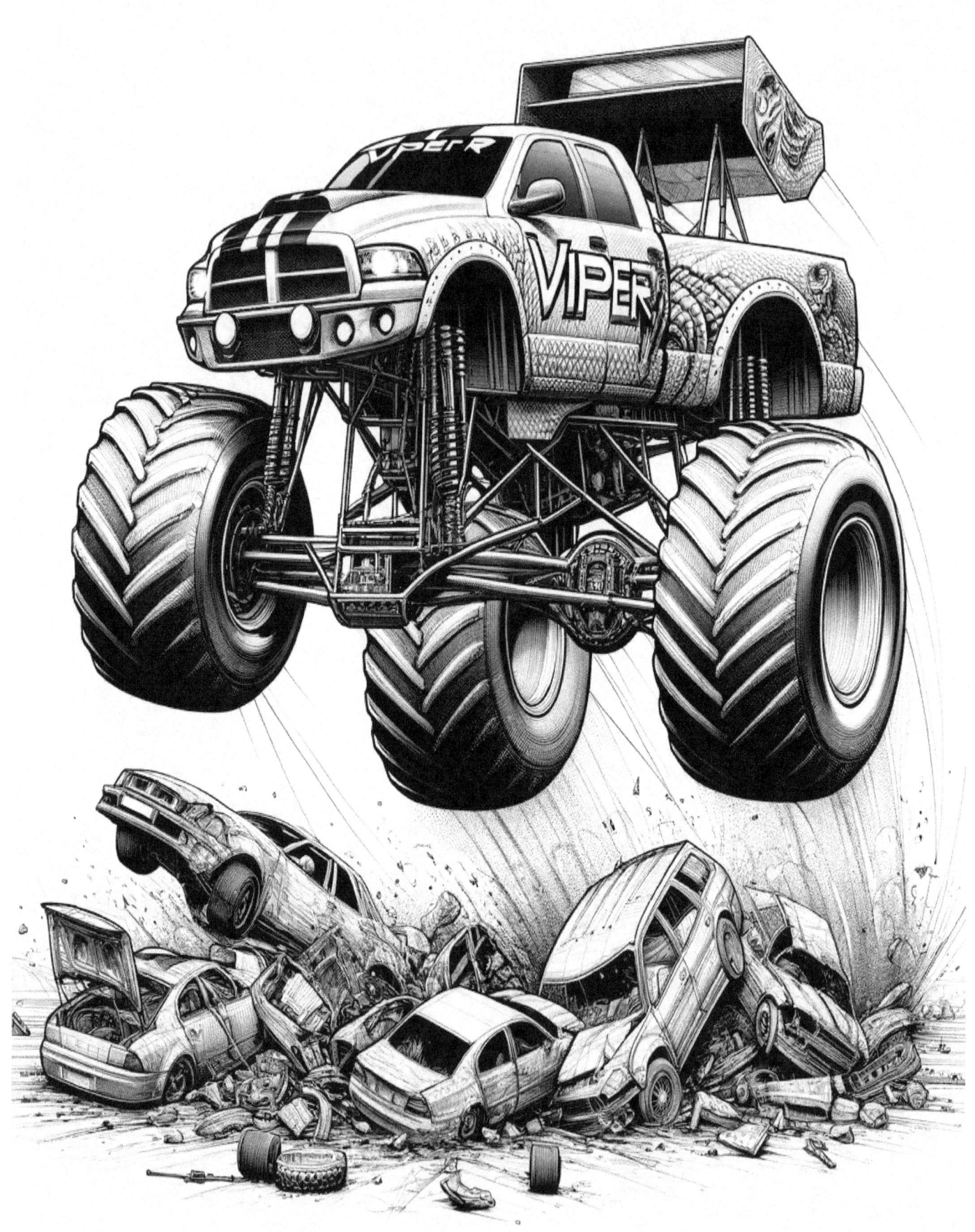

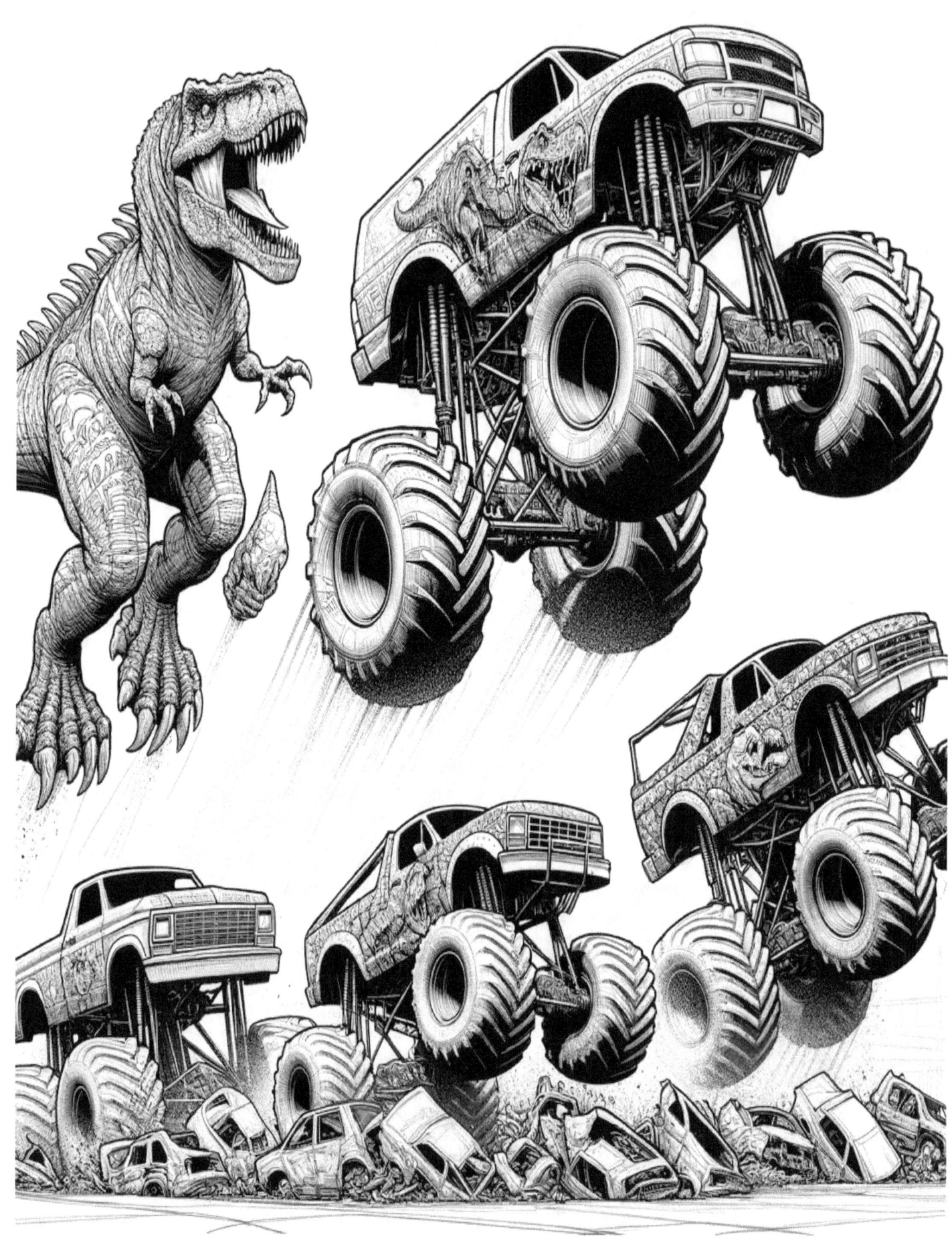

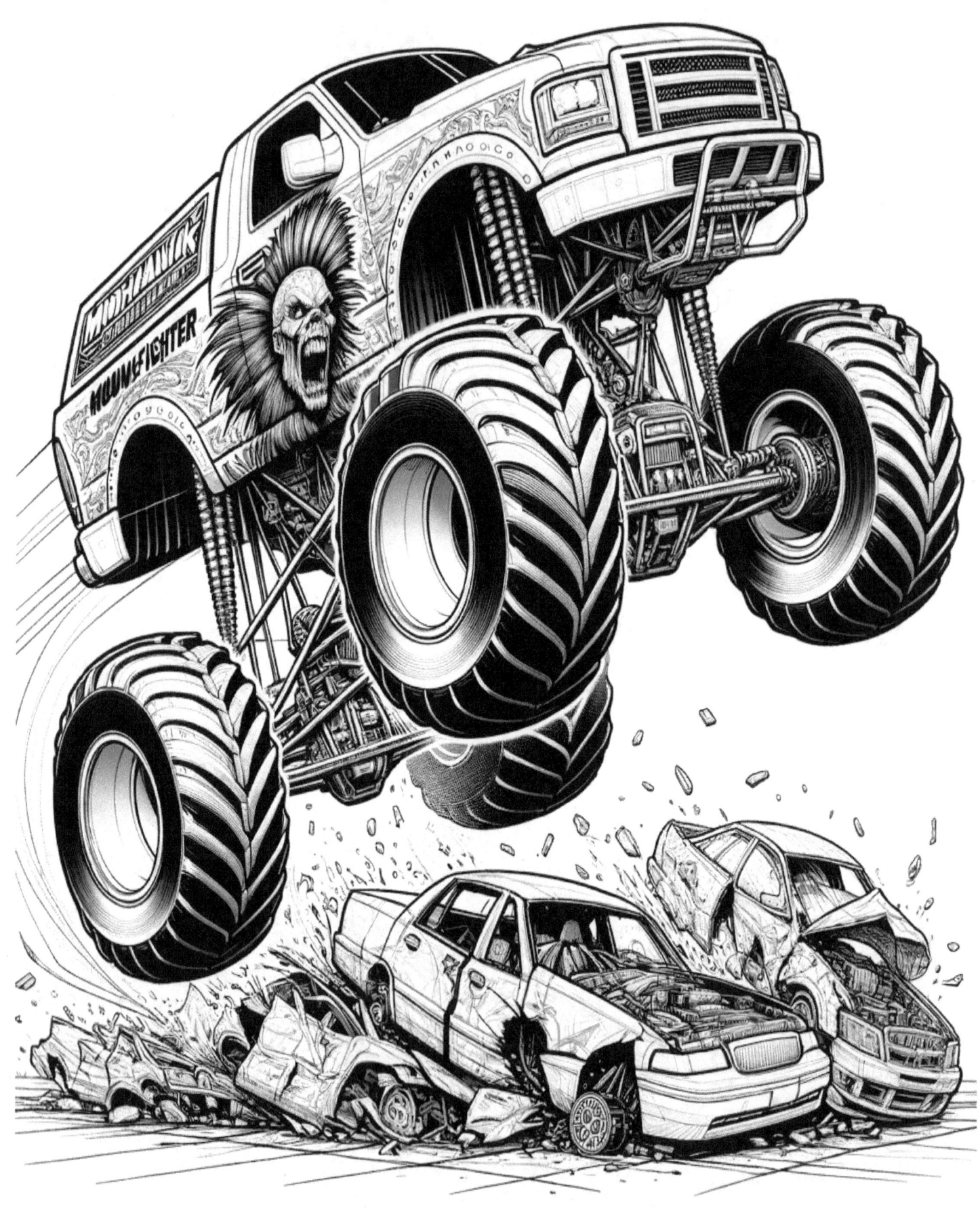

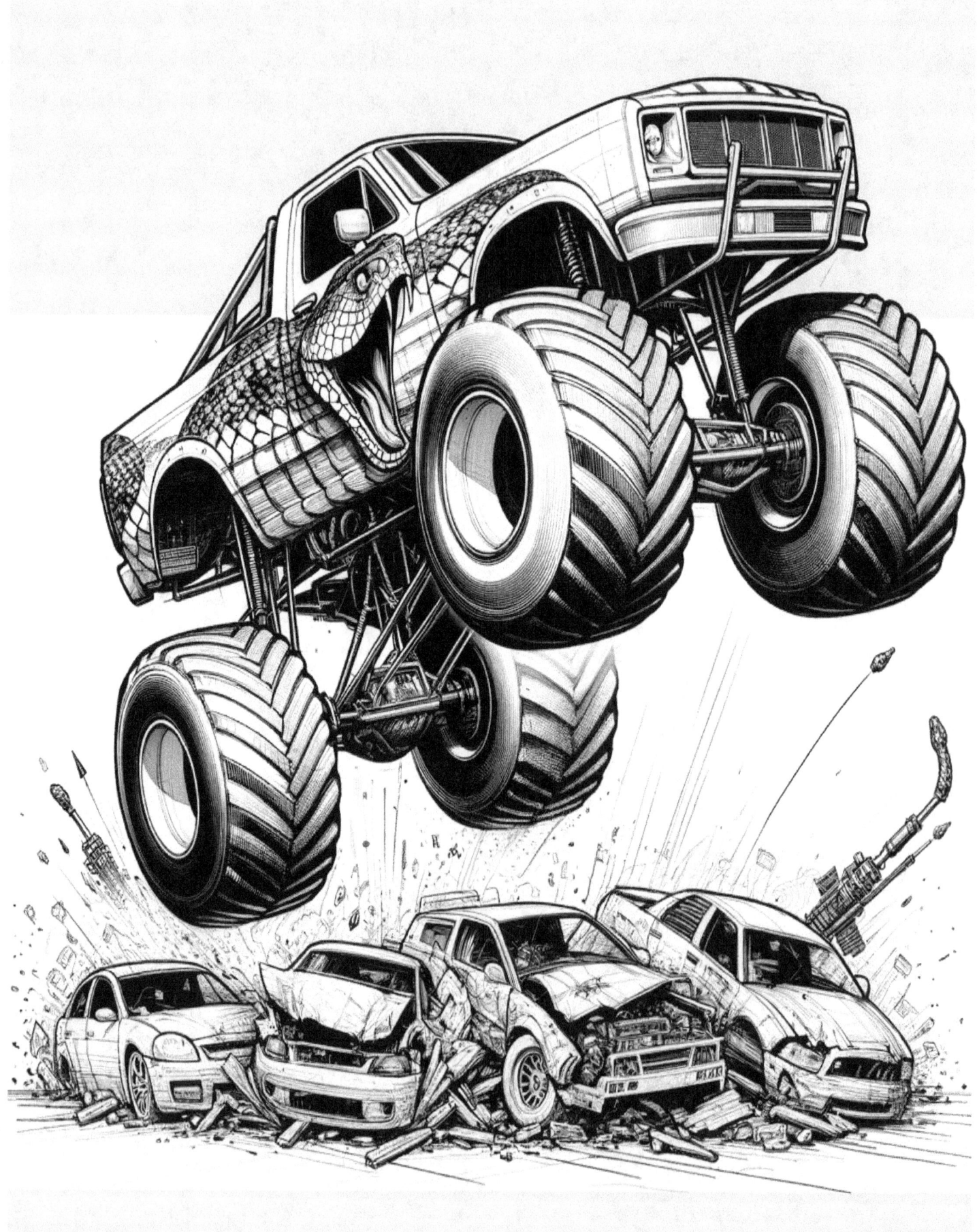

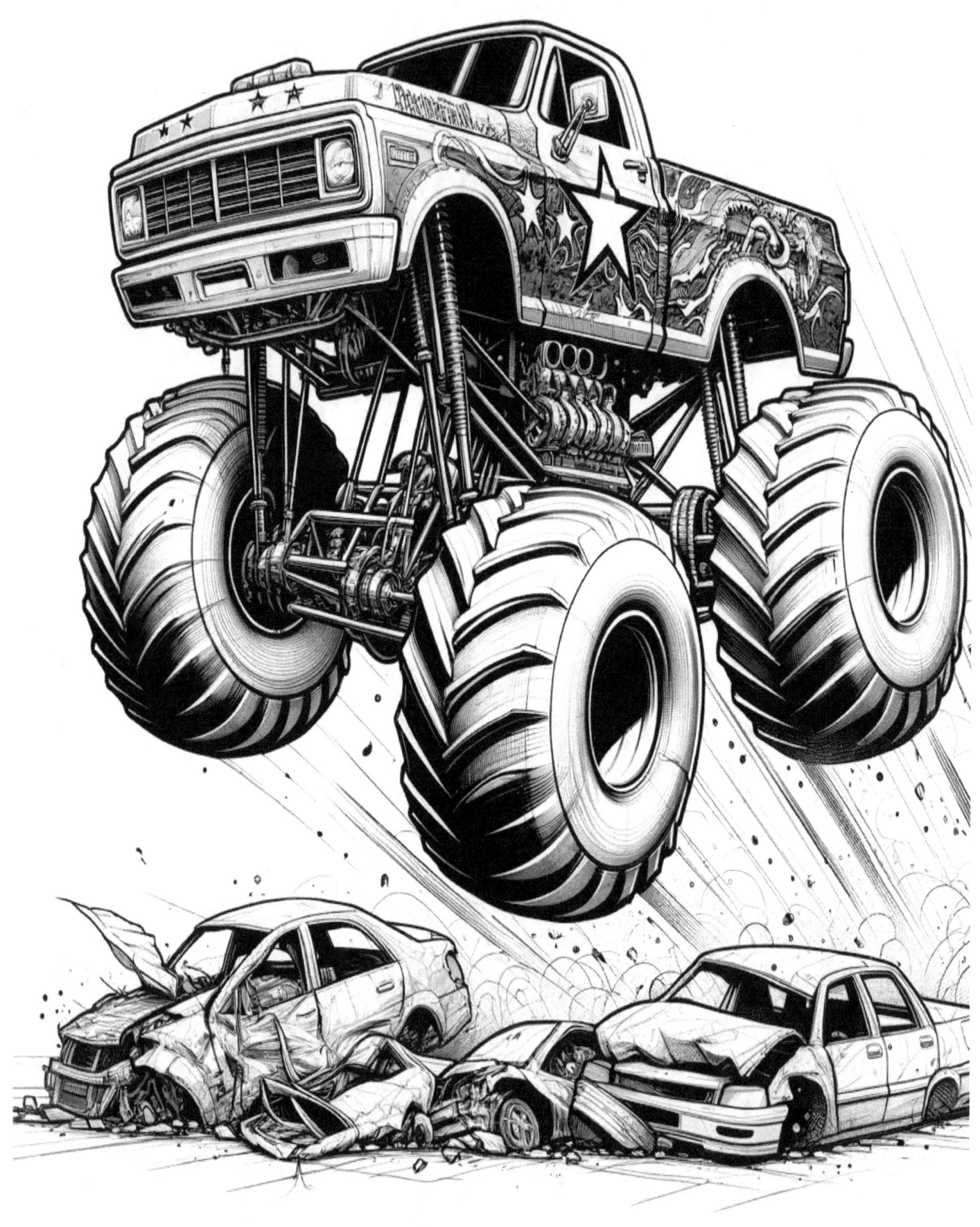

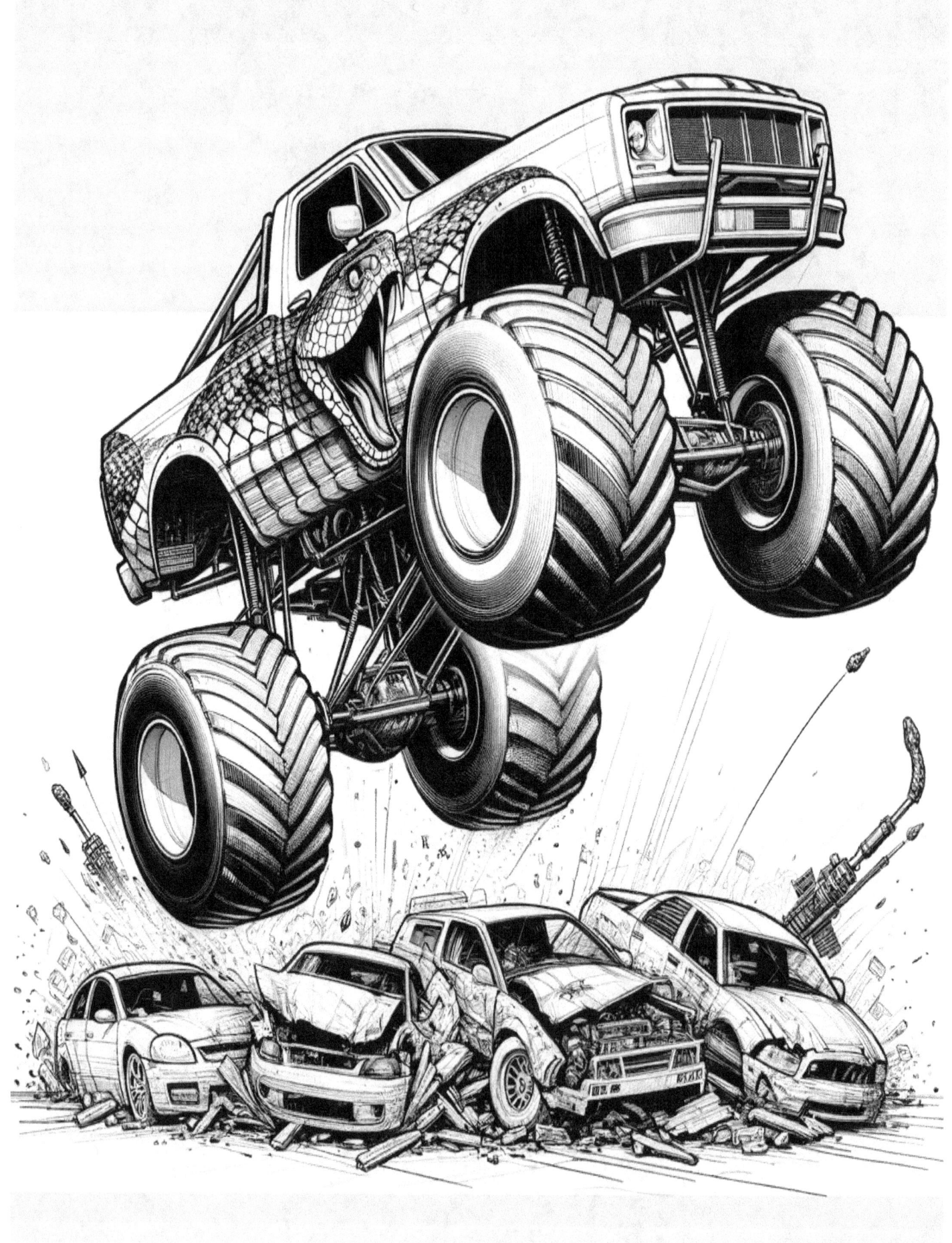

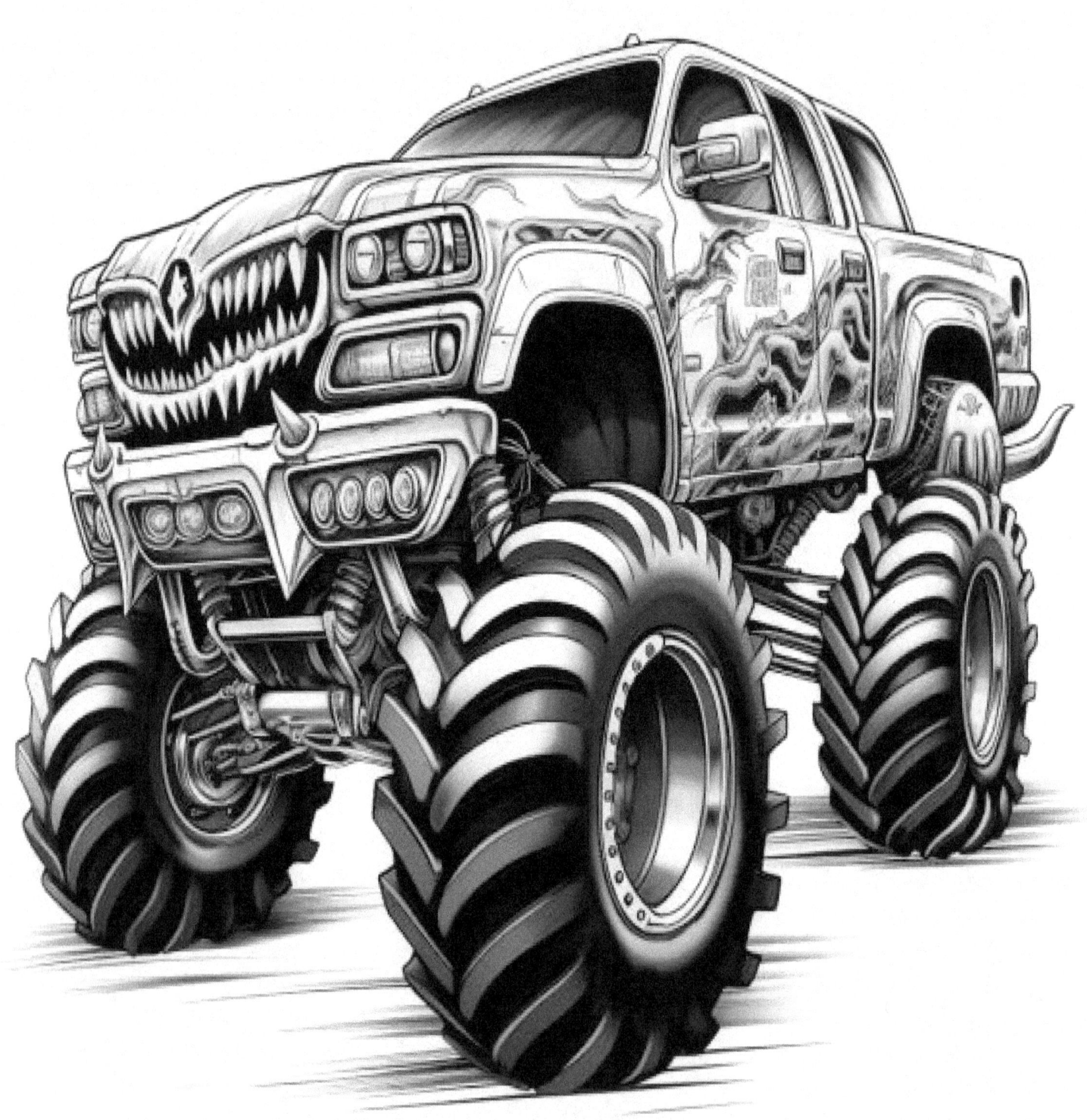

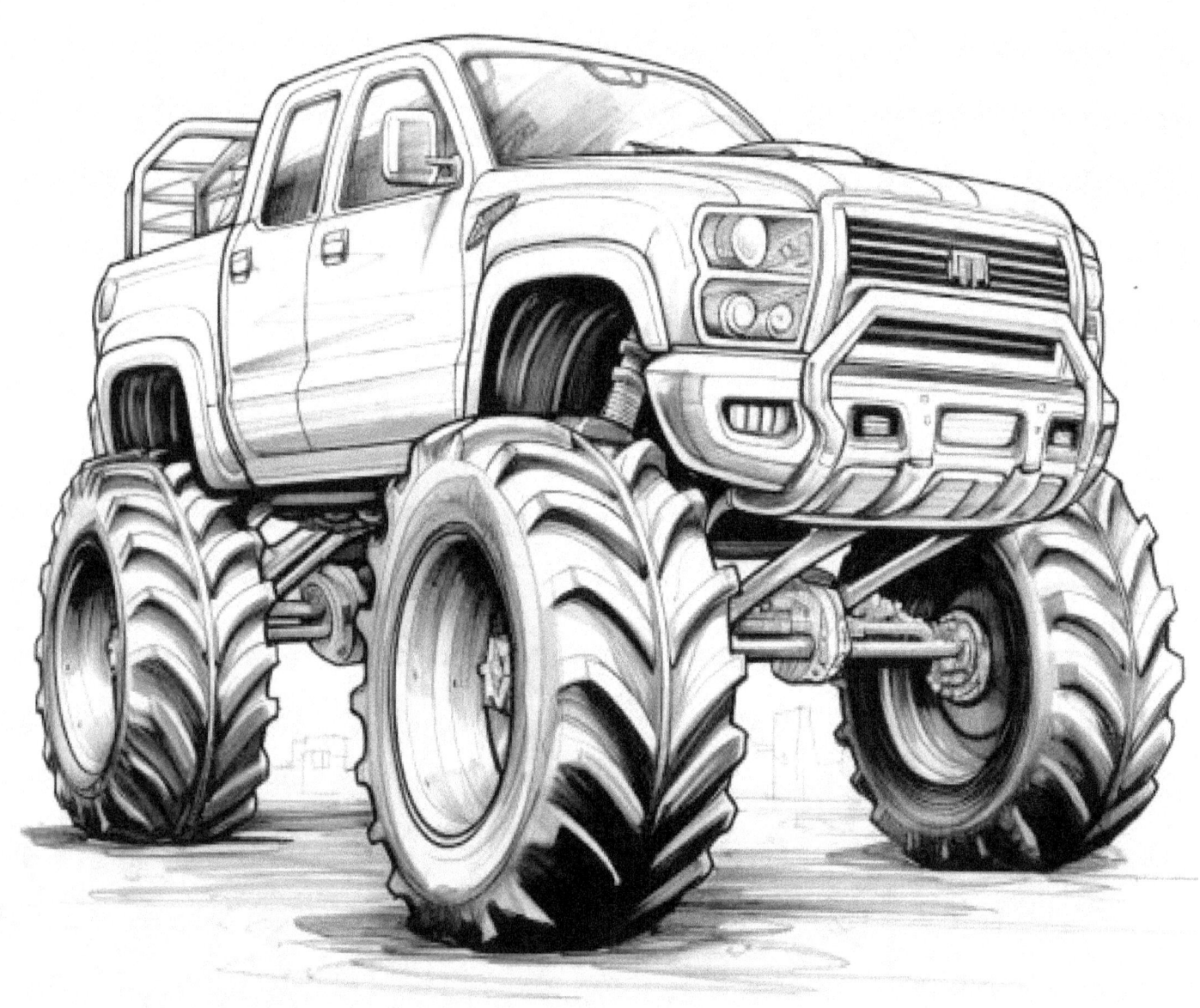

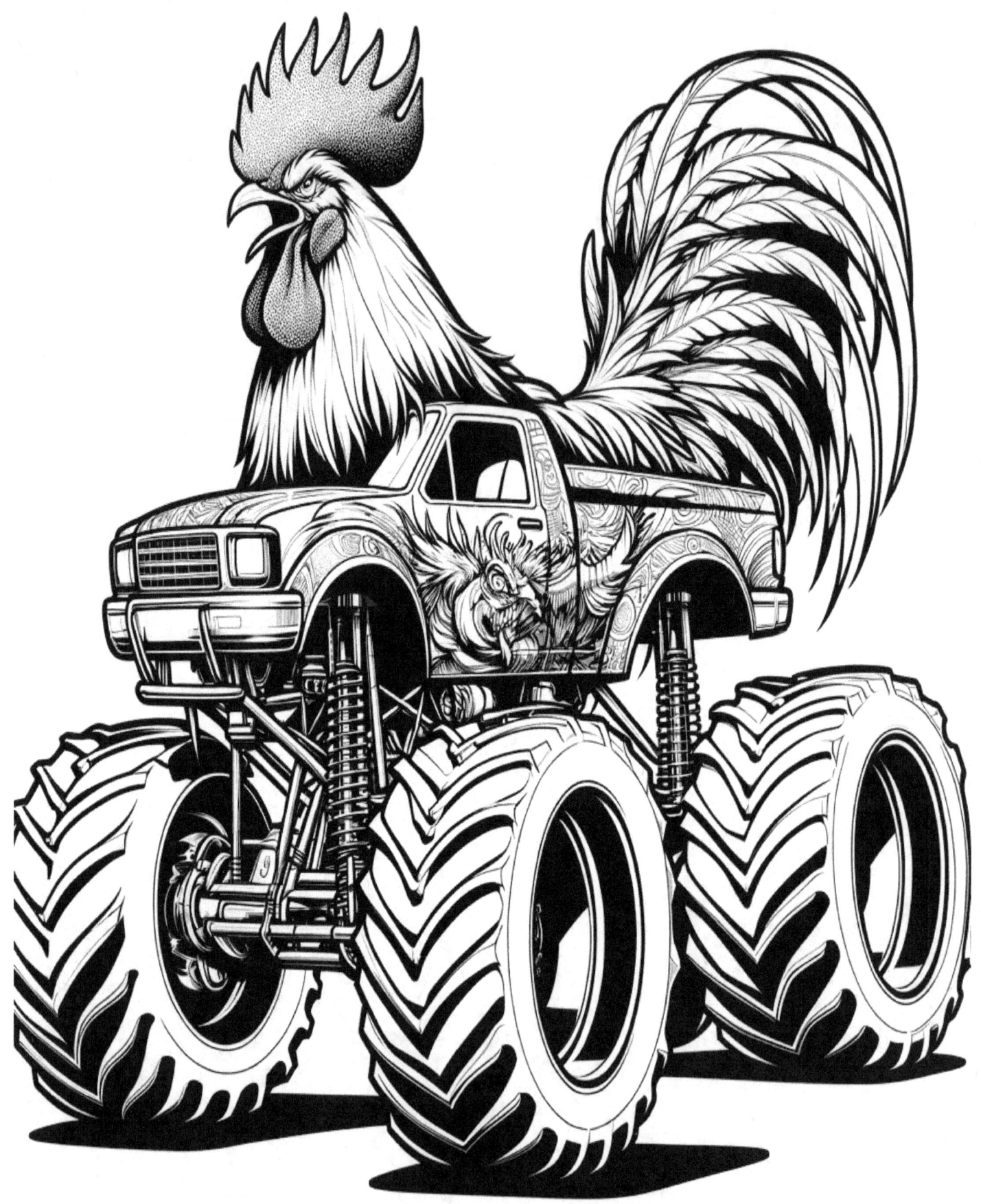

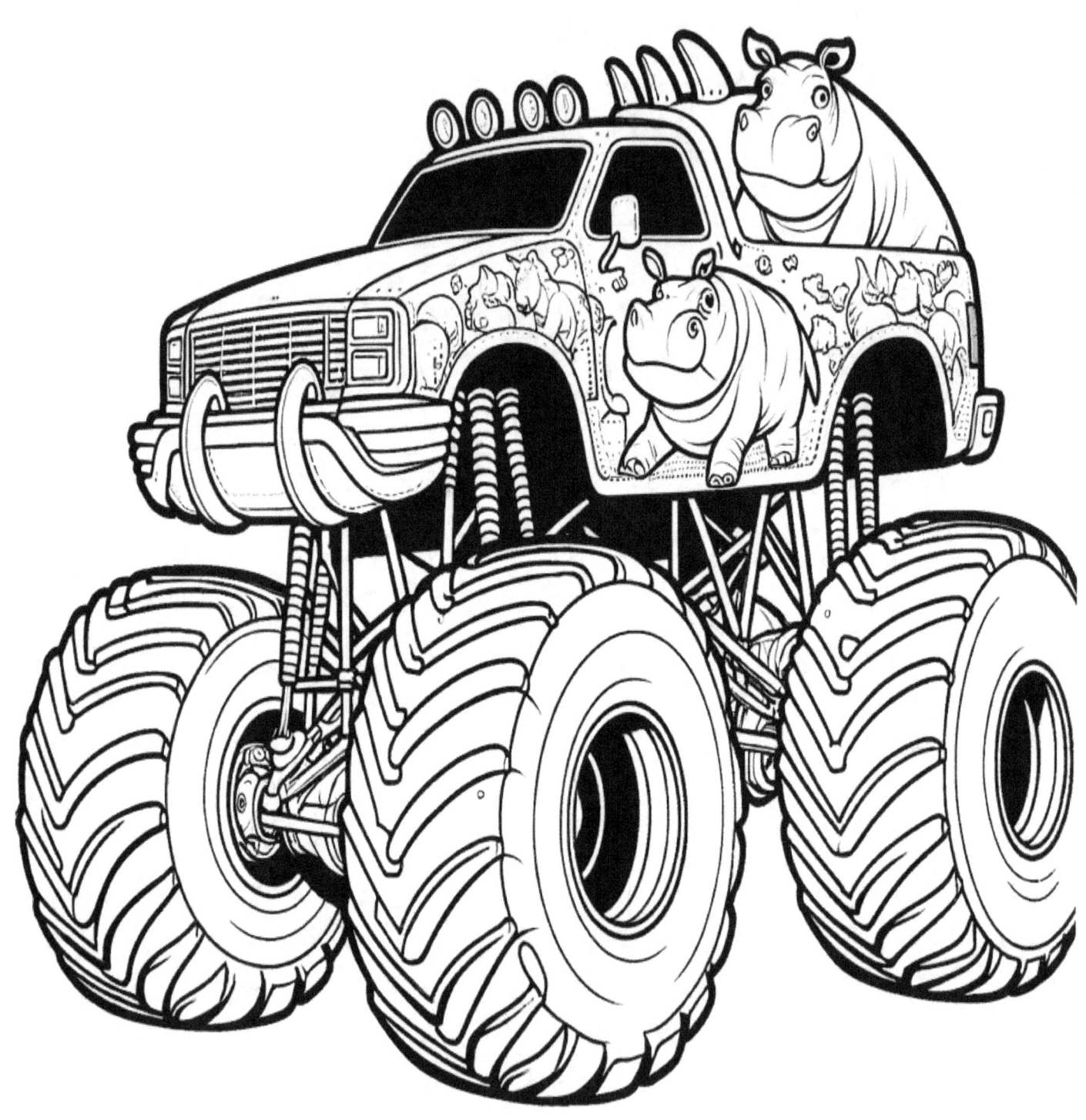

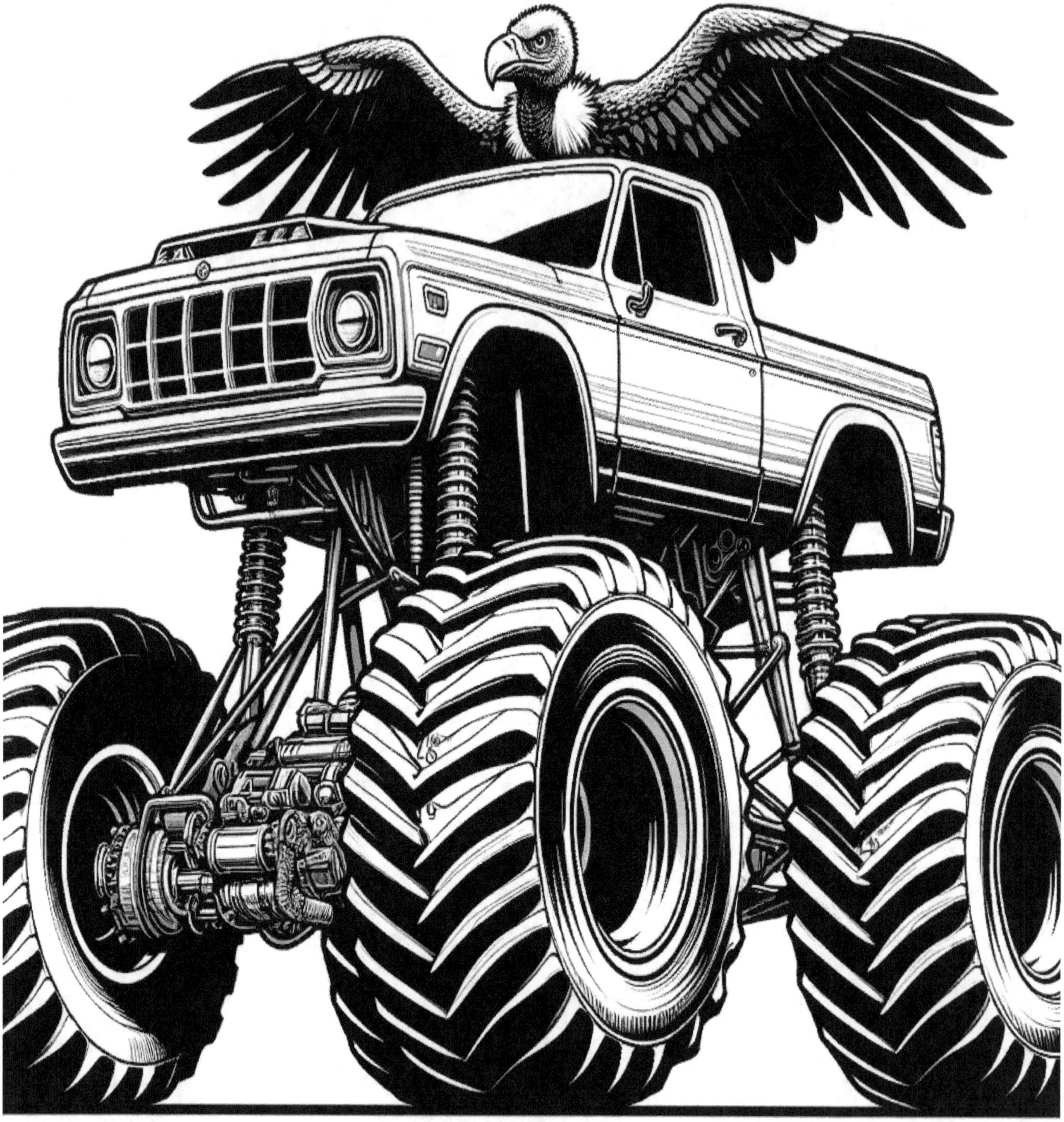

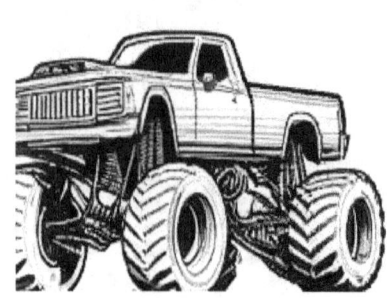
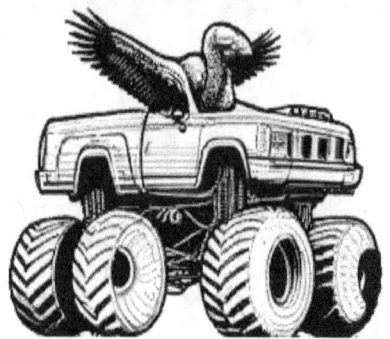
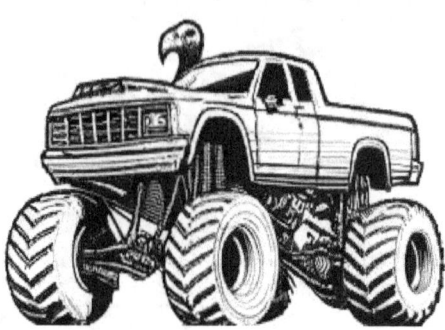

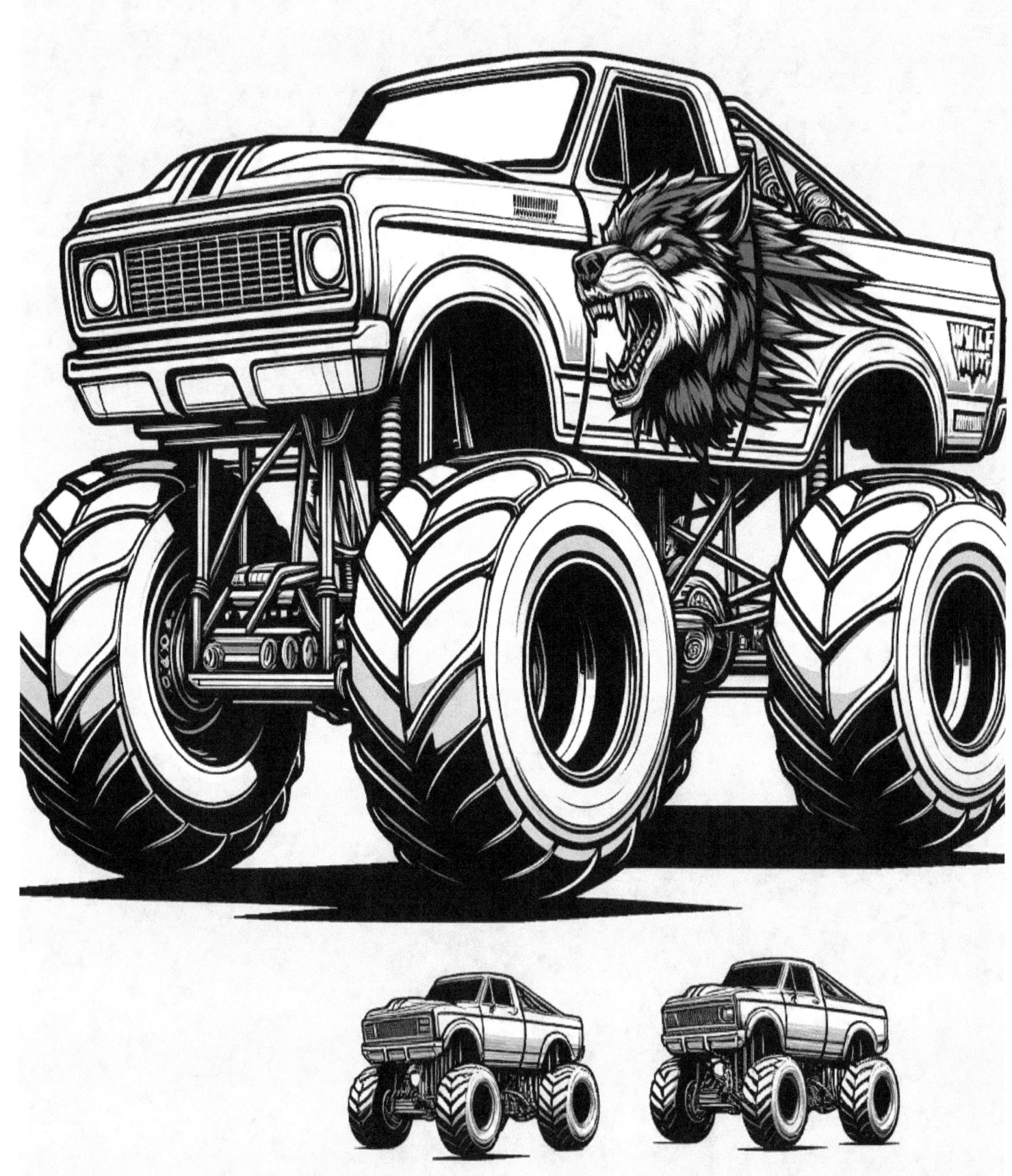

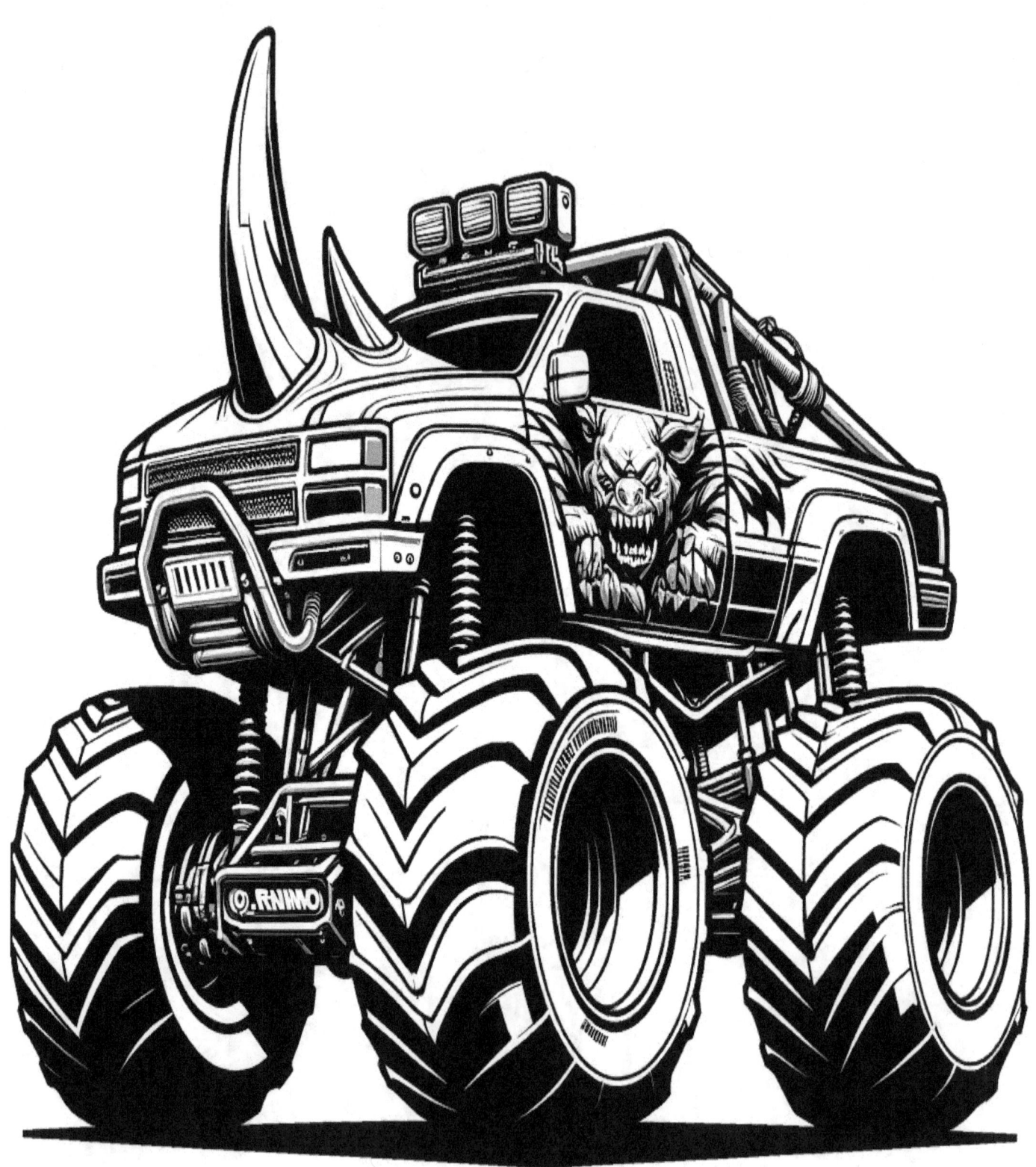

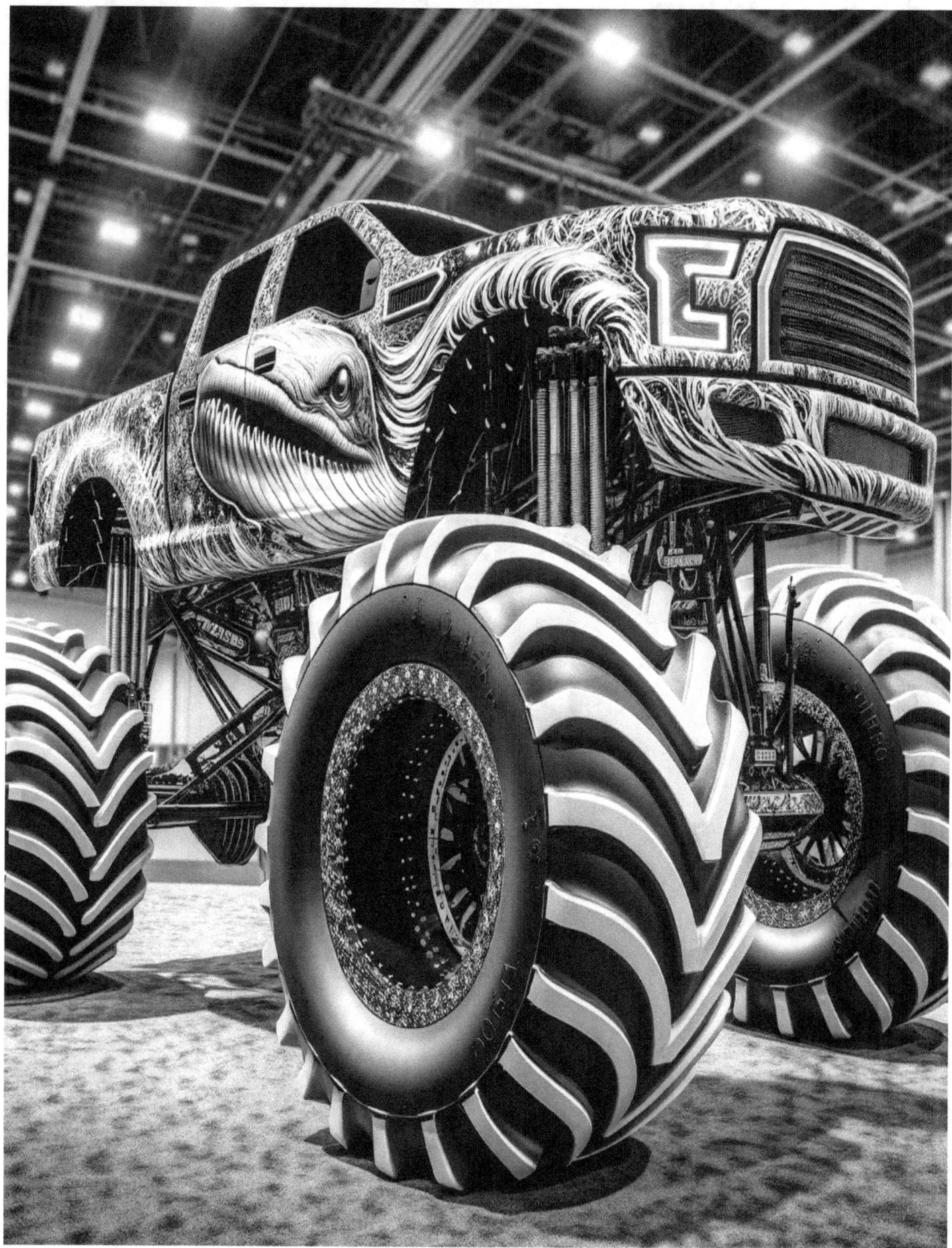

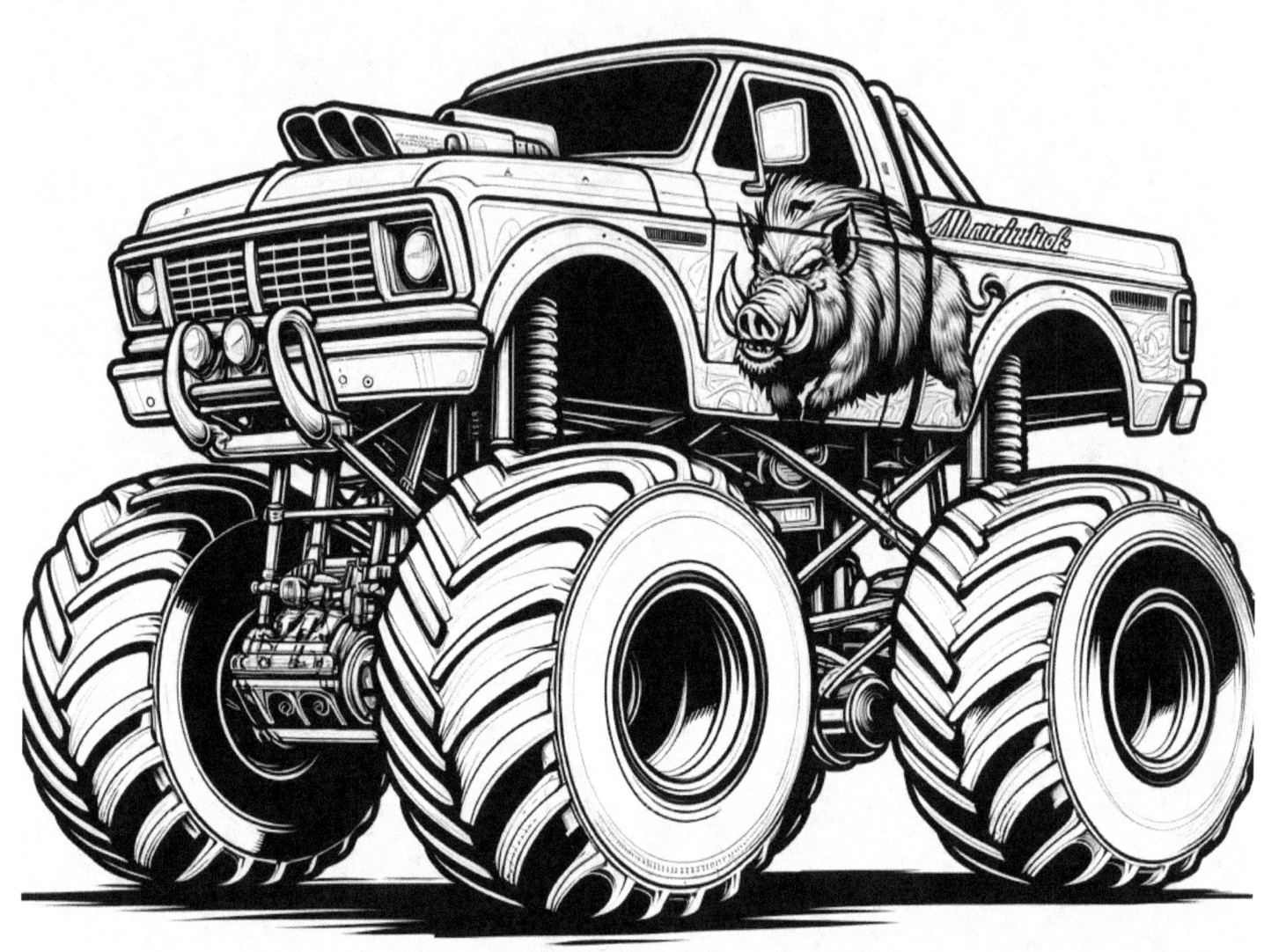

www.ingramcontent.com/pod-product-compliance
Lightning Source LLC
Chambersburg PA
CBHW080945290526
45795CB00009B/2920